THE COMPLETE HERB GARDEN

THE COMPLETE HERB GARDEN

JOHN STEVENS

THE READER'S DIGEST ASSOCIATION, INC.
Pleasantville, New York/Montreal

To Louise, Nikki, and Charlie

A READER'S DIGEST BOOK

The acknowledgments that appear on page 192 are hereby part of this copyright page.

Designed and edited by Collins & Brown
Editorial Director: Sarah Hoggett
Editors: Katie Bent and Catherine Bradley
Editorial Assistant: Robin Gurdon
Art Director: Roger Bristow
Senior Art Editor: Sarah Davies
Assistant Designer: Sue Metcalfe-Megginson
Photography: Jacqui Hurst and Sampson Lloyd
Illustrations: Eric Thomas
Cover Illustration: Clare Roberts

Library of Congress Cataloging in Publication Data

Stevens, John, 1937–
The complete herb garden / John Stevens.
p. cm.
"A Reader's digest book"—T.p. verso.
Includes index.
ISBN 0-89577-876-9
1. Herb gardening. 2. Herbs. 3. Herb gardening—Pictorial works.
4. Herbs—Pictorial works. I. Title.
SB351.H5S72 1996
635'.7—dc20 96-12463

READER'S DIGEST and the Pegasus logo are registered trademarks
of The Reader's Digest Association, Inc.
Printed in Italy

Many herbs that have valuable medicinal properties are unsafe for home use and are in some cases poisonous. The medicinal information in this book is for general interest only and is in no way intended to be a substitute for the advice of a physician or a qualified herbal practitioner. None of this information is intended to be used for home or self-treatment.

Contents

Origanum vulgare 'Aureum' Golden marjoram

Salvia officinalis 'Aurea' Golden sage

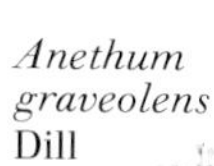

Anethum graveolens Dill

Introduction

FOR CENTURIES HERBS have been highly valued for their many practical uses as culinary, medicinal, and dye plants as well as for their decorative beauty and scent. The incredible variety and adaptability of herbs make these plants a perfect choice for today's gardeners. In addition to their many traditional uses herbs are a delight to grow for their bright and delicate flowers, their textural and colorful foliage, and often wonderful fragrances.

There are herbs for all situations and all seasons. This book helps you to make the most of your existing garden, giving practical advice on propagating and cultivating herb plants, identifying different habitats, and suggesting planting designs to suit any garden.

This introduction describes how to use the book to the best advantage, enabling you to create a beautiful garden of herbs. It also briefly identifies how to make the most beneficial use of their many decorative, medicinal, and culinary values in the home.

Introduction

HERBAL PLANTS have been valued in the garden for many hundreds of years, but they have no clear-cut definition: there is no botanical connection between them, not all are fragrant, and they are found in every continent, every climate, and every habitat. There are many plants that we instantly recognize as herbs – thyme, sage, and rosemary, for example. More surprisingly, some well-known, decorative garden plants, such as the old-fashioned favorites pinks, primroses, and hollyhocks, are also categorized as herbs.

The word "herb" comes from the Latin *herba* "green plants," from which the modern term "herbaceous" is also derived. In Elizabethan times herbs were put into four groupings: salat (salad) herbs, sweet herbs (flavorings), simples (medicinal plants), and pot herbs (green and root vegetables). Today, it is the medicinal and culinary uses of plants that are the main criteria for calling them herbs. However, those plants that are fragrant and those used for dyes are also often classed as herbs, as are those that have insecticidal properties and offer a safe alternative to chemical pesticide sprays. Yet other herbal plants are those employed in the production of cosmetics, perfumes, and potpourri. The valuable essential oils extracted from many herbs are widely used in aromatherapy. Wild plants, such as chicory, cress, lamb's-lettuce, and purslane, are often classed as salad herbs, some

A spring perspective RIGHT
This planting makes use of all the natural features of the existing garden. Low-growing colorful herbs are offset by the varied foliage of sweet cicely, golden lemon balm, and bronze fennel, and the flowers of Spanish broom.

Salvia officinalis
'Purpurascens'
Purple sage

A sheltered site RIGHT
The striking foliage of purple sage and golden marjoram is offset by the pink and purple blooms of the surrounding herbs in this colorful sheltered border.

being of medicinal value too. Spices are dried aromatic seeds, bark, or root used for seasoning only and include the seeds of the herbs caraway, coriander, dill, fennel, and saffron. Many other spices have valuable medicinal properties and would, therefore, also be classed as herbs.

Herbs are essentially plants with a specific use and have been cultivated ever since we ceased to be nomadic people. Long ago, herbs were grown and appreciated for their curative and magical powers, for their perfume, for their seasoning properties and food value, and for dyes; they have always been admired for their beauty and fragrance.

Gardening with herbs

When you choose to grow herbs you are following a tradition that has its roots in antiquity. From the geometrically laid-out gardens of the ancient civilizations of Egypt and Rome, to the colorful informal displays of the Victorian cottage gardens, herbs have always played an important role. It is fascinating to learn that the herbs that flourish

A lightly shaded border ABOVE
White-flowered herbs, such as the sweet rocket featured here, are enhanced in partial or light shade. *See chapter 3, "Designing with Herbs," for more ideas on using color.*

Mediterranean colors RIGHT
An exuberant planting of sun-loving Mediterranean plants. The soft gray-green leaves of the phlomis are a wonderful backdrop for the exquisite purple flowers of French lavender.

A walled garden BELOW
This lovely old wall provides a perfect backdrop for the vibrant blooms of red valerian and colorful spires of burning bush. See chapter 1, "How to Grow and Raise Herbs," for instructions on planting into walls and dry areas of the garden.

Centranthus ruber
Red valerian

Vibrant colors LEFT
This bright red valerian looks spectacular with the long-lasting spikes of blue flowers and soft gray-green foliage of Nepeta *'Six Hills Giant.'*

today were valued by people living thousands of years ago: the coriander plant had ancestors in the gardens of the pharaohs, where anise, caraway, mint, poppies, saffron, and wormwood were also cultivated. The delicate violets and crocuses that appear in spring were once beloved by the Roman emperors, who also valued sweet bay and myrtle. The Persians of the 5th century had a deep respect for the rose. They also grew such favorites as jasmine, irises, larkspur, hollyhocks, and lilies.

Apart from the historic importance of herbs, their own qualities commend them as ideal plants to grow in all parts of the garden. Most are simple in form. Even those that have been cultivated for centuries are still available in their near-to-wild state and those that have been "improved" by selection still retain many of their original qualities. They have blooms ranging from the smallest and daintiest, such as the tiny white stars of sweet woodruff, to the bold trumpets of lilies or superb thistlelike heads of globe artichoke. Many herbs have scented flowers and foliage.

A mixed border LEFT
This colorful planting of herbs, including ox-eye daisy, fragrant orange daylilies, and the purple spires of monkshood, creates a vibrant mixture in the border.

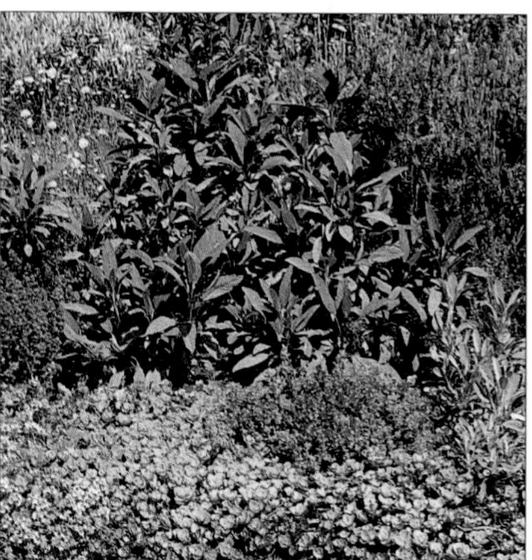

A sunny site LEFT
In this raised bed sages, thymes, sedum, and lavender thrive in the sun. Chapter 2, "Habitats in the Garden," describes open, dry habitats in detail.

Herbs are often grown for their foliage alone, which in many cases is especially beautiful. Fennel, for example, particularly the soft and feathery bronze variety, is a perfect foil for the wonderful range of gray- and silver-leaved herbs – santolinas, artemisias, and lavenders, among others. Herbs may be selected for their ample foliage – the great woolly leaves of mullein, for instance, or the large shiny leaves of acanthus. Some herbs have tiny delicate leaves; others are variegated or colorful, like those of the gold-variegated thymes, lemon balm, and marjoram or the purple-reds of perilla and purple sage. Attractive ground cover is provided by low-growing and carpeting herbs. This huge variation of foliage can be used to stunning effect in the garden in many combinations.

There are herbs suitable for all habitats: boggy areas, fertile beds and borders, shady woodland and hedgerows, dry rocks and gravelly sites, in pots and containers, and in wildflower gardens or meadows.

A terraced garden ABOVE
The flowers and foliage of sprawling catmint contrast dramatically with the dark green, clipped rosemary in the background.

Alchemilla vulgaris
Lady's mantle

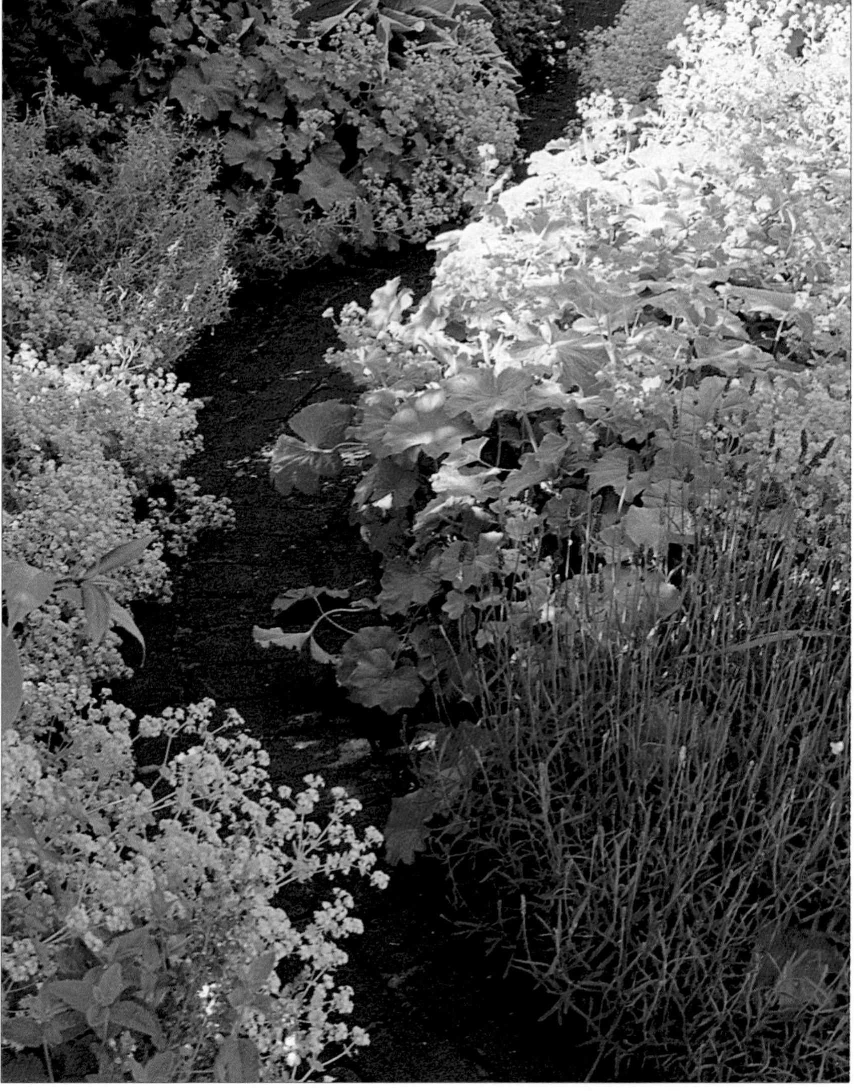

A cool path RIGHT
This shady winding path, bordered by silver, green, and golden plants, such as artemisia, lady's mantle, and lavender, is an effective planting making use of the varied foliage without the need for bright flowers.

Herbs are such a diverse group that they offer an enormous choice. There are herbs for every garden situation, providing a variety of foliage and flowers, many aromatic, and include shrubs and trees, herbaceous, ground-cover, and climbing plants.

With so many marvelous qualities, herbs deserve to play a key role in the overall planting of any size garden. Their great diversity demands that they are not solely confined within a designated "herb garden" but rather that they are displayed with other plants throughout the garden.

Uses for herbs in the home

Since earliest times, herbs have been valued in the home. They were strewn on the floor to deter insects and mask smells, their medicinal properties were frequently relied upon, they were drunk in teas, employed in many recipes, and were used for cosmetic ointments and for washing fabrics.

Today, culinary herbs are still widely used to add flavor, for making aromatic oils, vinegars, and sauces, for enhancing soft and alcoholic drinks, and for confecting sweets and candies. As well as the more obvious qualities of flavor, they also contain many substances of nutritional and medicinal value, such as vitamins, minerals, trace elements, essential oils, and alkaloids.

Although many herb products and dried herbs for flavoring can be easily bought, it is much more satisfying to use your own herbs, freshly picked from the garden. For cooking, start with a varied selection of parsley, chives, oregano, thyme, French tarragon, spearmint, rosemary, and a bay tree. It is worth growing some annual herbs including basil, dill, coriander, and summer savory. For salads, grow sorrel, borage, salad burnet, perilla, and watercress.

Many herbs are beneficial for the skin or hair and can be used in various cosmetic preparations. Comfrey, marsh mallow, and sweet violet provide softening and soothing emollients; elder flowers, calendula, and chamomile are gentle cleansers, and lady's mantle and witch hazel contain astringents. Chamomile and elder flowers are also traditional conditioners for fair hair; greasy hair is improved by lavender and peppermint. Essential oils can be diluted for use in cosmetic preparations, and in baths and vaporizers. They are also invaluable for massage when combined with a carrier oil such as sweet almond or jojoba.

Other herbs are useful for dental hygiene. Wild strawberries whiten teeth and remove plaque, and sage and thyme are excellent antiseptics for use as a mouthwash. Peppermint and parsley will remove the odors of onions and garlic from your breath.

Viola tricolor
Heartsease

Culinary herbs LEFT
Fresh leaves, flowers, and dried seeds are all used for seasoning. This selection of fresh cut herbs includes chives, parsley, dill, basil, winter savory, and oregano. Some edible flowers, such as nasturtium and heartsease, can be used to decorate salads. Flavored vinegar and oils can also be produced from herbs such as French tarragon.

Dyed wools ABOVE
These subtle colors are derived from natural extracts of herbal dye plants, such as coreopsis, which yields yellows, bronzes, oranges, and reds. Elecampane root yields a blue dye.

Coreopsis tinctoria
Coreopsis flowers

Inula helenium
Elecampane root

Flower arrangements ABOVE
Both fresh and dried herbs can be used in flower arrangements. Here the soft glowing color of chrysanthemums is set off beautifully against artemisia, marjoram, muskmallow, wild carrot, and dried teasel heads. Around the jug are the plumed seed heads of travelers' joy.

The soft and rich colors of herbal dyes are much more beautiful than modern synthetic dyestuffs and can give an infinite number of subtle shades of any color. There is a tremendous revival of interest in natural plant dyes and, once the basic techniques are mastered, it is a fascinating craft. Most plants will yield a dye, although not all are fast. Wool is the best fiber for dyeing. Cotton and linen are more difficult and synthetic fabrics are best avoided.

Aromatic herbs are a marvelous way to perfume your home. A typical potpourri contains a mixture of herbs, including rose buds and petals, lavender leaves and flowers, lemon verbena, sage, rosemary, and oregano. Grated or powdered orris root fixes the scent. Sachets of scented herbs, filled with hop, lavender, rose petals, or woodruff, can be scattered in drawers or hung in wardrobes.

Herbs are ideal for flower arrangements. Their decorative flowers and foliage, both fresh and dried, can be used throughout the year. In the fall and winter, colorful berries and unusual dried seed heads add seasonal interest.

Many herbs repel insects and are much safer to use in the home than chemical sprays. Place sprigs or bags of southernwood, santolina, rosemary, or lavender among your clothes to deter moths. To discourage flies, hang up bunches of tansy, eau de Cologne mint, pennyroyal, rue, or southernwood.

Medicinal uses for herbs

Herbs are used in a wide range of holistic medical treatments including homeopathy, aromatherapy, and herbal medicine. They also play a significant part in orthodox medicine. Many important drugs are derived from plants, including quinine for malaria, morphine, codeine, and methadone from opium poppies, and aspirin from meadowsweet. The Madagascar periwinkle, which contains many alkaloids, is used in the treatment of leukemia.

Herbal medicines can be prepared in several ways. The simplest is an infusion or tea, which employs the soft green parts and flowers. Herbal teas have many beneficial properties, for example lemon verbena tea is soothing for indigestion. A decoction is used to prepare bark, root, or seeds. A tincture, to extract the plant chemicals, is made from water and alcohol. Herbal oils can be made by macerating fresh herbs in pure vegetable oil.

Warning: always consult a qualified herbal practitioner before using any herbs for home treatment. Many of the herbs that have valuable medicinal properties are unsafe for home use and are in some cases poisonous.

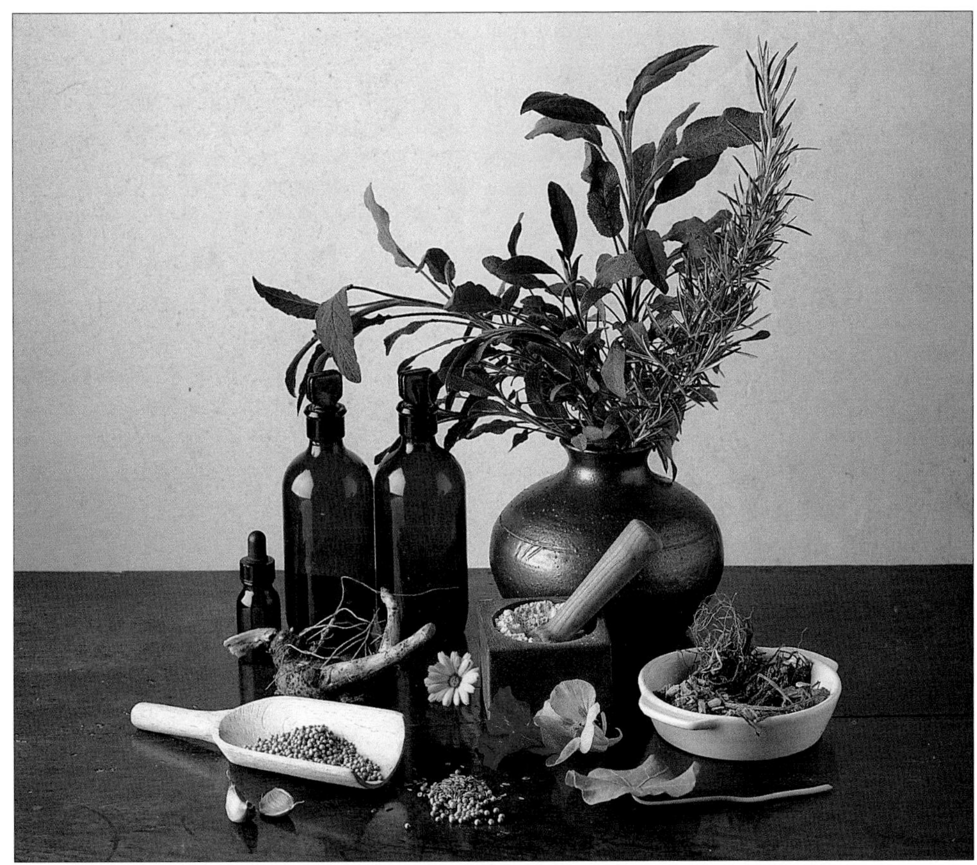

Herbal apothecary LEFT
The leaves, flowers, seeds, stems, roots, and bark of herbs are used in various herbal preparations. This selection of medicinal herbs includes rosemary, purple sage, fresh elecampane root, dried valerian roots, pot marigold flowers, garlic bulbs, and dill seed. Infusions or teas are made from herbs such as lemon verbena.

Aloysia triphylla
Lemon verbena

HOW TO USE THIS BOOK

THIS BOOK PLACES EMPHASIS on an ecological approach to gardening. Most plants are adaptable and surprisingly tough, but they all have specific conditions under which they will thrive best. Woodland herbs, for instance, planted in a shady site with woodland-type soil, will grow well and look natural together. However, a plant from an open habitat will struggle in such a situation. Despite being a simplification of what happens in nature, this principle can be applied successfully to growing all plants, not just herbs. Looking at this principle in more depth, this book describes how to provide the best conditions for all your herbs.

For those new to gardening with herbs, or in need of more detailed information, chapter 1, "How to Grow and Raise Herbs," covers all the practical techniques. The most suitable methods of propagation are explained with clear step-by-step photographs, along with advice on how to maintain and improve your soil, how to care for plants, and how to harvest your herbs. It describes how to make full use of the habitats in your garden, or how to introduce new ones. Chapter 2, "Habitats in the Garden," looks in more detail at a range of habitats describing their characteristics and those of the plants that naturally thrive in them. Once you have established which habitats exist in your own garden, selecting the most appropriate plants is simplified. Chapter 3, "Designing with Herbs," helps you to create attractive plantings. This chapter not only gives ideas for herbs that are particularly well suited to the sites that you have, but also shows you how to produce gardens that maintain their interest throughout the year. Full descriptions of these plants and many others are found in the "Herb Directory," which contains all the information you need to cultivate a huge range of herbs.

Herbs come from all over the world, from all climates and from virtually every habitat so finding some to suit the particular conditions in your garden, wherever you live, should not be difficult. By following the advice in this book you will be able to cultivate a wide range of plants, and will appreciate their beauty in a setting that approaches their natural habitat.

How to Grow and Raise Herbs

THIS CHAPTER LOOKS AT the best ways of growing healthy plants, how to care for them, and how to harvest the seeds and herbs for home use. The most commonly used methods of propagation are explained with clear step-by-step illustrations.

A healthy soil is the key element for growing successful, disease-free plants. Described here are the most environmentally friendly ways of improving the soil and for dealing with pests and diseases, should they occur.

Methods of preparing and planting different habitats are described. It is important to plant herbs in the most appropriate habitat: each of these is illustrated and described in detail in chapter 2, "Habitats in the Garden."

Soils and Manures

SOIL IS THE MOST important ingredient of any garden, and in order to grow plants successfully you need to understand a little about its structure and composition.

Soil is divided into three layers: topsoil, subsoil, and bedrock. Topsoil is the humus-rich, dark colored layer that contains a proportion of decaying vegetation and broken-down organic matter teeming with living organisms including worms, soil bacteria, and fungi. These organisms break down the organic material converting it into food that plants can use. It is from this top layer that plants obtain most of their nutrients.

Subsoil contains fewer nutrients but holds reserves of moisture and minerals and is much lighter in color. Through cultivation, topsoil may become mixed with subsoil, so there is not always a clear division. Deep-rooting plants penetrate the subsoil for minerals and moisture and help to break up and aerate the subsoil.

Beneath the subsoil is the bedrock, which, depending on its composition, may or may not provide good drainage and can affect the pH of the soil above (see "Assessing your soil" opposite).

Topsoil can be considerably improved by applying organic material, which adds nutrients, lightens the soil for easier root penetration, and helps conserve moisture. Subsoil can be improved in several ways so that its structure is open, providing better drainage and easier root penetration.

SOIL TYPES

The main soil types are clay, sand, peat, and loam. Other soil types are silt and chalk. Silt soils have similarities to clay. They are smooth, sticky, and airless when wet and need the addition of coarse grit and organic material to improve drainage and workability. Chalk soils have a high pH. They are poor and free-draining, often containing stones, and need organic matter to improve them and retain moisture.

Sandy soil LEFT
Light and usually free-draining, sometimes gravelly, sandy soil is easily worked in winter and very dry in summer. It needs plenty of organic matter to help retain moisture and increase the nutrients. Sandy soil has a coarse, gritty texture.

Loam soil LEFT
Loam, the most common garden soil, is a combination of clay, silt, and sand. Heavy loam has a large proportion of clay and may become waterlogged in winter. Sandy loam drains well but may lack moisture in hot summers. Loam is usually crumbly.

Peat soil LEFT
Because peat soil has a low pH, many plants cannot grow in it without the addition of lime. Although usually fertile and well drained it can become waterlogged. In extremely dry conditions the soil may shrink and require irrigation. Peat is spongy in texture.

Clay or heavy soil LEFT
Made up of minute particles, clay is usually fertile and retains moisture. It is difficult to work in winter, slow to warm up in spring, and bakes hard in summer. The addition of plenty of organic matter and grit improves drainage and aeration.

Assessing your soil

In order to assess your soil, dig a hole 1 foot (30 cm) deep in the garden and slice cleanly down one side of it with a spade. You should clearly see the extent of your topsoil, which normally varies in depth from several inches (cms) to 2 feet (60 cm) or more. An ideal garden soil is a medium loam composed of sand, silt, and clay with a free-draining stony subsoil beneath.

As well as finding out what type of soil you have, you also need to establish its acidity or alkalinity, as this may be a factor in determining which plants you can grow (see right). Acidity and alkalinity are measured on the pH scale. The scale goes from 0 to 14: the higher numbers indicate a soil with a high lime content (alkaline), 7 is neutral, and between 0 and 6 is acid. Most soils have a pH between 4.5 and 8.5. The majority of herbs prefer neutral to slightly alkaline conditions.

If you have acidic soil, the best way of raising the pH is to add dolomite limestone, which also contains magnesium, or better still, incorporate calcified seaweed, which is long-lasting, contains magnesium and other plant nutrients, and unlike limestone does not wash away through the soil. The only way to lower the pH of alkaline soil is to add organic matter, which is slightly acid.

It is better, if possible, to select herbs that enjoy the conditions natural to your garden than to make significant adjustments to the pH value of the soil. However, many herbs are adaptable.

Improving and feeding the soil

To make healthy growth plants require nitrogen, phosphorus, and potassium (NPK) and other trace elements. Plants normally absorb these substances from the soil, but in poor soils you may need to provide them in the form of fertilizers or manures.

Poor, light soils need plenty of organic matter to provide nutrients, to encourage the soil bacteria that make plant foods available, and to increase the moisture-holding capacity. Homemade compost is by far the best material, but there are plenty of other forms of organic matter, including well-rotted horse or cattle manure, spent mushroom compost, leaf mold, and various waste organic products, as well as regular use of green manures.

There are various ways of improving heavy, badly drained soils. If the soil is waterlogged, special drainage will be required before any planting and it might be best to get professional help. Adding organic materials, especially compost, helps to break down heavy clay, as does planting deep-rooting green manures (see page 22) and working grit and small stones into the soil. Constant cultivation of a clay soil can form a "pan" of compacted soil a few inches below the surface, that is impenetrable to water. This can be broken by working a fork as deeply as possible into the soil or by growing deep-rooting plants that penetrate the soil so improving aeration and drainage.

SOIL TESTING

Carrying out a soil test, using a kit available from most garden centers, tells you whether your soil is acid or alkaline.

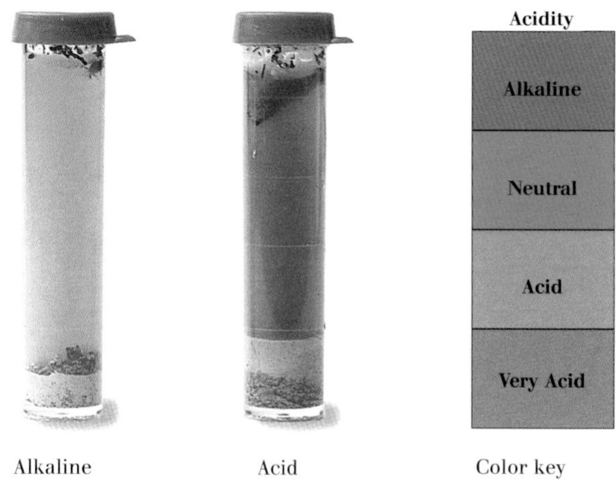

Test tubes ABOVE
Put a soil sample in the test tube and follow the instructions on your kit. The solution changes color and can be matched to the color key supplied.

Soil meter ABOVE
A soil meter is a simple instrument with a metal probe that is placed in the soil and produces a pH reading on the dial. An advantage of the meter is that readings can easily be taken at different sites around the garden.

Compost

Composting is the breaking down of waste plant materials to a crumbly soillike substance that provides nutrients for the soil. Adding compost to the soil also encourages beneficial soil fungi and bacteria that make it possible for plant roots to absorb many nutrients from the soil.

You can make your own compost from a varied mix of kitchen and garden waste. Small quantities of compost can be made in a commercial compost maker; larger quantities are best made using a homemade compost box. Avoid using animal wastes, especially meat, which will attract rats and other scavengers. Put a thick layer of coarse material including stems and stalks, in the bottom of the compost box to aerate the heap. Mix rough, twiggy material with weeds, grass mowings, and other waste, to keep the material from packing down and excluding air.

Composting requires air, heat, and moisture to break down the raw material. To accelerate the composting process turn the heap or add an activator. The best activators are natural ones, such as animal manures (especially from poultry), and seaweed meal. Extra moisture may be needed especially when the heap is turned.

The finished compost will be ready in about six months. Ideally, it should look dark, crumbly and soillike. Some of the organic material may have only partially rotted; however it will continue breaking down in the soil.

Compost box ABOVE
A compost box is usually made of wood. It has no bottom, is fitted with a detachable lid, and has a front made up of planks that can be slotted in as the compost box fills up. Cover the heap with black plastic or even old carpet to keep in heat and moisture and keep out the rain.

GREEN MANURE PLANTS

Listed below is a selection of the most beneficial green manure plants. Although usually cut before flowering, several green manures are very decorative if allowed to flower and some are also excellent bee plants.

Fagopyrum esculentum
Buckwheat

Medicago lupulina
Trefoil

Medicago sativa
Alfalfa

Phacelia tanacetifolia
Phacelia

Sinapis alba
Mustard

Trifolium pratense
Red clover

Trigonella foenumgraecum
Fenugreek

Green manures

Green manures are quick-growing crops, providing dense ground cover and suppressing weeds. When dug in they also improve the soil's fertility. This is an excellent way of covering bare soil, protecting it from the effects of heavy rain and baking sun.

A green manure can also be used to maintain the soil in a good condition. Some green manures (leguminous plants such as clover) are nitrogen "fixers"; their roots support bacteria that "fix" nitrogen in the soil, making it available to the following crop. Others produce deep and extensive roots that break up heavy ground, bringing up available minerals from the subsoil.

If you grow a perennial green manure, mow it regularly through the season, keeping it about 6 inches (15 cm) tall to prevent the growth of woody stems that are difficult to break down and which use up nitrogen that is required by the next crop. Leave the cuttings to rot where they are; they will add organic matter to the soil. When the ground is needed, simply dig the crop in.

Annual green manures should be dug into the ground when they are soft and green. These, too, can be mowed down before they are dug in.

Using natural fertilizers

There are many natural fertilizers on the market including seaweed, calcified seaweed, and various natural rock fertilizers, such as rock phosphate and rock potash; there are also animal-waste products,

GROWING A GREEN MANURE

Broadcast or drill the seed into well-prepared soil. Rapid germination provides dense ground cover.

1 *Cut down the crop just before it flowers (or earlier if required). Use a mower, scythe, or shears. Cuttings may be left on the surface to rot down before digging in.*

2 *Incorporate the cut foliage into the top few inches of soil using a spade or a cultivator. The green leaf will decompose rapidly, thus improving soil fertility.*

such as dried blood and bonemeal. Liquid seaweed provides foliar and soil feed.

If the soil is healthy, chemical fertilizers are unnecessary. Chemical fertilizers can easily produce too much soft growth on a plant, making it more susceptible to diseases and less hardy over the winter. Feeding the soil, thus building up a huge population of soil bacteria (estimated at millions per gram of soil), is the best and most ecologically friendly way of producing healthy plants.

A good way of feeding plants directly, especially if some deficiency is suspected, is to spray foliar feed onto the leaves. Liquid seaweed is often used as a foliar feed because it contains NPK and a wide range of trace elements.

Homemade liquid manure can be made using comfrey and stinging nettles in a proportion of half and half by volume. Press them into a bucket, cover with water, and stir occasionally. Over a few weeks a black liquid is produced, making an excellent liquid fertilizer that can be applied to the soil or sprayed onto the leaves.

MULCHES

Mulches are used to cover the soil in order to suppress weed growth, retain moisture in the soil, and sometimes to add nourishment. They can also modify soil temperature and improve soil texture. The best mulching materials, particularly in a flower garden, are those that look attractive. Suitable materials are spent mushroom compost, gravel, chipped wood bark, hay and stem, and leaf mold.

Hay and stem
Lay hay and stem mulch to a depth of 6 inches (15 cm) or more. After rain this mulch will break down to a denser layer, suppress weeds, hold moisture, and eventually decompose into the soil.

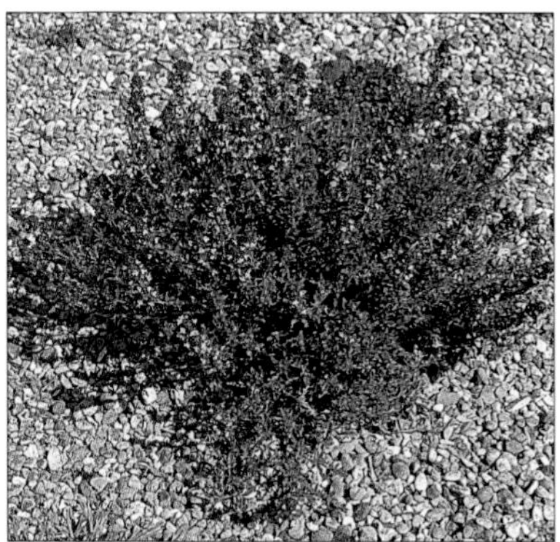

Stones or gravel
Small stones or gravel make an ideal mulch for a rock garden, where they keep the leaves of low-growing herbs free of the soil, and retain moisture in the soil beneath. In hot climates they also reflect heat.

Bark chippings
The Joe-pye weed shown here is surrounded by a mulch of dried bark chips. Bark chippings break down slowly and are efficient at suppressing weeds and keeping moisture in the soil.

Spent mushroom compost
Spent mushroom compost still contains some nutrients and is usually alkaline in nature. It is an excellent mulch and soil conditioner.

Growing from Seed

Seed is the means by which most flowering plants reproduce themselves. Among all the methods of propagation, growing from seed is the most common. It is much less expensive than buying already established plants, although the disadvantage is the amount of time involved: it will often take a whole season, and sometimes more, to produce a substantial plant.

Herbs normally grown from seed are annuals, biennials, and many of the herbaceous perennials. Herb seeds can either be sown directly into the ground or sown in pots or seed trays (flats) and transplanted later. Seed packets will advise you on which method is most suitable. Growing from seed is generally straightforward but it is important to understand a little of their requirements.

Seed requirements

Seeds have certain basic requirements in order to germinate and grow:

• Moisture is supplied by moist compost or soil. Larger seeds can be soaked overnight to speed up their germination time.

• Oxygen is available in a well-aerated seed or potting compost, or in soil that is well cultivated. Waterlogged or compacted soil can cause failure.

• Warmth is required in varying degrees for successful germination. The optimum temperature is 68°F (20°C).

• Some seeds, particularly those of wild plants, require light to germinate. As a general rule most small seeds should be surface sown or only lightly covered. Bury larger seeds to their own depth.

DIRECT SEEDING

For many annuals and biennials (details are given on seed packets), it is best to sow seed in situ, *where the plants are to grow, since they do not like being transplanted. Most biennials should be sown in early summer to allow them time to get established before the winter; some, especially umbellifers (carrot family), also require a period of cold to trigger germination and they should be sown in the fall. Annuals are normally sown in the spring or, if they are hardy, in late summer. Most perennials are best sown in spring – unless they need cold treatment (see opposite), in which case a fall sowing is essential.*

1 *Prepare a seedbed by clearing any existing weeds, making a reasonably fine bed without too many soil lumps or stones.*

2 *Sprinkle seeds over the soil. Dustlike seeds should be scattered on the surface. Larger seeds should be pressed into the soil, to the same depth as the seed size. Sow sparsely to avoid having to thin out the seedlings.*

3 *If the seeds need to be covered (see step 2), use your fingers or a small fork to work them lightly into the soil. Firm the soil down lightly. Sprinkle pale-colored sand over them so that you can see where they are.*

4 *Water with a fine rose to make sure the seed is in close contact with the soil. Once the seedlings emerge, water regularly until they are established, ensuring that the top 2 inches (5 cm) of soil is moist.*

Germination time

On average, germination takes up to 30 days, but some seeds may take 90 days or more. If your seeds do not come up in reasonable time, take a look at them to find out what has gone wrong. In some cases the seed may have rotted or gone soggy, in which case start again. If the seed is hard, it is still alive and is in dormancy, awaiting the right conditions to germinate. Seeds do this in order to give themselves the best chance of survival: without such safety mechanisms they might germinate during drought or when temperatures are too high or too low for survival. To improve their chance of survival, wild herb seeds do not always germinate all at the same time. This may give rise to erratic germination over a long period.

Breaking dormancy

There are several ways of breaking dormancy in order to get seeds to germinate. See the "Herb Directory" (pages 100–77) for the most suitable methods for specific herbs.

Cold treatment or stratification Some seeds will not germinate until they have been through the low and freezing temperatures of winter. In this way, nature ensures that they germinate in spring, when weather conditions are most favorable for growth. Sow these seeds in the fall, cover the tray with glass to protect against mice and birds, and leave it outside or in a cold frame over the winter. Germination will take place in early or late spring.

Alternatively, mix the seed with moist peat or sand in a plastic bag and leave outside over the winter (or in the refrigerator for approximately eight weeks). In the spring, sow as normal.

The seeds of some shrubs and trees, such as rose hip and elder, are contained in a fleshy coating. To germinate, the seed coat has to be broken down. In nature this happens when the seed passes

INDOOR SOWING

Because many herbs have tiny seeds and germination can take many weeks, even months in some cases, it is not always practical to sow in situ. *Vermin or birds may take the seed; more usually, weed growth overtakes the sowing area, and distinguishing between weed and herb seedlings can be difficult. It is often best to germinate small seeds in controlled conditions indoors, in a seed tray (flat), rather than in the open ground.*

1 Prepare the seed tray (flat) with special seed and sowing compost, level it off ¼ inch (0.6 cm) below the rim. Water with a fine rose until moist throughout.

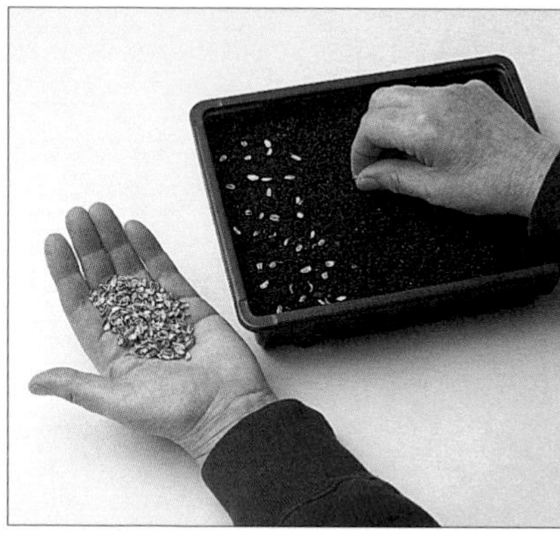

2 Pour the seeds into the palm of your hand, pick some up between your thumb and forefinger, and sprinkle thinly and evenly over the surface of the seed tray. Do not sow too thickly.

3 Lightly cover with fine seed compost sieved through a plastic pot or sieve. Cover larger seeds to their own thickness or press them into the seed compost. Tiny seeds germinate best uncovered. Water gently with a fine rose.

4 Cover the seed tray (flat) with a sheet of glass. This keeps moisture in, eliminates the need for further watering, and prevents pests attacking the seeds and emerging seedlings. Keep in the shade.

through a bird's intestine. If you want to grow such seeds yourself, they should be stratified over winter, although some may take two seasons to germinate.

Scarification Seeds with tough, hard coats are often unable to take in moisture to start germinating. To break down the hard coating, scarify the seed by rubbing it gently between two sheets of sandpaper. Alternatively soak the seed in warm water for 24 hours. Many of the seeds with hard coats are from the Leguminosae (legume) and Geraniaceae (cranesbill) families. The seeds of *Helianthemum* (rockrose) also fall into this category.

Caring for seedlings

Seeds sown *in situ* After direct sowing, always mark the area with sticks or stones or by sprinkling clean sand over the seeded area and label with the date and plant name.

If the season is windy, hot, or cold, you should cover the area with "fleece" to protect the seeds and prevent the soil from drying out. A featherlight, translucent fiber covering fleece creates a warm microclimate and allows rain through; it also keeps off birds and pests. As the seedlings grow, the fleece rests on top of the plants.

Seed sown indoors Seed trays (flats) should be kept in the shade, never in direct sun. Keep them in a warm place in the house or in a greenhouse, where you can maintain the correct temperature.

When the seeds start to germinate, remove the glass cover. Do not overwater the seedlings or allow the seed compost to dry out. Keep them out of direct sun; high temperatures encourage spindly growth and "soft" plants.

Because the seedlings have been growing in a protected environment, they need to be gradually acclimatized to conditions out of doors. This process is known as "hardening off." For a period of two to three weeks move the seedlings from the greenhouse to a closed frame or open the frame during the day, putting them back in the protected environment at night.

Transplant the seedlings into small pots when they are large enough to handle (see opposite). Allow them to become well rooted before planting.

Self-seeding

Many herbs will self-seed if the flower heads are left for the seed to mature. In any natural or ecological planting this is desirable. Unwanted seedlings can be transplanted or hoed out.

TRANSPLANTING SEEDLINGS

When seedlings are large enough to handle, they are ready to be transplanted. If they have been sown thinly they can be left slightly longer. Transplant seedlings into small pots filled with a suitable potting compost.

1 *Starting from one corner, loosen the soil and ease out the seedling, holding the first leaves between thumb and finger. Hold the stem of larger seedlings. Ensure plenty of root and soil come away with the seedling.*

2 *Make a hole in the potting compost large enough to accommodate the root system of the seedling. Drop the seedling into the hole, making sure that it is planted at the same depth as before.*

3 *Cover the roots with potting soil and fill the hole. Press the soil firmly around the plant so that it is stable.*

4 *Finally, water well with a fine rose to settle the soil into contact with all the roots. Label your plant.*

Propagating Plants

GROWING A PLANT from seed is not always appropriate or even possible. A number of herbs either do not set seed or do not come true from seed. These include many varieties with variegated or decorative foliage, or particular flower colors, and the large number of decorative thymes, most of which cannot be grown from seed. Also, as in the case of shrubs, producing a mature plant from seed is often a slow process. There are also methods of using an established plant to reproduce further identical ones; these can sometimes be planted into their permanent growing positions immediately. The only means of reproducing the parent plant exactly is by vegetative propagation, which is most commonly done by cuttings.

CUTTINGS

A cutting is a length of stem that under suitable conditions is able to produce its own roots and form a new plant. The different types of cuttings include softwood, greenwood, semiripe, hardwood, and water. Softwood cuttings root quickly but easily wilt; greenwood cuttings are preferable. Woody shrubs can be propagated by hardwood cuttings taken during the fall or early winter and rooted outside in a sandy trench.

GREENWOOD CUTTINGS

This is the best type of cutting to take from most herbs. Greenwood cuttings are taken when the soft spring growth has firmed up in late spring or early summer. Take the cutting from the tip of a healthy stem; it may vary in length according to the plant. The tip of the cutting will be floppy and the base just firm enough to insert into the cutting medium.

1 *Select cuttings 2–4 inches (5–10 cm) long from the tip of a healthy, non-flowering main stem. Take them before the sun is hot.*

2 *Strip the leaves off the lower half of the stem. Any leaves that touch the cutting medium will rot.*

3 *Keep the cuttings turgid and moist by carefully spraying them with a fine mist of water.*

4 *Using a length of wire or a stick, make holes in the cutting medium the same size as the stems.*

5 *Insert the cuttings, taking care not to crowd them. Water well with a fine rose. Place a hoop of wire as shown to support a plastic bag.*

6 *Fix a plastic bag around the pot with a rubber band or string to keep moisture inside. The cuttings should need little watering until they have rooted.*

7 *Cuttings require good light (not direct sun) and a temperature of about 70°F (21°C). Rooting usually takes 1–5 weeks. Transplant cuttings once rooted.*

8 *Repot each cutting in a small pot large enough to hold the root system without restriction. Firm the compost around the plant, and water.*

SEMIRIPE CUTTINGS

Trees and shrubs are usually propagated from semiripe wood. Semiripe cuttings, like this sweet bay, should be taken in mid- to late summer when the shoots are starting to ripen and become harder. Rooting hormone powder encourages the cutting to root and is available from garden centers. These cuttings will normally root by the following spring.

1 *Take 4–6 inch (10–15 cm) cuttings from the current season's growth. Strip off any leaves from the lower part of the stems.*

2 *Insert the base of the stem in rooting hormone powder; knock off any excess. Insert approximately 1 inch (2.5 cm) into the compost.*

3 *Space the cuttings at intervals around the edge of the pot. Keep the mixture damp; cover with a clear plastic bag to retain the moisture.*

Rooting cuttings

Most cuttings can be rooted into pure coarse sand, but for better results use one of the following mixes: equal amounts of peat (or peat substitute) and sharp sand; equal amounts of peat and perlite (made from volcanic rock); or equal amounts of peat, perlite, and coarse sand. Peat retains moisture and encourages roots; perlite retains moisture and air; and sand aerates the mix and supplies bulk and density, making the inserted cutting more secure.

Cuttings must be kept turgid. Take them early in the day, before the sun is hot, and keep them sprayed with a mist spray before you insert them into the cutting mix. Once they are inserted, cover the container with a plastic bag to retain moisture until the cuttings have rooted.

ROOTING CUTTINGS IN WATER

Some plant stems – particularly mints and other moisture-loving plants – can be rooted in water. Roots tend to develop near the surface of the water, so keep the water level in the jar low.

1 *Cut non-flowering stems up to 6 inches (15 cm) long. The base of the cutting should be firm. Strip off the lower leaves so that none touches the water.*

2 *Put the cuttings in a glass jar of water and place them in full light (not in direct sun). Do not crowd too many into the jar.*

3 *Leave the cuttings in the water until a good root system has formed. Remove any leaves that drop off or turn brown before they rot or become diseased.*

4 *Plant the cuttings in individual pots filled with general-purpose potting soil. When they have formed a good root system plant them in the garden.*

PLANT DIVISION

Many herbaceous plants and some shrubs can be propagated by dividing the parent plant. The main advantage of this method is that you reproduce the mother plant exactly (with seed there is often some variation) and are provided with a good-sized plant that will quickly establish.

Select healthy specimens, free from imperfections or disease. The method of division depends on the type of plant and its root system. In most cases all or most of the plant will have to be dug, divided as required, and replanted into new soil. Fork compost into the area from which the plant was dug to revitalize the soil.

HERBS WITH A FLESHY CROWN

Divide crowns at the end of their dormant season as they start to shoot. Slice the crown vertically into several pieces, each with its own shoot or "eye."

1 *Either dig up the whole plant, or slice a piece off the crown, and divide it using a sharp knife. Each section of this sweet cicely must include a shoot.*

2 *This comfrey will produce new shoots and roots from any piece of root. Slice it into sections with a knife and plant in prepared soil.*

HERBS WITH FIBROUS ROOTS

Clumps of fibrous roots can be lifted and divided just after flowering or in early spring to form smaller plants each with plenty of roots and shoots.

1 *Using your hands or a knife, ease or cut pieces from the outside of the dug plant. The center of the plant can be replanted but discard old and woody centers.*

2 *Once the plant has been divided, either repot the small clumps or, in the case of large clumps, plant them direct in prepared soil.*

HERBS WITH A RHIZOME

Some plants, such as this mint, produce rhizomes – stems that run from the plant at ground level or under ground. Rhizomes produce both roots and shoots along their length that look like several separate plants but are, in fact, all connected. Divide rhizomes after flowering or in spring.

1 *Using a fork, dig up rhizomes with young shoots away from the main plant. These shoots have their own root system and will produce good-sized plants within the same season.*

2 *With garden scissors or pruners, cut the rhizomes into short lengths, each with some healthy roots and a green shoot. These will quickly grow into strong new plants.*

3 *If the plant has a good root system, plant into prepared soil outside. Otherwise, plant the sections into pots to grow further and produce more roots before planting in the garden.*

OTHER METHODS OF PROPAGATION

Sowing seed, division, and taking cuttings are the most common methods of propagating plants, but some herbs lend themselves to the other techniques described below. These include layering, by runners and suckers, or by division of bulbs and corms. See the "Herb Directory" (pages 100–77), for methods suitable for individual plants.

Layering, one of the oldest of all propagation techniques, uses the natural tendency of some woody plants to develop roots and new shoots at points where their stems come into contact with the soil. Suckers are produced by some shrubs and trees, such as roses and sweet bay. They originate from the underground root system or at the base of the main stem of a mature plant and may appear as leafy shoots near the base of the parent plant or as much as several feet away. They produce their own root system and can be detached from the parent plant, dug up, and planted as new plants.

Many herbs, such as crocuses or chives, grow from bulbs or corms. These multiply over the years to produce a clump that can then be split up into individual bulbs and planted to make new plants.

LAYERING

Layering is a traditional method of propagating woody plants. It involves pinning down a long, low-growing stem from a parent plant into a specially prepared soil; where the stem touches the soil a new root system will be produced. Once established the new plant can be detached from the parent and planted in a different site. Layering is a good alternative to taking cuttings.

1 *First, prepare the soil by lightly forking over and mixing in some coarse sand so that drainage is improved. Select the longest stem growing from the base of the plant. Remove any leaves in the way.*

2 *About 6 inches (15 cm) from the tip, pin the stem down into the prepared site with a U-shaped wire. Cover with soil and press down firmly so that a section is buried beneath the soil. Water well.*

3 *When the shoot has produced roots of its own and is starting to grow, cut the stem attaching it to its parent. Transplant to its permanent place in the same season, before the root system becomes too extensive.*

RUNNERS

A runner is a specialized overground stem that develops from the axil of a leaf at the crown of the plant. Plants develop at intervals along the stem, putting down their own roots. The strawberry is a typical example of a plant with runners.

1 *Take a runner and place the roots in a small pot. Fill with soil and pin the runner down into the pot. Continue potting other runners around the plant.*

2 *After a few weeks a healthy-looking, new plant will have rooted well into the pot. At this stage, cut off the runner stem near the new plant. You can then transplant it elsewhere.*

Preparation and Planting

BEFORE YOU PLANT a new area or habitat in the garden, assess your soil and its requirements (see page 21). All persistent perennial weeds must be eradicated (see page 43). Annual weeds are easily dealt with by hoeing. Thorough preparation is essential. By cultivating the soil you can improve its aeration and drainage and, with the addition of organic matter, its fertility. Ideally, choose a site with well-drained and easily workable soil, but which still retains moisture in summer.

Your choice of plants will depend to some extent on the conditions prevailing in your garden, although these can always be modified, if not changed. Some plants do require specific conditions to thrive and all do best in a situation similar to their natural environment. However, they are surprisingly adaptable, especially in the garden where conditions are less extreme than in the wild.

Planting

Planting is best done in spring or fall, although container-grown herbs may be planted year-round as long as conditions are suitable. Avoid planting when the weather is harsh or if the ground is

BUYING PLANTS

When selecting plants, look for healthy, disease-free top growth, a good overall shape, and small roots just emerging through the base of the container. They should not be too large with lush growth, as this indicates a soft plant that will not establish well. Plants should be well labeled with both the common and the Latin name, their eventual height and spread, their flower colors, and the type of site and soil required.

Large root system
The large root system appearing from the pot base indicates that this rosemary should have been planted before now; the top is beginning to die off, indicating stress.

Poor shape
Avoid plants like this rosemary, which has a poor shape, is very spindly, and will not grow into a good specimen.

Stunted growth
This marjoram has been in the pot too long, resulting in stunted, woody growth on top and old roots coming through the pot base.

Poor root system
This plant is not ready for sale. It has only recently been potted and has little root system.

A well-grown plant
This well-grown marjoram has fresh, healthy top growth and no large roots growing out of the pot base.

A healthy plant
An excellent specimen. It has good top growth and shape, and a few small roots just coming through the base.

frosted, and also during intensely hot weather or a prolonged dry period.

Prepare the soil and plant new purchases as shown below. Herbs do not require feeding after planting if the soil has been properly prepared beforehand and garden compost, lime, and other fertilizers added as required (see pages 21–3).

All plants require moisture to grow, including plants that are described as enjoying dry, hot conditions: in the wild these plants start life from seed in the rainy season and are well established before drought sets in. Water plants before planting and keep them watered in dry weather until they are established and growing.

PLANTING

Fork over the top 6 inches (15 cm) of soil, breaking down any lumps and removing all weeds. Add compost as a general soil conditioner. Thoroughly water the plant in its container well before planting, or if it is bare-rooted, soak the roots for approximately 15 minutes in a bucket.

1 *Dig a hole slightly larger than the container. Loosen the soil at the bottom of the hole; if dry, pour water into the hole and allow it to soak away. Remove the plant from the pot and place in the hole.*

2 *Return the soil around the plant and firm down with your hands. Water the plant to consolidate the soil around its roots. Water regularly until established.*

Preparing borders and island beds

Herbaceous borders and island beds are ideal for growing a wide range of plants. Borders are often set against a background of some kind, either natural or humanmade; island beds are normally more central and usually surrounded by grass.

Siting As far as possible borders should be sited in full sun, although there is no reason why your border should not be in the shade to show off woodland and woodland-edge plants. Suitable backgrounds include a wall, fence, or hedge; and for a more ecological planting, a wild hedgerow, shrubs, or trees. When choosing a new site, make sure that the soil drainage is good. Poor drainage restricts the range of plants that will thrive. Many herbs will not survive having wet roots, especially over the winter when they are dormant. On heavy soils consider putting in a drainage system.

A bed that is too wide can be difficult to maintain and is complicated to plant, so always tend toward a narrower rather than a wider design. An asymmetrical border or island bed is often effective, especially for more natural plantings, providing its design is simple.

Use a garden hose or rope to outline the area. Then mark the shape directly on the grass using sand or whitewash.

Soil preparation If you are cutting out a bed from an existing lawn, first remove all the turf by dividing it into manageable pieces and then lifting them up with a sharp spade. If the turfs are not required elsewhere, stack them grass-side down in a neat heap and let them rot. Removing the turf removes most of the weed seeds.

Dig heavy soil or fork over if it is light, and remove all perennial weeds. Whenever soil is turned over, weed seeds are brought to the top; see page 43 for methods to combat weeds.

Incorporate some garden compost (see page 22), if available, in order to provide a balanced slow-release source of nutrients. An alternative is a general organic fertilizer; seaweed meal is suitable but may be expensive, and spent mushroom compost (preferably organic) makes an excellent conditioner but is low in nutrients. Apply fertilizers when the soil is warming up in spring.

Preparing an open, dry area

Certain garden features, such as rock gardens and gravel beds and even walls, can provide open, dry habitats (see pages 62–5).

Siting Paths made from bricks, stones, or concrete slabs, bedded on a layer of sand, are ideal locations for some herbs, provided the foundations allow for sharp drainage. Low-growing and carpeting herbs, such as creeping thymes and chamomile, do well here. If you have little space, a stone sink or small trough is perfect for a miniature rock garden. Where drainage is poor, you can construct a raised bed with walls of brick, stone, or logs, 1–2 feet (30–60 cm) high.

Soil preparation After any new construction allow the soil to settle for at least a week before you begin to plant. Break up any large lumps of earth and make sure that there are no air pockets without soil around the rocks. If the soil is dry, water the area to be planted and the herbs, at least a few hours before planting. To prepare a raised bed, fork over the soil at the base of the bed to assist drainage, then cover it with 6 inches (15 cm) of stones and rubble. Finally, fill to the top of the walls with a rock-garden soil mix of loam, sharp sand, and grit.

Planting The most suitable seasons to plant herbs in a rock garden, or dry area, are in spring or from late summer to early fall.

Rock garden ABOVE
This rock garden has only recently been planted. Note how the plants have been spaced out and planted to take account of their habits and growth.

An established rock garden ABOVE
Rock garden plants quickly spread over the rocks. Cover the soil with small stones or gravel to retain moisture and keep weeds down.

PLANTING IN A ROCK GARDEN

Planting in the rock or dry garden is normally done in late summer or early fall. In areas that have hard or wet winters, however, late spring is preferable as this allows the plants time to establish well before winter sets in. Follow these planting instructions for rock, gravel, or scree gardens, a rocky outcrop, or a raised bed.

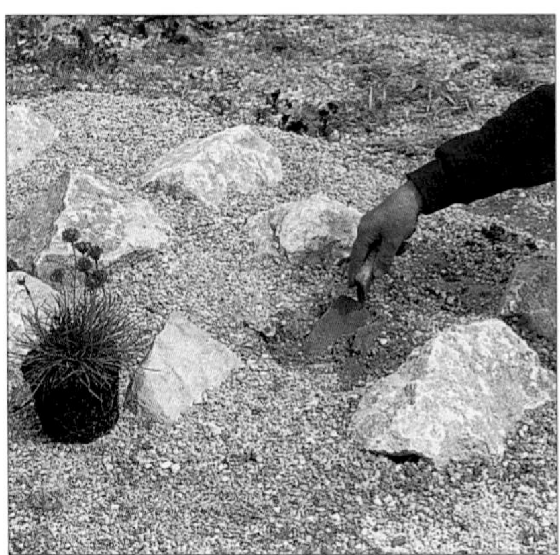

1 *Dig a hole slightly larger than the plant. Loosen the earth at the base to allow the root system to establish quickly and to improve drainage.*

2 *If the soil is dry, fill the hole with water and allow to drain away. Place the plant in the hole to the same depth as in the container.*

3 *Fill the soil in around the plant and firm down with your hands. Using a fine rose, water the plant well. Cover the soil with gravel or stones.*

Before finalizing your planting scheme, place new plants, still in their containers, in their approximate positions. Try to imagine how they will look when they are mature – how tall and wide they will grow. Remember that some plants will grow up between the rocks and others will naturally cascade over them. Also consider the effects of color and foliage (see pages 76–7).

PLANTING IN A WALL

Choose small plants so there is minimal root disturbance and plant them in the wall in cool, wet weather to give the roots a chance to establish in this difficult environment.

1 *Use soil with some clay content that is not too dry and crumbly. Push enough soil into the wall crevice to enable the plant roots to establish.*

2 *Place your plant upright in the wall crevice. Press more soil around it firmly, so that it is held securely; make sure the roots are fully covered.*

Seeding into dry areas Where planting into walls and between rocks in rock gardens is difficult, direct seeding of herbs such as wild wallflower, ivy-leaved toadflax, and sedums is the answer. Drop or firm soil into crevices and press or sprinkle a few seeds into it. Seed gaps in stone or brick paths in a similar way with creeping thymes and chamomile. Regularly water herbs growing in walls until they have developed strong root systems to search out moisture and nutrients.

Preparing a pond and wetland area

Water features can range in size from a small wooden barrel to a large natural pond. No garden is too small for a pond or wetland area of some sort.

Siting a pond Before creating a water garden, decide what you want to achieve. Do you want a natural pond blended with other landscape features, or do you prefer a formal structure with a hard surface surround possibly near the house or patio? However small it is you should always relate it to other garden habitats. Ponds associate well with a boggy area, rock features, woodland edge, and wild areas. In a formal setting, a pond can be incorporated into a paved area near the house and bog plants grown in containers around the edge.

PLANTING IN A POND

In a small pond put plants in a special pond basket to prevent them from taking up too much space. In a larger pond plant this marsh marigold out of its basket directly into the pond mud and allow it to spread.

1 *Select an appropriate area at the pond edge where the water will remain shallow, and where there is enough space for the plant to spread as it grows.*

2 *Press the plant basket into the pond bottom. Make sure the plant is upright and stable. The plant will quickly root itself through the holes in the basket.*

Construction Decide whether the pond is to be naturally constructed with either a puddled clay bottom (trampled smooth and compact when wet) or lined with a flexible plastic liner, or whether a rigid plastic mold sunk into the ground is more appropriate. Unless you are using a rigid mold, the shape of your pond can be first marked out on the ground with a hose or rope.

In all but the smallest ponds the depth should range from shallow to deep so that plants requiring different levels of water can be accommodated. Generally you will need a shelf about 4 inches (10 cm) deep, with a second shelf about 9 inches (22 cm) deep. Varying depths can also be obtained by including a gently sloping side.

The base of the pond should be covered with an inch or two of damp sand and a liner of butyl rubber or plastic laid on top. Soil is not normally used in a small pond and is not required if plants are kept in planting baskets. If you are planting directly into the soil add a layer of up to 6 inches (15 cm) of clay/loam soil depending on the size of the pond. In smaller ponds this can be topped with a 1 inch (2.5 cm) layer of gravel.

If possible, include an area of marshy ground. Extend the pond liner into a shallow depression filled with soil. Puncture the liner to allow slow drainage so that the soil remains firm but moist.

Siting a wetland area Normally a wetland or boggy area is sited adjacent to a pond, although you can create a suitable area elsewhere, as described above, by using a dripping hose to keep the soil moist. A wetland area would associate well with a wild meadow or an area of trees and shrubs. Other areas that can provide effective wetland are ditches and stream margins.

Pond plants These can be grown either in baskets, which will prevent them spreading and is by far the best method for small ponds, or in a layer of planting soil spread over the bottom of the pond. If the latter method is used, avoid plants that spread too rapidly and constantly have to be thinned out.

PLANTING IN A WETLAND AREA

Yellow flag and cardinal flower are plants that grow along pond margins and in wet meadows and are ideally suited to any ground that retains moisture through the dry months of the year. A good time for planting is in summer when the water level is low but moisture is still available. Make sure that the plants are in moist compost before planting.

1 *Select a suitable site and space plants to allow room for them to spread. Dig a hole slightly larger than the plant. It will probably fill with water.*

2 *Make sure the plant is in damp compost or water it well before planting. Then carefully remove it from its container.*

3 *Place the plant in the hole you have prepared, ensuring it is planted at the same depth as it was in the pot.*

4 *Gently fill in the hole around the plant with damp soil and then press the surface firmly.*

Preparing and planting a shaded area

A shady habitat will already occur in a well-established area of the garden where shade is cast by mature trees and shrubs, or in an area on the shady side of the house or against a wall or fence.

Siting The best way to create a shady habitat is to plant suitable trees. Choose trees that are decorative and grow to an appropriate size for the garden. Often a single tree will provide enough shade and a simple planting underneath can look charming. For woodland planting, select deep-rooting trees that do not rob the upper soil of nutrients and moisture. Avoid shallow-rooting trees such as birch, poplar, willows, and false acacia, as most plants will not do well near them.

Soil preparation An established area is more like a natural woodland or woodland edge where shade is heavy in summer and lighter in winter. Over the years fallen leaves will have formed a nutrient-rich soil that requires no digging, topped by a leaf layer that keeps the soil relatively free of weeds. These areas need little preparation except for the removal of any weeds. Woodland-type soil with layers of humus should be left uncultivated.

Any other area that is to be planted with shade-loving plants (see pages 53 and 57 for lists of suitable herbs) should be prepared if possible with well-rotted leaf mold or spent mushroom compost, which should be worked into the top 6 inches (15 cm) of soil, together with seaweed meal or a general fertilizer that is low in nitrogen.

PLANTING A SMALL TREE OR SHRUB

This narrow-leaved bay is to be planted in an area that is partially shaded by trees. Always water the plant in its container before planting.

1 *Dig a hole a few inches larger and deeper than the size of the container. Fork over the base of the hole to aid root penetration and drainage.*

2 *Add a sprinkling of bonemeal to the bottom of the hole. If the ground is dry, fill the hole with water and wait for it to drain away.*

3 *Tip the tree out of the container and plant it, making sure the stem is at the same level in the ground as it was in the pot. Fill in the soil around the root ball.*

4 *Use your feet to firm down the soil, then water well. If the area is very dry, regular watering will be required for several weeks until the tree is established.*

Preparing a partially shaded area

Light or partial shade is ideal for many herbs that enjoy a "woodland edge" habitat including ground-cover plants and many attractive climbers. Many woodland species that tolerate full shade will also grow well in these conditions provided they are shaded from the hot midday sun.

Siting Most gardens have an area of partial shade under or near lightly foliaged trees, shrubs, or hedges or provided by walls and fences that cast shade for part of the day. Even a single tree will provide dappled shade. Additional areas of partial shade can be created by further planting of trees, hedges, and suitable shrubs.

Soil preparation Woodland-edge plants enjoy an undisturbed soil that is covered every fall in leaf litter. Leaf litter adds nutrients and humus, making a loose, friable soil. When creating a new area of partial shade that does not have the benefit of annual leaf fall, add plenty of organic material – particularly leaf mold – and work it into the top 6 inches (15 cm) of soil. Add an annual mulch of leaf mold or bark chips.

Planting a hedge A hedge provides shade in varying amounts, and is an excellent windbreak that provides nesting and shelter for birds.

Hedges should be planted in the fall or in winter in mild areas. Add to an existing hedge when the ground is moist. Container-grown plants can, in theory, be planted at any time, but if they are bare-rooted (much less expensive) they should be planted when dormant. Plant them the correct distance apart (ask your supplier for advice).

Mark the hedge line with string stretched between two stakes. Dig a trench 1–2 feet (30–60cm) deep and 2 feet (60 cm) wide. Fork the base over to improve drainage and assist root penetration, add 3 inches (7.5 cm) of well-rotted compost or manure, a layer of soil, and sprinkle with bonemeal. Leave for about a week before planting. Water container-grown plants or soak the roots of bare-rooted plants in tepid water for 15 minutes before planting. As you plant, spread the roots and fill in with topsoil. Water well.

PLANTING A NATURAL HEDGE

Sweetbrier makes a dense and decorative hedging plant that bears flowers in early summer and brilliant hips in the fall. This sweetbrier will eventually grow into a substantial plant and become part of the wild hedgerow.

1 *Water the container well. Dig a hole close to the hedge. Make it a little larger and deeper than the size of the container.*

2 *Fork over the base of the hole to aid root penetration and drainage. Add a sprinkling of bonemeal. If the soil is dry, fill the hole with water and allow it to drain away.*

3 *Tip the plant out of the container and place it in the hole. Fill in the soil around the roots and firm down with your feet. Water well.*

A sweetbrier hedge RIGHT
Sweetbrier rose, like several other rose species, makes a decorative and impenetrable hedge. Roses can either be planted as a hedge on their own or integrated into a mixed hedge of other suitable shrubs.

Protecting Plants

AREAS PROTECTED by glass, plastic, or netting provide a sheltered environment in which to grow plants. These include greenhouses, conservatories, tunnels, cold frames, and cloches; all have advantages for growing herbs. As well as offering protection they all extend the growing season for many herbs. Tender herbs can be grown year-round, winter protection provided for half-hardy herbs, and young seedlings and plants sheltered in the spring.

Greenhouses and conservatories In a greenhouse or conservatory, heat and light can be regulated, enabling plants that cannot withstand frost and cold temperatures to be grown all year round or to be protected overwinter.

A conservatory has the advantage of being attached to an already warm house. Tender herbs from all over the world can be grown here including lemon verbena, pineapple sage, and the full range of scented-leaved pelargoniums. Grow aromatic culinary herbs in pots such as sweet bay, oregano, parsley, sage, and thyme. Over the summer, basil will thrive here.

Seed sowing and propagating are often done in a greenhouse, where the temperature can be controlled and, for cuttings, humidity can be provided. If tender plants are to be kept in the greenhouse over the winter, consider some form of insulation to save on heating. Shade is easily provided by spraying the glass with white shading wash or by installing blinds to pull down if the summer sun is too hot.

A heated sand bench in your greenhouse on which to place seed trays (flats) of seeds requiring bottom heat for germination is invaluable. It is also worth installing a small mist unit for cuttings. Although this might seem rather sophisticated, it does mean that a much wider range of cuttings can be rooted far more quickly and with greater success.

A conservatory ABOVE
A conservatory provides warmth and protection for many tender herbs, such as scented-leaved pelargoniums, lemon verbena, and basil. They all grow well in containers.

Tunnels A tunnel made up of a series of metal hoops and covered tightly with clear plastic provides the perfect climate for growing many perennial and annual herbs but will keep out only a light frost and is therefore not suitable for overwintering frost-sensitive plants.

At only a fraction of the cost of a greenhouse of similar capacity, tunnels are readily available from good garden centers and home stores.

A tunnel is ideal for growing healthy herbs and vegetables. Apart from those that are frost tender, herbs can be grown all the year round in most areas. In a particularly severe climate, the growing season can be greatly extended. In areas with very hot summers, shade and controlled irrigation are easy to provide.

Annual herbs that thrive in a tunnel include dill, coriander (cilantro), and basil. Perennial herbs from Mediterranean climates, such as lavender and rosemary, that might not survive outside in winter, also flourish. They enjoy the comparative warmth and freedom from icy winds and need the drier soil conditions that a tunnel provides.

Cold frames Small frames are like mini greenhouses and are indispensable for starting seeds and for protecting seedlings and any plants that are not completely hardy. Seedlings and plants can be transferred into a frame from a heated greenhouse for hardening off before being planted into their permanent sites in the garden. Frames also protect plants from birds and other pests. Once the weather warms up in spring, the frame can be left open in the day and closed at night and later kept open all the time. If birds are a problem, netting can be draped over the open frame; this also gives the plants some shade.

The cold frame ABOVE
Cold frames or similar constructions have long been used by gardeners to protect plants and seedlings from the weather and pests. Seedlings can be started earlier in a cold frame than outside and hardened off before planting.

Cloches These are of great benefit for early crops and bird protection. Cloches are portable and can be positioned over plants or seedlings growing in the soil or constructed before seeding or planting. This enables seedlings, such as coriander (cilantro), dill, and summer savory, to be given an early start with protection from pests and the extremes of spring weather. Cloches give hardy herb crops, such as parsley, shelter from cold winds and heavy rain well into the fall. Rigid cloches, often in attractive designs, are available for covering individual plants.

Overwintering

In early fall tender and half-hardy herbs should be prepared for overwintering in the greenhouse or conservatory, and hardy culinary herbs may be brought in to provide fresh leaf over winter and early spring. During winter when plants are growing in enclosed conditions they are much more susceptible to disease. Make sure that your plants remain healthy by cutting off dead flowers, leaves, and branches and by spacing them well apart. Watering during winter should be sparse and plants must never be permanently wet. On sunny and frost-free days, open windows to allow air to circulate freely.

THE CLOCHE

Cloches come in many forms, some homemade. This tunnel cloche, which can be bought as a simple kit, has long-lasting plastic ribs and a clear plastic cover that is stretched over it and anchored at both ends. Netting is also provided for shade or bird protection.

Closed cover ABOVE
At night and in bad weather, the cloche is closed to provide protection from cold winds, light frost, heavy rain, and pests, such as rabbits.

Open cover ABOVE
On fine days, the cover is lifted to allow air to circulate and to stop excessive heat building up. The atmosphere inside a cloche quickly becomes humid on warm days.

Caring for Herbs

GOOD GARDENING PRACTICE and a healthy soil are the key elements for producing healthy plants. Plants can be damaged or destroyed by pests and diseases, so it is important to keep an eye on your herbs for the first signs of trouble and treat any problems as soon as they occur. Plants are more likely to succumb to disease if they are under stress from lack of moisture or nutrients.

Good gardening practice

The health of plants can be affected by many environmental factors, chief among them being soil moisture (either too wet or too dry), availability of nutrients including minerals and trace elements, temperature and humidity, rainfall, and wind. All these can be controlled to some degree in a garden situation by providing shelter and protection from: rain, wind, frost, cold temperatures, and hot sun, by adding nutrients to the soil, and by spacing plants so that sufficient air can circulate around them. See "Gardening Checklist" on page 44 for general maintenance tips. Make sure your plants are growing in a suitable environment, see chapter 2 "Habitats in the Garden."

Companion planting

Over many centuries it has been observed that some plants appear to promote the growth of others and some may protect those growing nearby from insect attack or disease. The deliberate positioning of such plants near each other in the garden is known as companion planting.

French marigold with tomatoes ABOVE
The strongly scented French marigold produces root secretions that deter whitefly. It is probable that the root secretions are taken up by the tomato plants, thus making their foliage unpalatable to pests.

Features of companion plants

- Taller plants, sometimes with large leaves, provide shade for other plants and shelter from winds, and may create a mini environment.
- Deep-rooting herbs bring up valuable minerals from the subsoil that are made available to other plants when their leaves and stems rot down into the topsoil.
- The flowers of many herbs attract pollinating insects, especially essential for fruit trees.
- Some plants attract beneficial insects, such as hover flies, into the garden where their larvae consume large quantities of aphids.
- Ground-cover plants are excellent companions of clematis and other plants that require a moist root run. They keep the soil cool and prevent it from drying out.

BENEFITS OF COMPANION PLANTS

The herbs listed below are a selection of those plants that have beneficial properties, especially in the vegetable patch, attracting or deterring pests and disease.

Allium schoenoprasum Chives	Deters carrot rootfly, helps prevent black spot on roses and scab on apples.
Anthemis Chamomile	Improves health, yield, and flowers of other plants and attracts beneficial hover flies.
Hyssopus Hyssop	Attracts bees, generally beneficial to grapevines and helps repel cabbage white butterfly.
Origanum Marjoram	Attracts bees and is a good companion in the vegetable garden.
Salvia Sage	Repels cabbage white butterfly, generally beneficial to vegetables.
Tagetes minuta Mexican marigold	Chokes weeds, discourages wireworms and millepedes, kills eelworms and attracts hover flies.
Thymus Thyme	Attracts bees, strongly scented foliage stimulates other plants.
Tropaeolum Nasturtium	Deters aphids, especially whitefly, squash bugs, woolly aphids, attracts blackfly to itself.

Pests and diseases

Although there are many chemical preparations available for combating every sort of pest and disease, many people now prefer to use natural methods. Poison chemical sprays can completely upset the balance of the garden and may kill off useful predators along with the pests.

Controlling diseases You can limit the chance of disease in your garden by growing healthy plants, removing pests, and making regular checks on plants as they grow. Many diseases can be controlled by removal of the infected part. If the whole plant is affected dig it out and destroy it. Where mint rust (see below) is persistent, cleanse mint beds at the end of the season by setting fire to straw piled on the beds; this kills the spores. Never put diseased plant material on the compost heap; it is usually best burned to prevent the problem spreading to other plants. Avoid over crowding and over watering plants, and clear away any debris.

Controlling pests Of the many plant pests, the most common ones, likely to be in every garden, are aphids and slugs. Aphids in particular are to be discouraged, as they can spread virus diseases between plants. Spray them with a solution of soft soap or use a pyrethrum spray, which is also very effective but is not selective. Spray in the evening when bees and other beneficial insects have stopped flying. Pyrethrum is harmless to humans and animals and is nonpersistent. Encourage predators, such as hover flies, that feed on pests (see companion plants opposite).

Seedlings and young plants are most vulnerable to slugs. There are many traditional methods of disposing of slugs: collect them by hand after dark with a flashlight; sink an open can of beer upright in the soil – they will crawl in; surround specific plants with sharp grit or gravel, which will deter them. Warning: regular slug bait is highly poisonous to animals and birds; a completely safe alternative is widely available.

COMMON PESTS AND DISEASES

Symptoms of diseased or infested plants often include distorted and discolored leaves. Be vigilant; treatment is always most effective at the start of the problem. Seedlings may die from damping off, a common fungal disease, which results in yellow leaves and blackened stems and is caused by over crowding, over watering, and poor ventilation. Remove diseased seedlings immediately. Below are some of the common pests and diseases that may affect your herbs.

Leaf scale
Tiny waxy scales on back of leaves and on leaf ribs. Remove by rubbing before insects emerge in summer. A common problem of bay trees, especially in a greenhouse.

Powdery mildew
Shows on the leaves as powdery white patches. Plants are susceptible when roots are dry and there is poor air circulation. Remove infected leaves and spray with sulfur.

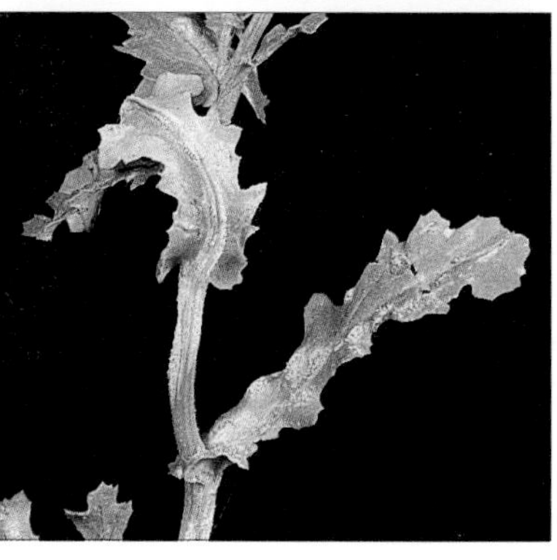

Rust
Red or rust-brown pustules on leaves and stems. Common in mint. Cut out and burn infected parts or cut plant to the ground. Dispersable sulfur spray may be used safely.

Black spot
A fungal disease that affects rose leaves, causing them to drop off. Spray with dispersable sulfur and burn infected leaves. Grow chives around roses to help prevention.

Wilting or dieback can be caused by pests, such as wireworms and flea beetles and their larvae, which attack the plant roots and sometimes the leaves. Predators, which feed on such pests, include birds, toads, and some beetles. Weed control (see page 43) and clearing of plant debris are essential for control. Grow wormwood as a companion plant to discourage flea beetles.

Encouraging predators One of the most effective ways of controlling pests is to encourage predators that feed on them. You can do this by selecting plants that will attract predators into the garden. Pot marigold and French marigold for example, attract beneficial insects, including hover flies that live on aphids. Gardens with suitable habitats, such as wooded areas and ponds, encourage frogs, hedgehogs, toads, and birds that devour slugs and insects. Ladybirds consume large quantities of aphids.

There are now biological controls available to the gardener. For example, in greenhouses or tunnels whitefly can be rapidly controlled by the introduction of a tiny wasp (*Encarsia formosa*). Lemon verbena is prone to infestation by red spider mite that can also be controlled biologically by a predatory mite (*Phytoseiulus persimilis*).

MAINTENANCE

Regular maintenance throughout the year, such as trimming and weed control, is important for keeping the garden looking tidy and ensures that plants are growing in a healthy environment. The "Gardening Checklist" on page 44 gives a summary of the different tasks you need to carry out in order to grow herbs successfully.

Trimming

Regular cutting down and trimming keeps woody herbs looking good for years and prevents herbaceous plants from becoming straggly. Most plants that have become untidy or unruly can be cut back or trimmed. Use a sharp pair of garden scissors or pruners (secateurs). Sharp is the key word, as stems damaged by blunt blades are more likely to become diseased.

Trim plants after they have finished flowering. Remove all the flowering stems unless you plan to collect the seeds or dry the seed heads for use in flower arrangements (see pages 45–7), in which case leave some stems to mature on the plant. Trim shrubs lightly after flowering; harder pruning can take place in spring. If santolina is being used as a hedge, it should be trimmed about three times a year to keep it a neat shape.

TRIMMING

Trimming of both woody and nonwoody herbs is best done when flowering is over and before the plants set seed. Trimming back herbaceous plants often encourages them to flower again later in the season. Trimming of woody shrubs like lavender and santolina encourages new growth and gives them a neat shape.

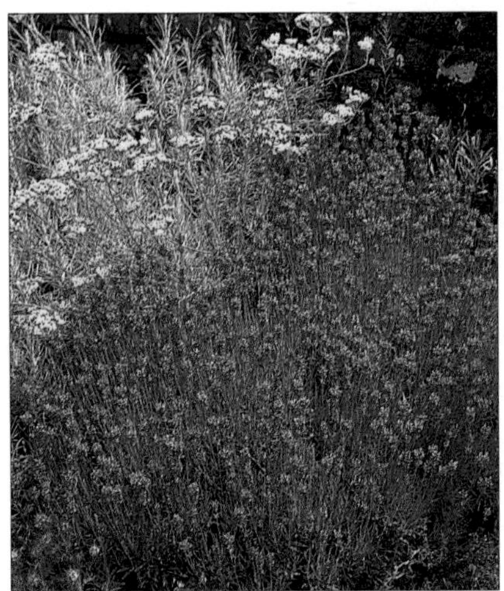

1 *Summer trimming is done to tidy up the plant after flowering or, in the case of this lavender, to harvest the flower heads for drying.*

2 *Using sharp garden scissors or pruners (secateurs), cut the heads in bunches held in one hand, as shown. Cut every stem back to the main growth of the plant.*

3 *The plant is now a neat bushy shape, ready to put on some new growth before the winter.*

Cutting back

Shrubby herbs should be cut back in spring to keep them bushy. Lavender, for example, should be cut back in midspring and pruned into the last season's growth by an inch or so. Annual cutting back of shrubs prevents them from becoming straggly with a lot of bare wood. A very misshapen plant is usually best replaced, although pruning back into the old wood might revive it. Santolina can be pruned much harder in the spring, to within a few inches of the ground. Rosemary is best left to grow to its natural size and shape, although it can be lightly trimmed after flowering to maintain a good shape; it will not withstand hard pruning.

Herbaceous plants Some herbaceous plants that flower in early summer, such as catmint, will bloom again in fall if cut back hard after the first flowering. Other early-flowering plants can be easily persuaded to bloom later in the season if they are cut back when their flower buds are forming. Some biennial herbs can be saved for another season if they are cut back before they flower or seed.

Controlling weeds

Weed control is necessary for maintaining healthy plants. Weeds use up essential nutrients and water and may also harbor pests and diseases (see page 41). Even after careful cultivation, the soil is full of weed and grass seeds waiting to germinate. After cultivation, wait several weeks, if possible, for weed seedlings to emerge, then hoe them out. Do not cultivate or turn over the soil again, as more weed seeds will be brought to the surface.

Weeds will inevitably appear among plantings. They should be pulled out at an early stage of growth. If herbs are being allowed to self-seed, selective weeding will be required. The creeping roots of weeds, such as bindweed, creeping thistle, and quack grass, must be dug out with a fork before affected soils are rotovated or tilled. Alternatively kill the weeds with an herbicide.

An effective alternative to cultivation is covering the area of soil with a sheet of black plastic. Leave the sheet down for several months if possible – over the winter is a good time. When it is removed, most weeds will have died and the roots of the creeping invasive varieties will have spread around under it, so that they are easy to see and fork out. The soil underneath will be loose and easy to cultivate. See also "Mulches" page 23, which among other benefits, also suppress weeds.

CUTTING BACK

Unless kept in good shape by annual light pruning, most shrubby herbs require reasonably hard cutting back every two or three years to retain a good shape and prevent tall, woody growth. Do this in spring when new growth is just starting. Cut back up to three-quarters of the last season's growth.

1 *Although it appears healthy from one angle, this santolina has been neglected and has become woody and lopsided.*

2 *Cutting back hard will encourage the plant to put on new growth from the base and regain a regular form.*

3 *Mulch with compost. Although the plant now looks unsightly, it will quickly grow back into a good shape with fresh foliage.*

4 *Later in the season the plant has produced plenty of new growth. This can be kept in shape with light but regular annual trimming.*

MAINTAINING A TIDY GARDEN

To keep your shrubby herbs looking good over the winter, get rid of straggly growth once flowering is over. This keeps the plants a neat shape.

Straggly growth ABOVE
In late summer shrubby herbs, such as santolina, lavender, artemisia, and marjoram above, have finished flowering and look untidy.

A neat shape ABOVE
The same plants have been trimmed to a neat and compact shape. The plants will put on some new growth before the onset of winter.

GARDENING CHECKLIST

Outlined below is a summary of the main points to bear in mind to help you grow and maintain healthy herbs through the season.

Sowing Sow seeds of annuals and perennials in spring. In milder climates, without deep winter frost, perennials can be sown in late summer or early fall and will often overwinter as seedlings. Seeds that require stratification should be sown in late summer or fall. Sow biennials in early summer to flower the following year (see pages 24–6).

Transplanting Transplant seedlings grown in trays once they are large enough to handle. Plant into individual pots and allow to establish. Harden off seedlings before planting into permanent sites (see page 26).

Planting Water the plant well. Dig a hole more than large enough for its roots and deep enough to bring it to the same level in the ground as it was in the pot. Fill in the soil around the roots. Firm it down and water well (see pages 31–2).

Watering Water seedlings to keep them moist but do not overwater. Provide newly planted herbs with plenty of water until they are well established, particularly in dry weather. Water early in the day. Over or under watering will adversely affect your plants. If watering is necessary soak the soil thoroughly to make sure moisture reaches the roots. Allow the soil to become dry before watering again.

Feeding Herbs that are planted into a well-prepared site should not need subsequent feeding except on poor soils for the first few years; incorporate garden compost or natural fertilizer into the soil before-hand. Mulch annually if necessary. Spray with a foliar feed if you suspect nutritional deficiencies (see pages 21–3).

Weeding Hoe or pull out weeds as they appear – avoid digging the soil as this turns up new weed seeds and allows moisture to escape. Deeper rooting weeds need to be dug out individually or killed with an herbicide (see page 43).

Trimming After flowering and before the plant sets seed, trim with sharp scissors or pruners to keep woody or herbaceous plants tidy. Cut back flowered stems to the main growth, leaving some stems for seed development if you want to collect seeds (see page 42).

Cutting back and pruning As growth starts in spring, remove up to three quarters of the previous season's growth on shrubby herbs that have become straggly or untidy. Do a light prune every year and a harder one every two or three years (see page 43).

Controlling pests Early and regular control of common pests and diseases prevents them from causing widespread damage. Encourage natural predators and keep plants healthy with good gardening practice (see pages 40–2).

Harvesting Collect ripe seed, clean it, and dry thoroughly before storing it clearly labeled in a cool, dry, dark place. Pick healthy foliage and flowers early in the day for drying, preserving in oil, or freezing (see pages 45–7).

The Herb Harvest

HERBS ARE VERSATILE plants and have many practical applications. Both fresh and dried herbs are valued for their culinary and medicinal properties; dried herbs are a major ingredient of potpourri and make wonderful flower arrangements. Herb seed heads can be used in winter arrangements, and their seed collected to produce new plants for the spring.

Seed collection and storage

Collecting one's own seed is very satisfying and quickly becomes an obsession. The advantages of collecting your own seeds are many: fresh seed will be of the best quality, and you can select which plants to collect from.

It is usually obvious when seeds are ripe because the seeds or the seed capsules turn brown and dry. In order to collect seed, you should be familiar with the different types of seed heads and their methods of dispersal. The plant family often gives an indication of how the seed is held on the plant and how it is distributed. The families listed below are some of the most common, showing a variety of different seed heads and methods of collection. These methods can be applied to other plants that have similar seed heads:

- **Borage family** (Boraginaceae) Seeds resemble small black nuts that ripen over a long period of time, one at a time making collection difficult. Lay a sheet of muslin under the plant to collect the seed as it drops.
- **Carrot family** (Umbelliferae) Seeds are held on a flat head and will stay on the head for some time. Cut off the heads when ripe and shake or rub into a bag or bucket.
- **Cranesbill family** (Geraniaceae) A catapult mechanism ejects the ripe seeds. Seed heads must be collected just before ripening and kept in a bucket covered in muslin until seed is released.
- **Daisy family** (Compositae) Seeds are often held on an open head and frequently have a pappus or feathery hairs attached to aid dispersal by wind. Collect heads before seed disperses and shake off into a container.
- **Pea family** (Leguminosae) Many members of this family hold their round seeds in a pealike pod. When the pod is dry and crisp (ripe), it splits and ejects the seeds. Collect pods when ripe but before they have opened.
- **Poppy family** (Papaveraceae) Poppies hold their tiny seeds in hard, often decorative, capsules at

RELEASING SEEDS

Many seeds can easily be released from their heads or capsules by simply shaking them out onto a flat surface like a tray or straight into a paper bag.

Soft seed capsule
Hollyhock seed is held in a hairy, brown, circular capsule that opens when the seed is ripe. The flat circular seeds drop out in great profusion.

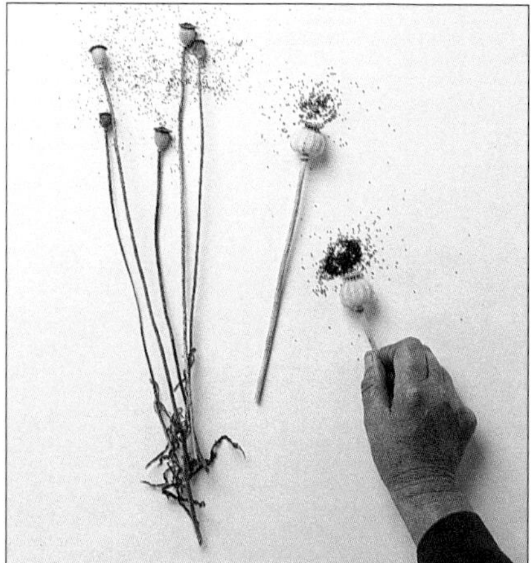

Hard seed capsule
Poppy seed is produced in a rigid brown capsule that develops holes in the top when ripe. The thousands of tiny clean seeds can be shaken out.

Seed pod
The seeds of larkspur are held in an elongated pod that splits after ripening. Pick the ripened pods just before they open.

the top of the flower stem. When ripe the capsule develops small holes in the top and the seed will rattle inside. To collect just shake the seed into a container.

- **Mint family** (Labiatae) Seed is often dustlike and ripens all at once. Wait until the flower head turns brown and rub the head to see if the seed is ready to drop out.
- **Primrose family** (Primulaceae) Seed is held in a seed case and remains inside until ripe. When case is brown and ripe shake out the seed.

Collected seed is often full of debris and, if small, needs to be cleaned (see below). After cleaning, dry the seed on a tray or lid in a warm room for a few days. It is now ready for storing until it is needed. Put it in clearly labeled paper packets or envelopes. For short-term storage these can be kept somewhere dry and dark like a desk drawer or a cookie tin, but they must be cool. For longer-term storage, over several years, seed can be kept in a sealed plastic container in the refrigerator (not the freezer). Seed for culinary use needs to be completely clean and free of debris.

Preserving herbs

There are various methods of preserving herbs. For culinary or medicinal use, or for potpourri and dried flower arrangements, drying is often the most suitable method.

CUTTING SEED HEADS

Cut ripe seed heads just below the head and put into a paper bag. Some seeds disperse the moment they ripen; cut a long stem just before they are fully ripe, and hang up with a bag tied over the head to catch the seed.

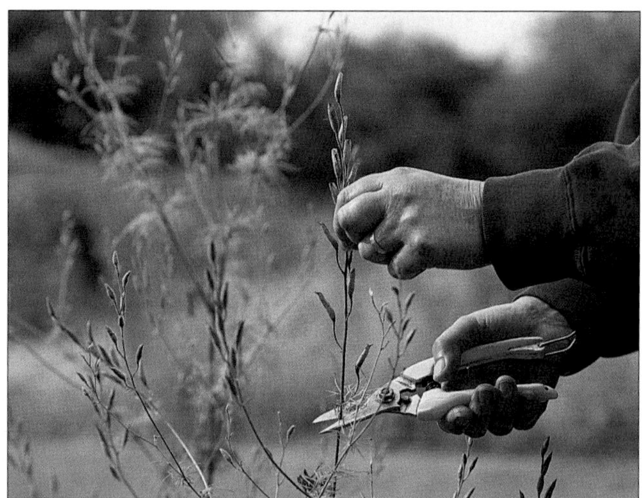

Collecting larkspur seeds ABOVE
Cut the stem below the ripening seed pods with pruners (secateurs). Carefully remove to dry further until the dried pods open.

Drying Herbs that are dried correctly retain their flavor, color, and healing properties. Successful herb drying requires warmth, air flow, and shade.

CLEANING AND STORING SEEDS

If seeds are to be collected and stored for use next season, they need to be reasonably free of debris. Many seed heads, such as those of lavender below, are cut on their stems and are ready for cleaning. It is most important to make sure that the seed is absolutely dry before storing.
Warning: *Asthma sufferers and those sensitive to dust should not clean seed. For others a simple face mask can be worn to protect from dust.*

1 *Remove the dried heads from the stems by rubbing between the hands. Pick out the stems, leaves, and larger pieces of debris.*

2 *Rub or shake the seed through a coarse sieve. Sieve through a finer mesh to clean the seed further.*

3 *Gentle blowing on a tin tray will remove any remaining dust. The seed is now ready for packing in a bag or envelope.*

4 *Label with the common name, the Latin name, and the date and store in a cool, dark, dry place.*

Leaves of herbs can be picked for drying at any time. Harvest them when there is plentiful healthy foliage, preferably before the plant flowers, before the heat of the day but after the dew has dried. They are best left on the stalk. After harvesting, remove them from direct sunlight, as this bleaches them and evaporates the essential oils. Divide and tie the stems into small bunches to hang upside down in a warm, dark, and airy place.

Dry herbs as quickly as possible – a temperature of 75–80°F (24–26°C) is ideal. Suitable places are a warm closet with good ventilation, a heated room with drawn curtains, a cool oven with the door left ajar, or in the microwave.

Drying time will vary. When dry, the leaves should still have a good fresh color and feel crisp. Rub them off the stem, keeping them whole if possible, and store in dark glass bottles or jars; for the shorter term they can be put in brown paper bags. Label and date the containers.

Flower heads gathered for decoration and flowers used for coloring and seasoning in cooking can also be dried in this way. The roots of medicinal herbs can be preserved by drying and should be collected at the end of the growing season when they contain maximum nutrients. Wash them thoroughly in cold water, then dry in an oven at approximately 120°F (50°C). Bark and roots should be dry enough to snap and must be stored in airtight containers.

Drying herbs ABOVE
Hang herbs in small bunches in a warm airy room, out of bright light. Hang bunches from a string suspended from the ceiling. When the leaves are crisp, rub them off the stalk and seal in a screw-top jar or store in a paper bag.

Other methods Herbs that do not dry well, or lose their flavor when dried, are best frozen or preserved in oil. Especially recommended for freezing are basil, tarragon, fennel, chervil, parsley, and chives; these can be stored in the freezer in sealed and labeled plastic bags. Chopped leaves and small flowers can also be preserved in ice cubes and look lovely if used in summer drinks.

DRIED SEED HEADS

Many herbs have decorative seed heads that can be dried to use in winter flower arrangements. (See page 184 for a list of suitable herbs.) Some herbs can be cut when in full flower and retain their color when dried. The selection of seed heads shown below illustrates a range of shapes and textures. Dry the picked stems in bunches as described above.

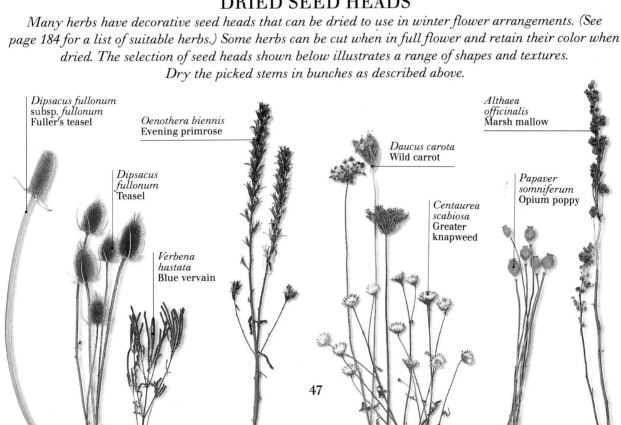

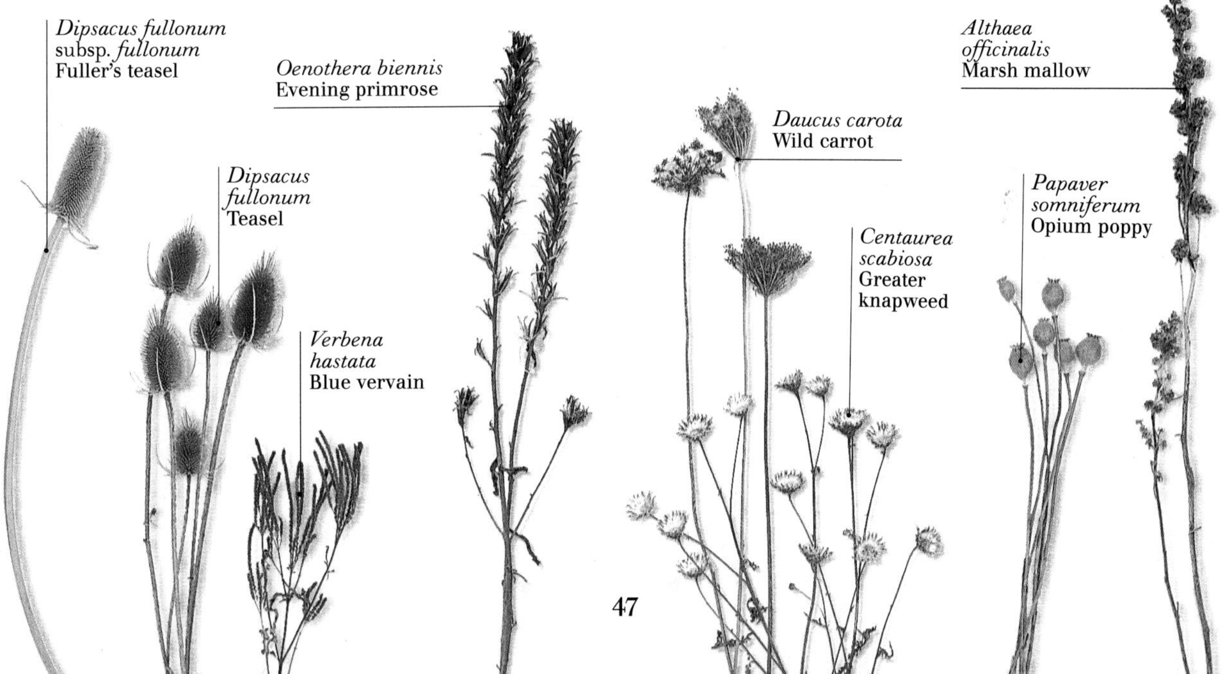

Habitats in the Garden

DIVIDING THE GARDEN into habitats and matching suitable plants to them is an ecological approach to growing herbs. In the wild, each plant flourishes in its own particular situation, which can often be found in the garden. In the right environment plants will flourish and require a minimum amount of maintenance. This chapter shows the gardener how to make full use of existing conditions in the garden and suggests new areas appropriate for specific groups of herbs.

The characteristics of six basic habitats are described, along with the particular traits and demands of the plants that grow there. The appearance of each habitat changes with the seasons; this is described here based upon the general conditions found in temperate zones. Comprehensive lists of herbs are given for growing in each habitat.

Fully Shaded Habitats

IN THE WILD, SHADED habitats are found where woodland has developed and there has been a gradual establishment of plants that enjoy its specific conditions, including the low light levels, sheltered climate, and type of soil. In the garden, shaded areas may exist under trees, but they may also be created by hedges, walls, fences, or the house.

Woods are warmer and more humid than the land outside and are sheltered from cold winds. Moisture levels vary according to the type of soil and underlying rock. Fallen leaves eventually rot to produce a crumbly, nutrient- and humus-rich topsoil. Shaded habitats are also characterized by changing light levels. Maximum light occurs in winter and spring; in summer, the trees produce a dense canopy of foliage that cuts out much of the light. In fall, light levels begin to rise again. Similar conditions can be found in any garden area that is subjected to long periods of shade and changing light levels throughout the year.

Woodland plants are able to tolerate a covering of dead leaves in fall and the low light levels in summer. Growth and flowering are chiefly in winter and spring, before light is excluded. The crumbly, loose topsoil is ideal for low-growing, ground-cover plants. Many woodland plants characteristically die down after seeding in early summer; and often have bulbs or rhizomes, enabling them to lie dormant during periods of unfavorable conditions.

WINTER

Winter is a time of renewal and preparation. Plenty of light and shelter from frosts provide perfect conditions for early flowering.

SPRING

Before the light is cut out by the canopy of leaves above, the woodland floor bursts into spectacular bloom, heralding the start of spring. Early-flowering plants such as primroses appear, and later bluebells may carpet the ground with a dazzling intensity of color. Growth activity is at its highest.

SUMMER

By summer, most shade-loving plants have set seed, and some have died down. But on the dappled woodland fringes and in sunny glades, many plants are now in flower. Ground-cover plants, such as creeping Jenny and skullcap, flourish in damper areas.

FALL

By now few plants are making new growth in the woodland, and it is the seed heads of taller plants, such as foxglove, that are prominent, along with the brilliant and varied colors of fall foliage and ripening fruit.

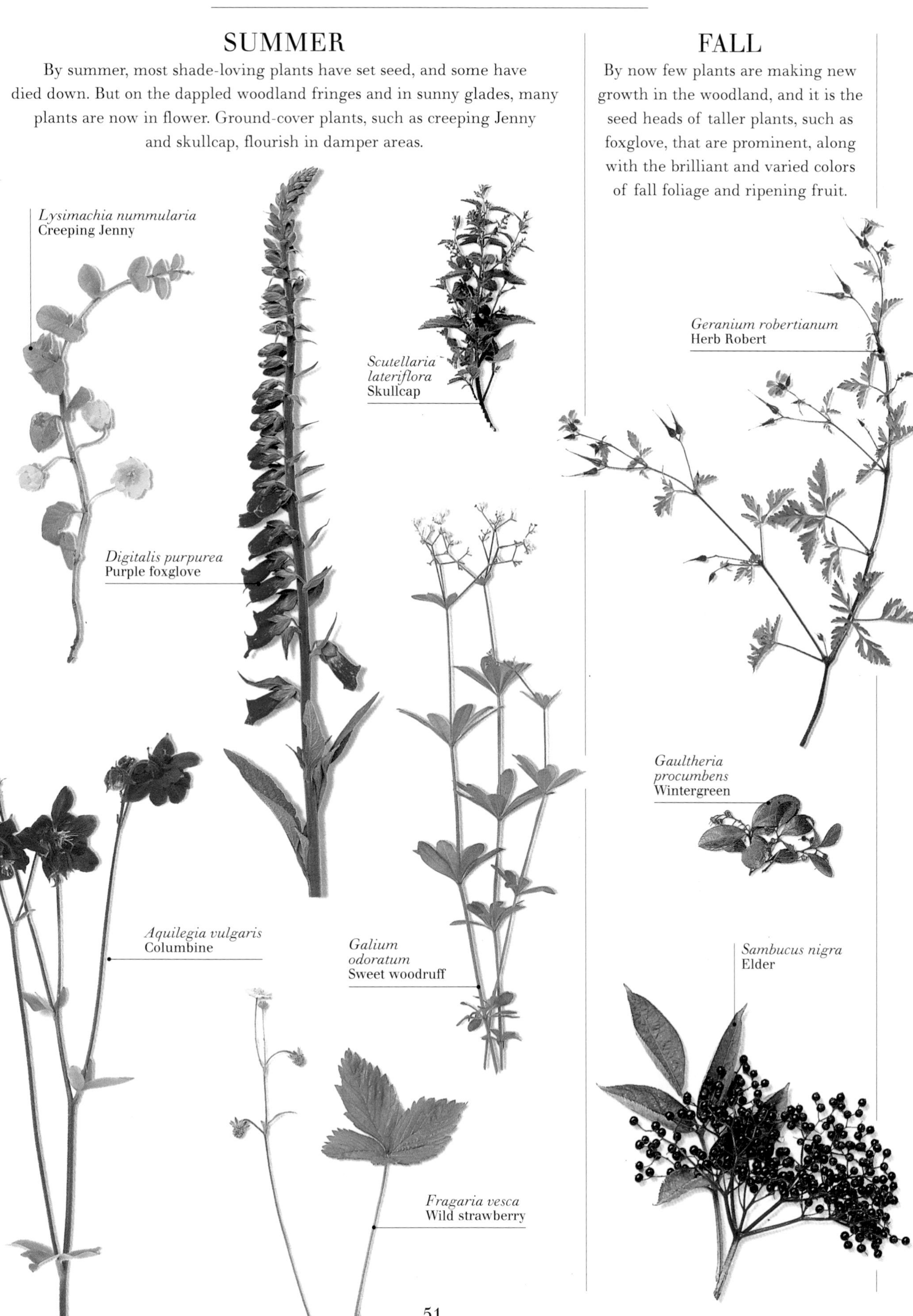

In the garden you can create new areas of shade (see page 36) or use existing ones. Like all plants, woodland species have particular soil preferences: some enjoy moisture, while others thrive in dry areas. Bear this in mind when deciding what to plant.

The miniature woodland

A single tree will produce enough shade to keep off the hottest sun and create a miniature woodland environment. Allow leaves to rot down naturally and, if possible, add extra leaf mold or garden compost to enrich the soil and retain moisture.

Dry and moist shade

The soil close to trees and shrubs is likely to be quite dry because their roots absorb surrounding moisture. However, there is usually plenty of moisture in spring, when woodland plants make their main growth and flower. Avoid watering except in extremely dry conditions.

Use areas of damp shade for plants that require moisture throughout the growing season. Many of these are ground-cover plants, such as bugle and sweet woodruff, which are grown as much for their foliage as for their flowers. If your shaded area is not particularly moist, consider creating the right conditions in the same way that you make a bog garden (see pages 34–5).

Shade from structures

Shade is cast by permanent features – such as a house, wall, or shed – in varying degrees according to the height and position of the structure and the time of year. Many woodland herbs may be grown successfully here as long as they are out of the hot summer sun. Prepare the soil before planting by adding leaf mold and other supplements (see pages 21–3). Keep planting designs simple to echo a real woodland, which is often characterized by areas dominated by a single species.

Maintenance

Shaded habitats created by trees require little maintenance, but cutting back may be necessary if the leaf canopy gets too dense. Other areas may benefit from extra leaf mold or garden compost. Thin out any plants that become too dominant.

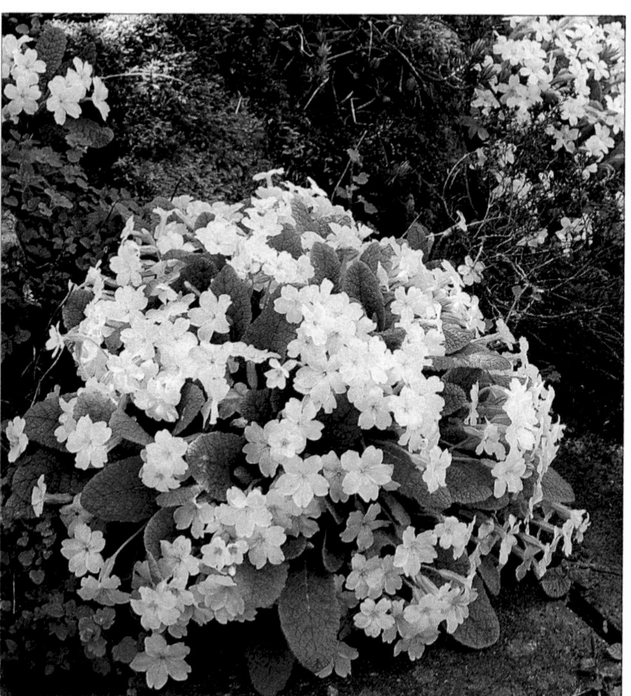

A woodland setting ABOVE
Primroses enjoy the cool shade of woodland and thrive in the rich leaf litter of the woodland floor. Here the ground is moss covered, indicating that there is plenty of moisture, which the primroses like.

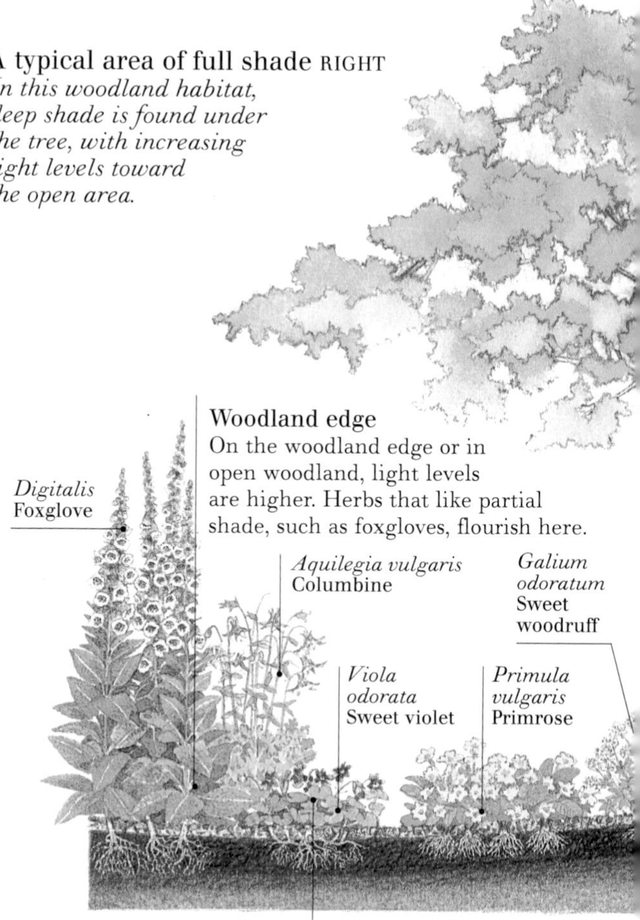

Woodland edge
On the woodland edge or in open woodland, light levels are higher. Herbs that like partial shade, such as foxgloves, flourish here.
Digitalis Foxglove
Aquilegia vulgaris Columbine
Galium odoratum Sweet woodruff
Viola odorata Sweet violet
Primula vulgaris Primrose
Ground cover
Many woodland plants form dense and decorative ground cover, on the humus-rich soil.

A typical area of full shade RIGHT
In this woodland habitat, deep shade is found under the tree, with increasing light levels toward the open area.

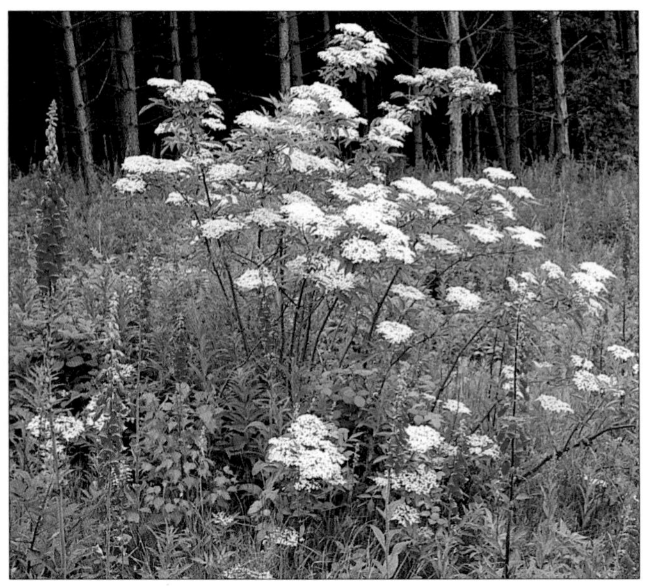

Elder and foxglove LEFT
Elders and foxgloves enjoy the woodland soil but prefer light shade and so usually grow in glades, where trees have been felled or coppiced, or on the edges of woodland. Unlike many woodland plants, foxgloves grow in deciduous and pine woods and don't mind an acid soil. Elders self-seed readily in open woodlands.

Tree
A single large tree can create suitable conditions for woodland herbs to naturalize.

Hyacinthoides non-scripta
Bluebell

Pulmonaria officinalis
Lungwort

Fragaria vesca
Wild strawberry

Soil
Woodland soil is characterized by an accumulation of leaf litter, which retains moisture and provides nutrients.

Dry shade
Soil in the immediate vicinity of trees is often dry. Select herbs that can tolerate these conditions.

SUITABLE HERBS

Pages 50–53 illustrate some of the most suitable and attractive plants for a fully shaded habitat. They are summarized below for quick reference. See the "Herb Directory" for more suggestions.

Aquilegia vulgaris
Columbine

Digitalis purpurea
Purple foxglove

Fragaria vesca
Wild strawberry

Galanthus nivalis
Snowdrop

Galium odoratum
Sweet woodruff

Gaultheria procumbens
Wintergreen

Geranium maculatum
Spotted cranesbill

Geranium robertianum
Herb Robert

Hyacinthoides non-scripta
Bluebell

Lysimachia nummularia
Creeping Jenny

Primula vulgaris
Primrose

Pulmonaria officinalis
Lungwort

Sambucus nigra
Elder

Scutellaria lateriflora
Skullcap

Trillium erectum
Birthroot

Vinca major
Greater periwinkle

Viola odorata
Sweet violet

Sambucus nigra
Elder

Partially Shaded Habitats

A PARTIALLY SHADED HABITAT is one that includes full shade for part of the day, or offers varying levels of dappled or light shade. In the wild, examples include woodland edges, scrub, and hedgerows. In the garden, partial shade may be provided by a few deciduous trees and shrubs, a hedge, or any other area that is partly shaded by a fence or small building, such as a shed. The main period of growth and flowering is longer than in more densely shaded habitats. Interest is provided by buds, bulbs, and new growth in spring, flowers in spring and summer, and leaf color, berries, and hips in the fall and winter.

Without the buildup of leaf mold that occurs in denser woodland, the soil is normally less fertile, but partially shaded habitats do offer protection from winter winds, and mixed hedgerows in particular supply havens for wildlife.

Among the herbs that flower here are such climbers as honeysuckle, hop, and clematis, which grow toward the light, and enjoy having cool, shaded roots. There is usually complete ground cover, but although grasses may be present, they do not grow as densely as they would in open habitats. This allows spreading plants, such as bugle and lesser celandine, and bulbs, like snowdrops, to thrive; many of the shade-loving flora also do well here. Although some plants that prefer light shade will grow in full sun, their colors and subtle beauty are always more effective in partial shade.

WINTER

Winter is a time of regeneration. Many buds are forming in preparation for spring, and there are a few flowers. February daphne blossoms before its leaves appear.

SPRING

With spring comes a wonderful variety of foliage, flowers, and textures. Ground-cover plants, such as bugle, spread quickly on moist soils; on lighter soils, plants like shrubby broom give brilliant splashes of color. Although many of the larger and taller herbs do not bloom until later in the season, their fresh foliage is continuously attractive.

SUMMER

A wide range of herbs thrive throughout the summer in the protection of hedges and shrubs, where the gentle shade provides adequate shelter from the hot sun and keeps roots cool. Growth is abundant now, with attractive foliage and many plants in full flower. Toward the end of the season, seed heads begin to form, many of them decorative.

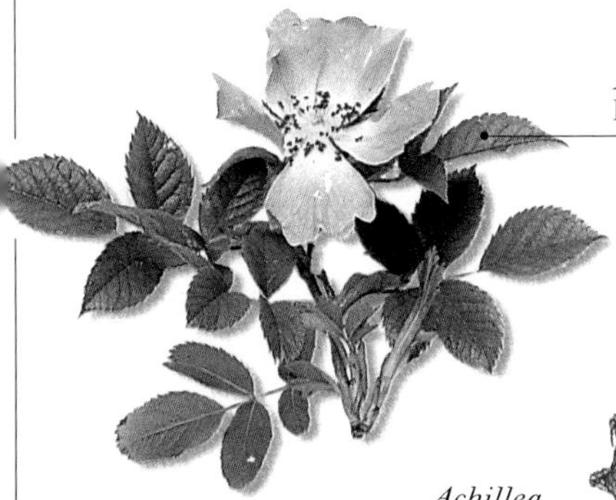

Rosa canina
Dog rose

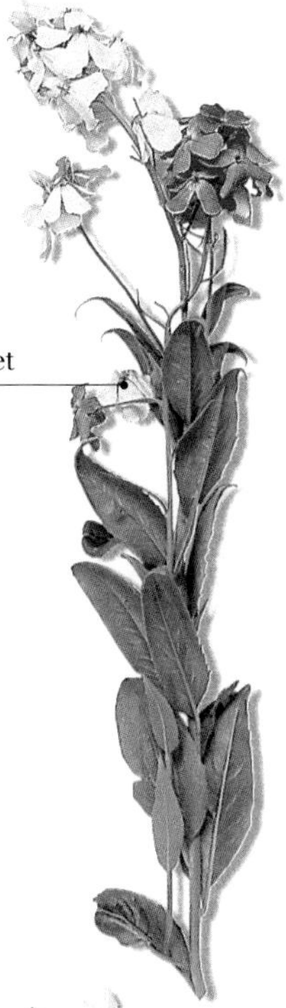

Hesperis matronalis
Sweet rocket

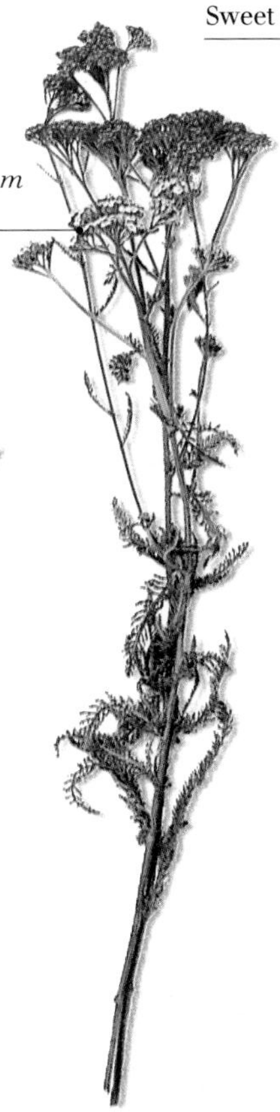

Achillea millefolium
Yarrow

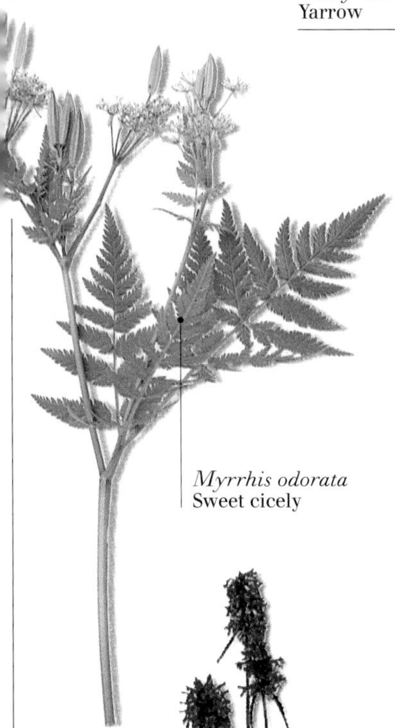

Myrrhis odorata
Sweet cicely

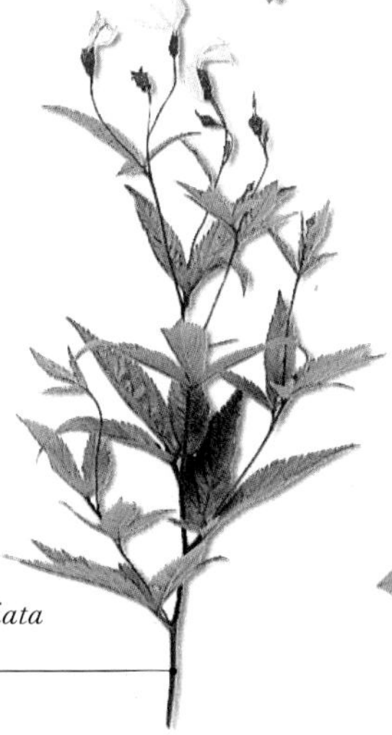

Gillenia trifoliata
Indian physic

Stachys officinalis
Betony

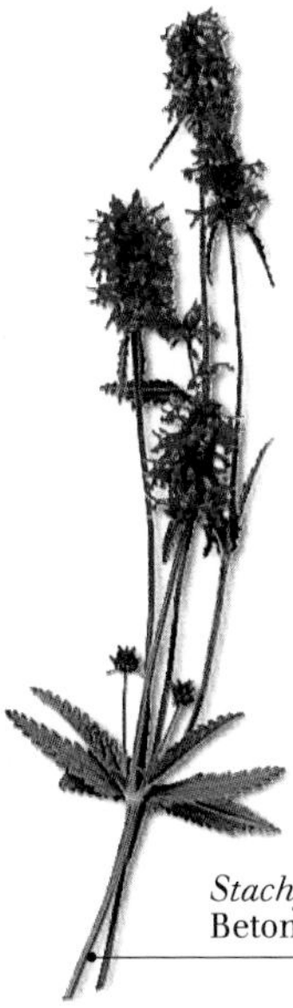

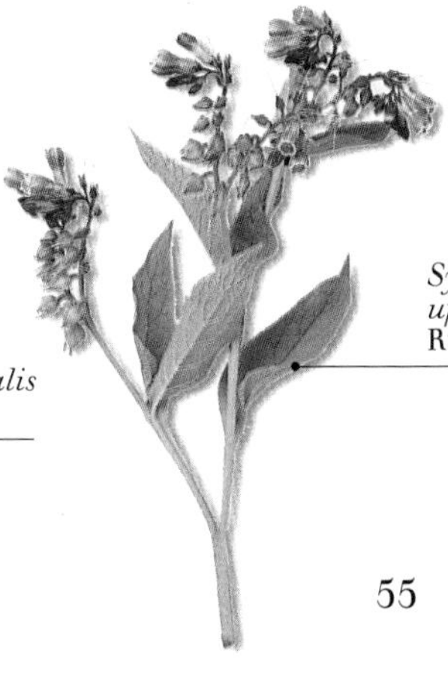

Symphytum x *uplandicum*
Russian comfrey

FALL

Often the most spectacular season in this habitat, fall is highlighted by the yellows, oranges, and reds of the foliage of many plants and shrubs. Although growth has slowed down, fruits and hips add further interest and color.

Humulus lupulus
Hop

Rosa eglanteria
Sweetbrier rose

Clematis vitalba
Travelers' joy

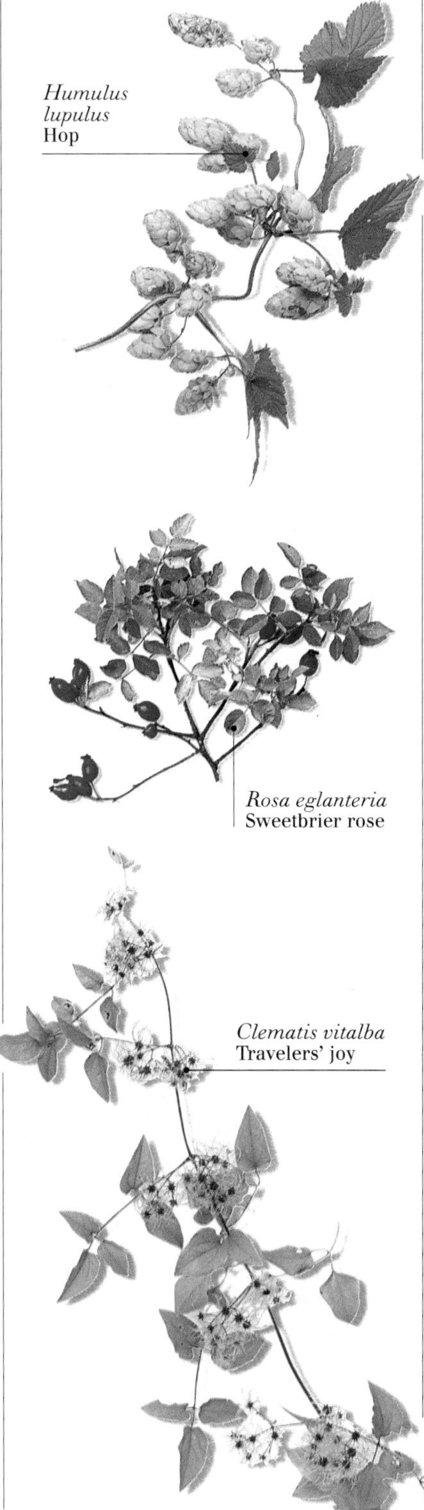

SURPRISINGLY, PARTIALLY shaded habitats tend to be the most neglected areas in the garden; many people do not realize that a wide variety of plants thrive in this environment.

Woodland margins

Woodland margins provide the ideal conditions for growing a varied and interesting range of herbs that prefer partial shade. These include daylilies, betony, peonies, and many ground-cover plants. By choosing your plants carefully you can have foliage and flowers well into winter.

Shrubs and hedgerows

Shrubs, particularly high-branching varieties, also create areas of partial shade. Here, many of the woodland-edge ground-cover plants, such as sweet violet, lungwort, and lesser celandine, provide ample decorative foliage and prevent weeds from colonizing. Bulbs such as snowdrop often thrive, providing interest before the shrubs come into leaf. Some plants that prefer moisture, such as creeping Jenny and bugle, may spread into surrounding grass areas; they will stand occasional mowing.

There are many types of hedge, from formal evergreens to more natural, semiwild hedgerows. The latter are the most interesting and beneficial type, containing a variety of mostly native shrubs that produce flowers and fruits, and provide a haven for wildlife. Climbing herbs can be grown through them, and in their shade a great variety of flowers, such as primroses and yarrow, will do well.

Garden structures

As with full shade, partial shade in the shadow of a house, wall, or shed can be adapted to form an environment suitable for some herbs. The addition of leaf mold or garden compost will help to create the right conditions, and plants chosen with care will flourish in these sheltered sites.

Decorative ground cover ABOVE
Dwarf comfrey, with its attractive foliage and lovely drooping cream and pink flowers in early spring, makes a dense ground cover in partial shade. This species of comfrey is especially drought resistant.

A typical area of partial shade BELOW
Many decorative herbs, including good ground-cover plants, thrive in partial shade, where the leaves of nearby trees and shrubs shade them from the hot sun.

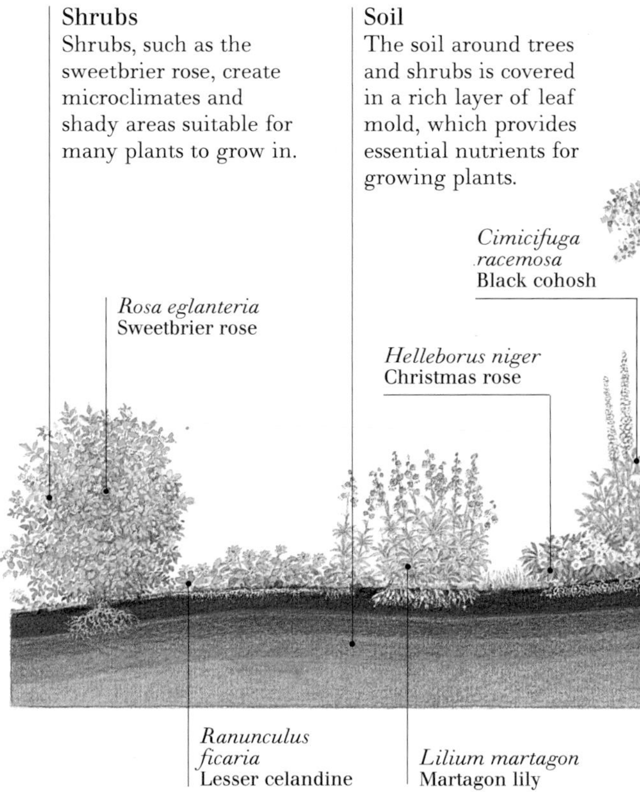

Shrubs
Shrubs, such as the sweetbrier rose, create microclimates and shady areas suitable for many plants to grow in.
Soil
The soil around trees and shrubs is covered in a rich layer of leaf mold, which provides essential nutrients for growing plants.
Cimicifuga racemosa
Black cohosh
Rosa eglanteria
Sweetbrier rose
Helleborus niger
Christmas rose
Ranunculus ficaria
Lesser celandine
Lilium martagon
Martagon lily

Maintenance

If the shade cast by trees becomes too dense, cut back branches or coppice in the dormant season. Shrubs and hedges can be trimmed to maintain their shape and increase light levels. To improve the soil, add leaf mold or garden compost in the fall.

Wildlife

Woodland habitats, whether fully or only partially shaded, benefit many kinds of wildlife. At ground level, rotting vegetation, decomposing wood, fallen branches, and undergrowth are used by wildlife for foraging and as places to hibernate. This dead and decaying plant material is essential for hedgehogs, mice, voles, and beetles. Above ground, trees and shrubs make good nesting sites for the many birds that may visit the garden.

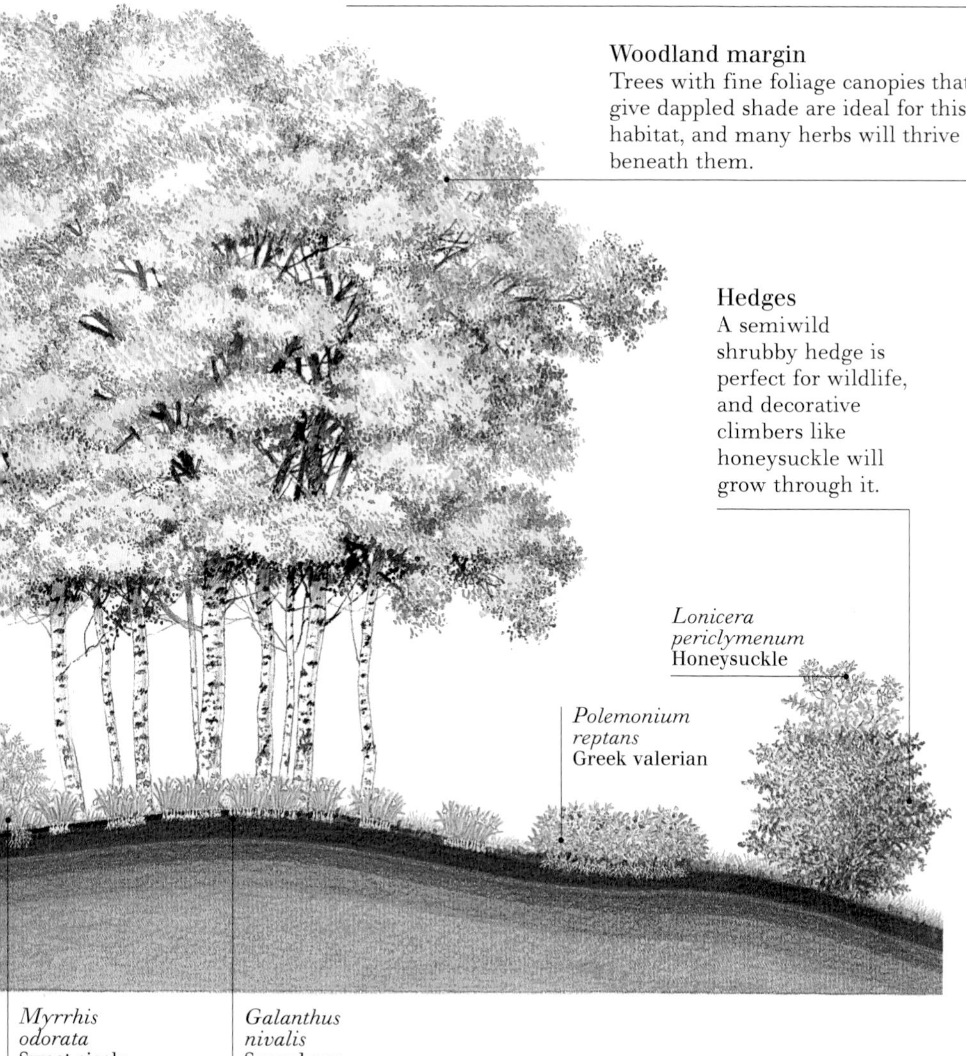

Woodland margin
Trees with fine foliage canopies that give dappled shade are ideal for this habitat, and many herbs will thrive beneath them.
Hedges
A semiwild shrubby hedge is perfect for wildlife, and decorative climbers like honeysuckle will grow through it.
Lonicera periclymenum Honeysuckle
Polemonium reptans Greek valerian
Myrrhis odorata Sweet cicely
Galanthus nivalis Snowdrops

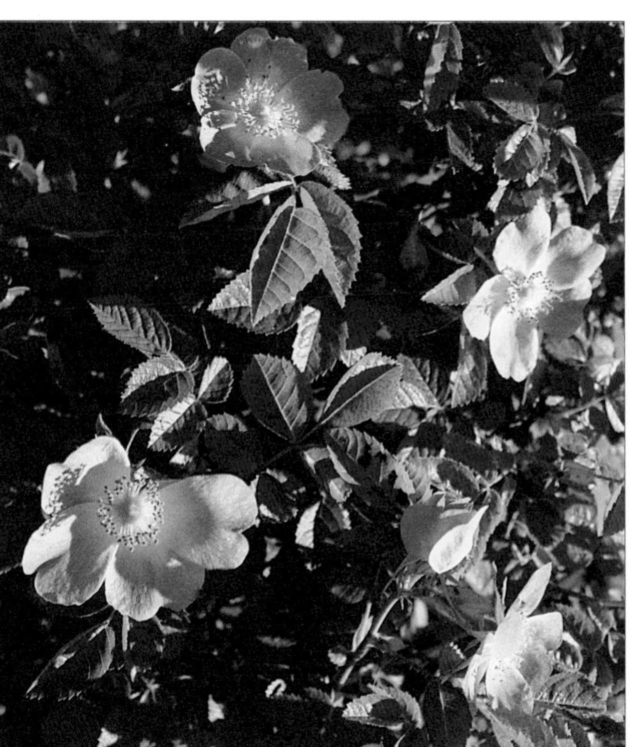

Hedgerow climber LEFT
This dog rose rambles through a hedge. In early summer it will be a mass of flowers. Later it produces brilliant scarlet hips, which will be greatly enjoyed by the birds in winter. Hedges themselves create areas of partial shade, as well as providing shelter from strong winds for plants growing beneath them.

SUITABLE HERBS

Pages 54–7 illustrate some of the most suitable and attractive plants for a partially shaded habitat. They are summarized below for quick reference. See the "Herb Directory" for more suggestions.

Achillea millefolium
Yarrow

Ajuga reptans
Bugle

Arctostaphylos uva-ursi
Bearberry

Berberis vulgaris
Barberry

Chelidonium major
Greater celandine

Cimicifuga racemosa
Black cohosh

Clematis vitalba
Travelers' joy

Cytisus scoparius
Broom

Daphne mezereum
February daphne

Galanthus nivalis
Snowdrop

Gillenia trifoliata
Indian physic

Helleborus niger
Christmas rose

Hesperis matronalis
Sweet rocket

Humulus lupulus
Hop

Lilium martagon
Martagon lily

Lonicera periclymenum
Honeysuckle

Myrrhis odorata
Sweet cicely

Polemonium reptans
Greek valerian

Ranunculus ficaria
Lesser celandine

Rosa canina
Dog rose

Rosa eglanteria
Sweetbrier rose

Stachys officinalis
Betony

Symphytum x *uplandicum*
Russian comfrey

Myrrhis odorata
Sweet cicely

Pond and Wetland Habitats

In the wild, water alone supports a restricted group of specially adapted plants. But wetlands, including wet meadows and marshes, contain a more extensive range. All wet habitats sustain a wide variety of wildlife. In the garden, the pond and bog area are the richest habitats of all. They teem with wildlife and are home to many lovely flowering and foliage herbs.

Pond and wetland habitats normally have silty, fertile soil with plenty of decaying plant material, and remain moist in summer. These conditions are required by many moisture-loving plants that grow on the pond margins, in ditches, or in boggy areas. Water offers winter protection for wildlife and for some plants growing in the shallows; cardinal flower, for example, might not survive freezing conditions in the soil outside. Many ponds and wet areas lie in open woods or under trees, and certain wetland plants prefer some shade.

Plants that grow in the water often have large floating leaves supporting the stem, which grows up from the bottom mud. Some plants do not require soil at all, but float on or under the surface, obtaining nutrients from the water. Others, often with stout stems and brightly colored flowers, grow in the shallows, and their strong vertical growth is characteristic of the vegetation. Wetland plants survive because their specially adapted root system is full of air canals that allow oxygen to diffuse into the underwater parts.

WINTER

Winter is a time of rest. Surface-growing plants have disappeared, marginal and bog plants have died down, and some new shoots are just coming through. Last season's decorative seed heads remain to add interest.

SPRING

In spring, replenished by rainfall and awakened by warmer weather, the pond brims with life. Early plants come into flower: marsh marigold with its stunning golden flowers, followed by the flag irises, with their spearlike foliage on the pond edge and lady's smock in wet meadows.

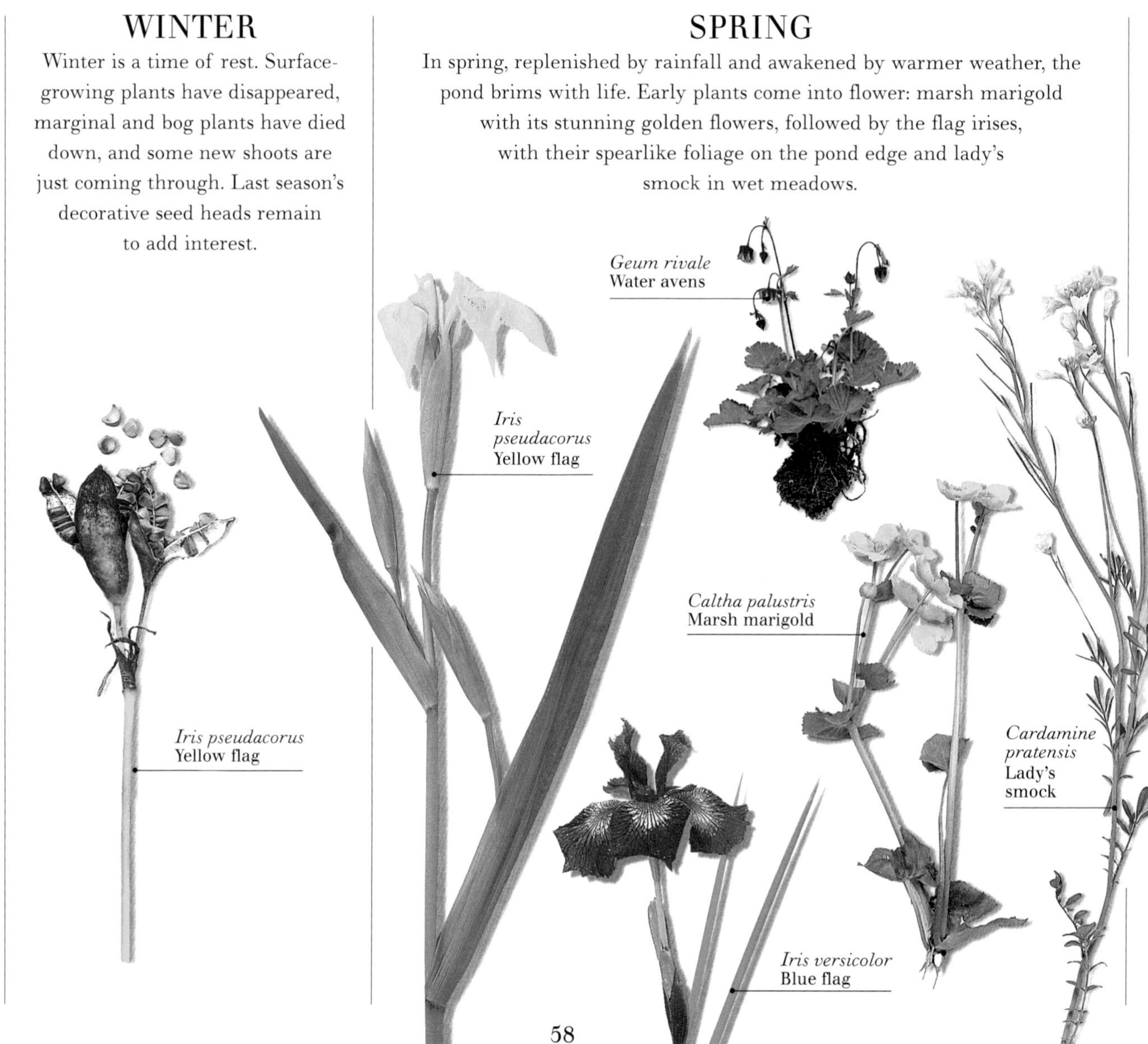

Iris pseudacorus
Yellow flag

Geum rivale
Water avens

Iris pseudacorus
Yellow flag

Caltha palustris
Marsh marigold

Cardamine pratensis
Lady's smock

Iris versicolor
Blue flag

SUMMER

With large floating leaves and spectacular white flowers, which open only on bright days, the water lily provides a focal point in the pond. Picturesque marginal and bog plants, like purple loosestrife, creamy white meadowsweet, and pale pink marsh mallow, also bloom in the summer.

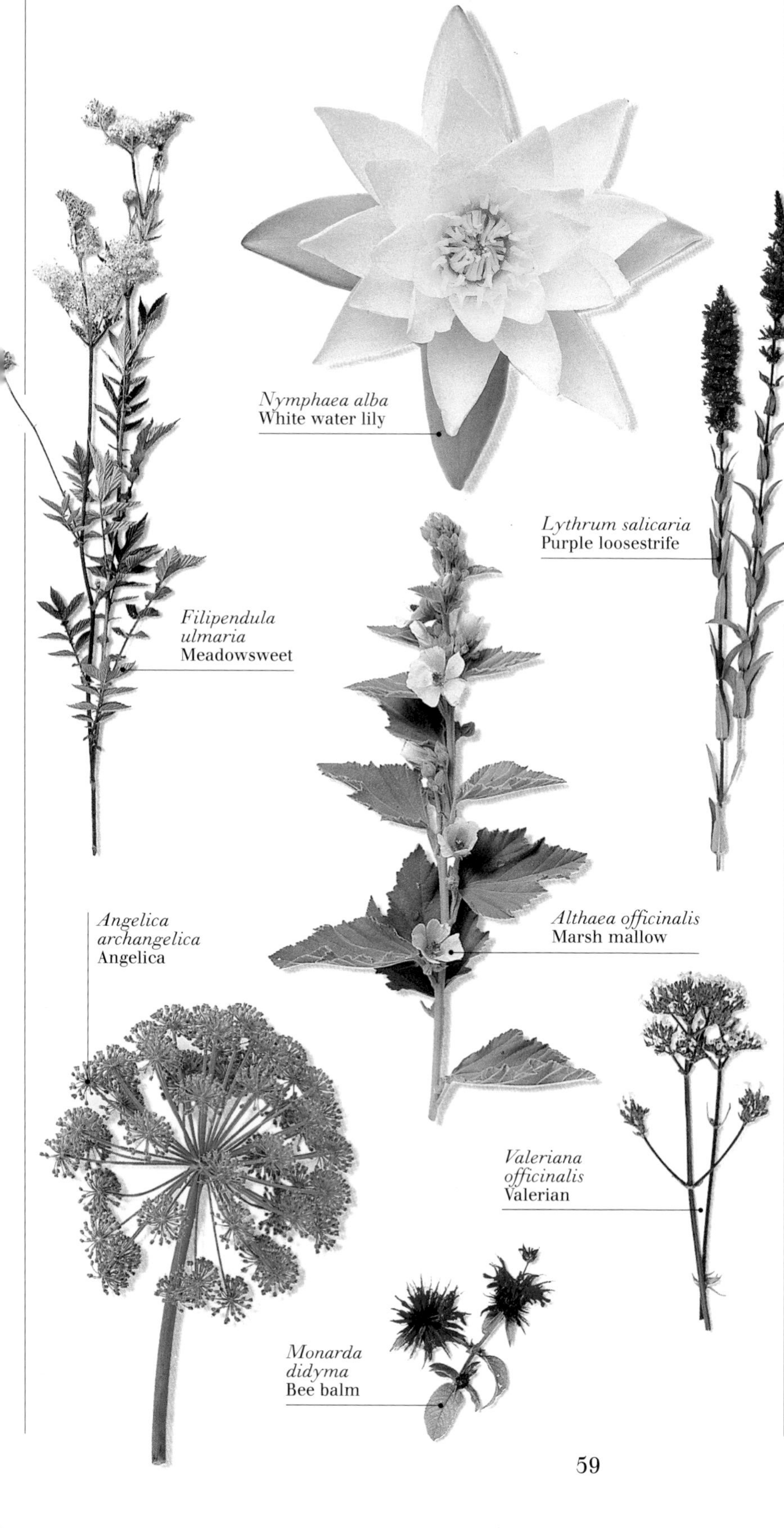

Nymphaea alba
White water lily

Filipendula ulmaria
Meadowsweet

Lythrum salicaria
Purple loosestrife

Althaea officinalis
Marsh mallow

Angelica archangelica
Angelica

Valeriana officinalis
Valerian

Monarda didyma
Bee balm

FALL

Many plants, such as the brilliant scarlet cardinal flower and Joe-pye weed, are still flowering on the moist pond margins. In the water, water mint is exceptional; its flowers attract bees and butterflies, and it quickly spreads to form dense, colorful fragrant drifts.

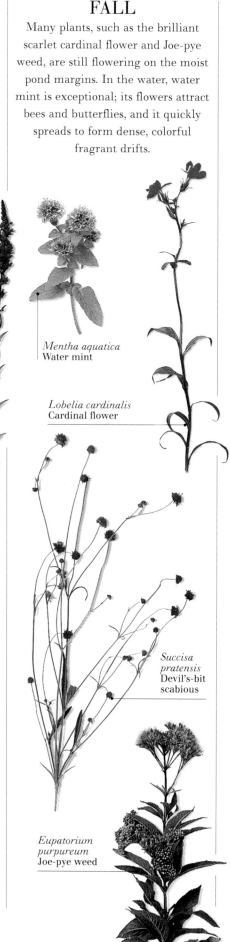

Mentha aquatica
Water mint

Lobelia cardinalis
Cardinal flower

Succisa pratensis
Devil's-bit scabious

Eupatorium purpureum
Joe-pye weed

YOU CAN CREATE a pond or wetland area in almost any garden (see pages 34–5). Even the smallest pond will provide a rich habitat for plants and will attract plenty of birds, insects, and small mammals. This is especially true if the wet area is positioned near another natural habitat, such as a wildflower meadow, woodland edge, or rock garden, where surrounding rocks and plants provide shelter and give access to the water.

Yellow flag LEFT
Yellow flag will establish itself densely on the margins of a pond, although its height and vigor make it unsuitable for small ponds. In early summer its glowing yellow flowers and spearlike leaves make a stunning sight.

Ponds and pond edges

In the pond, establish the oxygenating plants first. These keep the water healthy by releasing vital oxygen and absorbing the minerals that encourage algae. Introduce a selection of species; many are available from good water-garden centers. Most oxygenating plants float below the water surface and – with surface-floating plants such as water lilies – provide shade, which benefits pond life.

Many herbs thrive in the shallow water at the edges of ponds where the soil is moist year round. Make sure that banks, rocks, or plant foliage give wildlife access to and from the water (see box).

Marshy areas

Marshy areas look most natural when they are situated as an extension of the pond (see page 35). Plants enjoying a moist site such as this include meadowsweet, valerian, hemp agrimony, and great lobelia. Creeping Jenny and bugle will provide excellent ground cover where there is shade.

Maintenance

Oxygenating plants grow vigorously and need thinning at least once a year. Plants in baskets should be divided every few years. Most pond and marsh plants die down naturally in winter; clear away dead foliage and thin excess growth.

A pond with wetland margins RIGHT
This cross-section indicates the different depths of water required to grow the widest variety of plants. It also shows the pond related to other habitats at its edges.

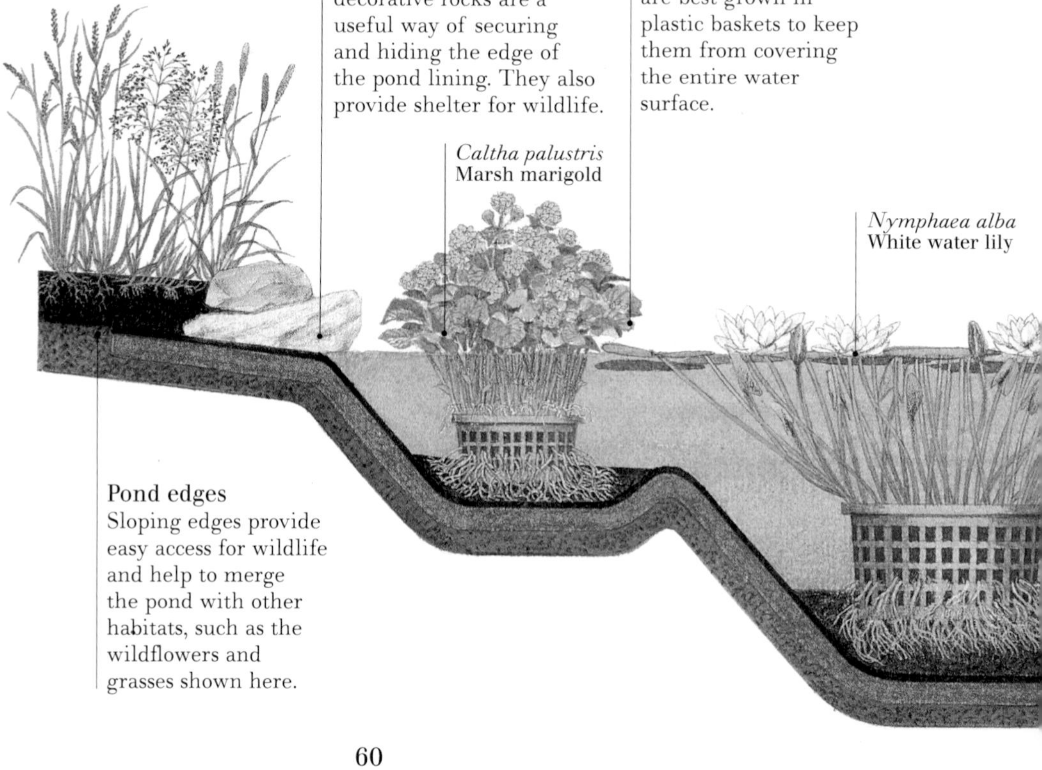

Rocks
Natural-looking and decorative rocks are a useful way of securing and hiding the edge of the pond lining. They also provide shelter for wildlife.

Water plants
Vigorous water plants are best grown in plastic baskets to keep them from covering the entire water surface.

Caltha palustris
Marsh marigold

Nymphaea alba
White water lily

Pond edges
Sloping edges provide easy access for wildlife and help to merge the pond with other habitats, such as the wildflowers and grasses shown here.

WILDLIFE

Within a few months of creating a pond, you are likely to see frogs or toads, newts, damselflies and dragonflies, water spiders, and beetles. The herbs planted in and around the pond will attract bees and butterflies, and, at the end of the season, seed-eating birds will have a feast, especially upon wild teasel. Moisture-loving herbs that attract butterflies are Joe-pye weed, hemp agrimony, devil's-bit scabious, and water mint.

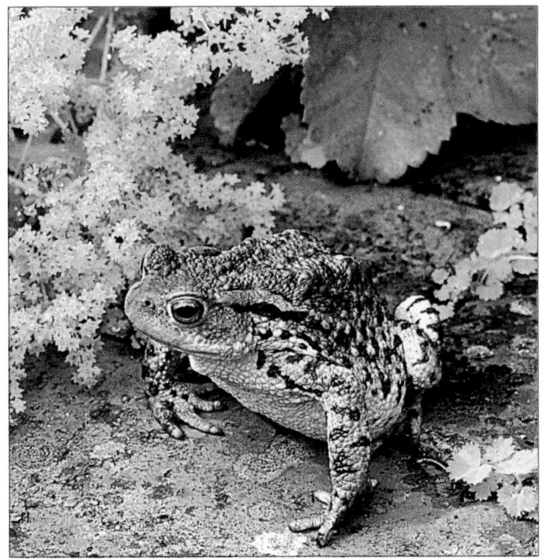

Toad with lady's mantle ABOVE

Warning

All ponds are potentially dangerous to small children.

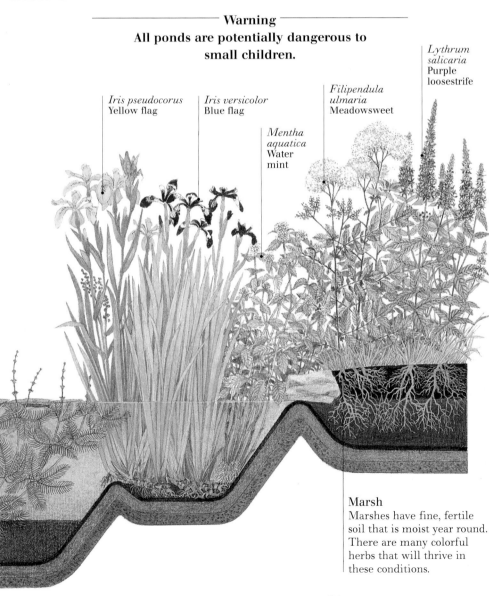

Iris pseudocorus
Yellow flag

Iris versicolor
Blue flag

Mentha aquatica
Water mint

Filipendula ulmaria
Meadowsweet

Lythrum salicaria
Purple loosestrife

Marsh

Marshes have fine, fertile soil that is moist year round. There are many colorful herbs that will thrive in these conditions.

SUITABLE HERBS

Pages 58–61 illustrate some of the most suitable and attractive plants for pond and wetland habitats. They are summarized below for quick reference. See the "Herb Directory" for more suggestions.

Althaea officinalis
Marsh mallow

Angelica archangelica
Angelica

Caltha palustris
Marsh marigold

Cardamine pratensis
Lady's smock

Eupatorium purpureum
Joe-pye weed

Filipendula ulmaria
Meadowsweet

Geum rivale
Water avens

Iris pseudacorus
Yellow flag

Iris versicolor
Blue flag

Lobelia cardinalis
Cardinal flower

Lobelia syphilitica
Great lobelia

Lysimachia vulgaris
Yellow loosestrife

Lythrum salicaria
Purple loosestrife

Mentha aquatica
Water mint

Monarda didyma
Bee balm

Nymphaea alba
White water lily

Succisa pratensis
Devil's-bit scabious

Valeriana officinalis
Valerian

Lobelia syphilitica
Great lobelia

Open, Dry Habitats

MOST HERBS THAT thrive in an open, dry situation occur naturally in the wild in a Mediterranean-type climate on rocky hillsides, dry grasslands or stony steppes. Plants are adapted for survival in this harsh environment. In the garden, open and dry habitats are created in rock gardens, walls, paths, and raised beds.

In spring in the natural habitat, there is usually plenty of moisture and cooler weather, but for much of the year, the surface of the ground is dry and the often thin soil is like dust. However, rocks and stones prevent moisture deeper in the ground from evaporating, keeping the soil comparatively cool beneath, and condensing any nighttime moisture from the air. Although the stony surface becomes burning hot in summer, scorching the leaves, the plant roots can survive. Winters are normally mild; in cold mountainous regions, where winters are severe, the alpine plants are protected by snow cover until the temperature rises in spring.

The plants that grow here are well adapted. Some, such as pasqueflower, bloom in the moist, cool spring. When the hot, dry weather comes, they set seed or die down to underground bulbs or rhizomes, remaining dormant until the following spring. Other plants have leaves specially adapted to retain moisture. These are often narrow, tough, and hairy or they may be gray in color; some leaves are succulent. These summer-flowering plants are able to survive the hot, dry conditions.

WINTER

In the dormant winter season, the foliage of evergreen herbs, such as purple and gold sage and the soft grays of santolina, provides continued interest and structure. Rosemary is often in full flower during late winter.

SPRING

Many herbs from hot, dry habitats provide a mass of color and fresh leaf in spring. Scented wild wallflower, growing in walls, flowers early and the beautiful purple pasqueflower, with its feathery leaves, is in full bloom by mid-spring. The foliage of golden and variegated marjoram looks its best at this time of year.

SUMMER

Summer produces a burst of color. The flowers and foliage of annuals like poppy and pot marigold are at their best. Shrubby perennials, including lavenders and thymes, are in full bloom from early to late summer. Taller plants – such as bronze fennel, with its finely cut foliage – provide a graceful backdrop for the brilliant summer flowers.

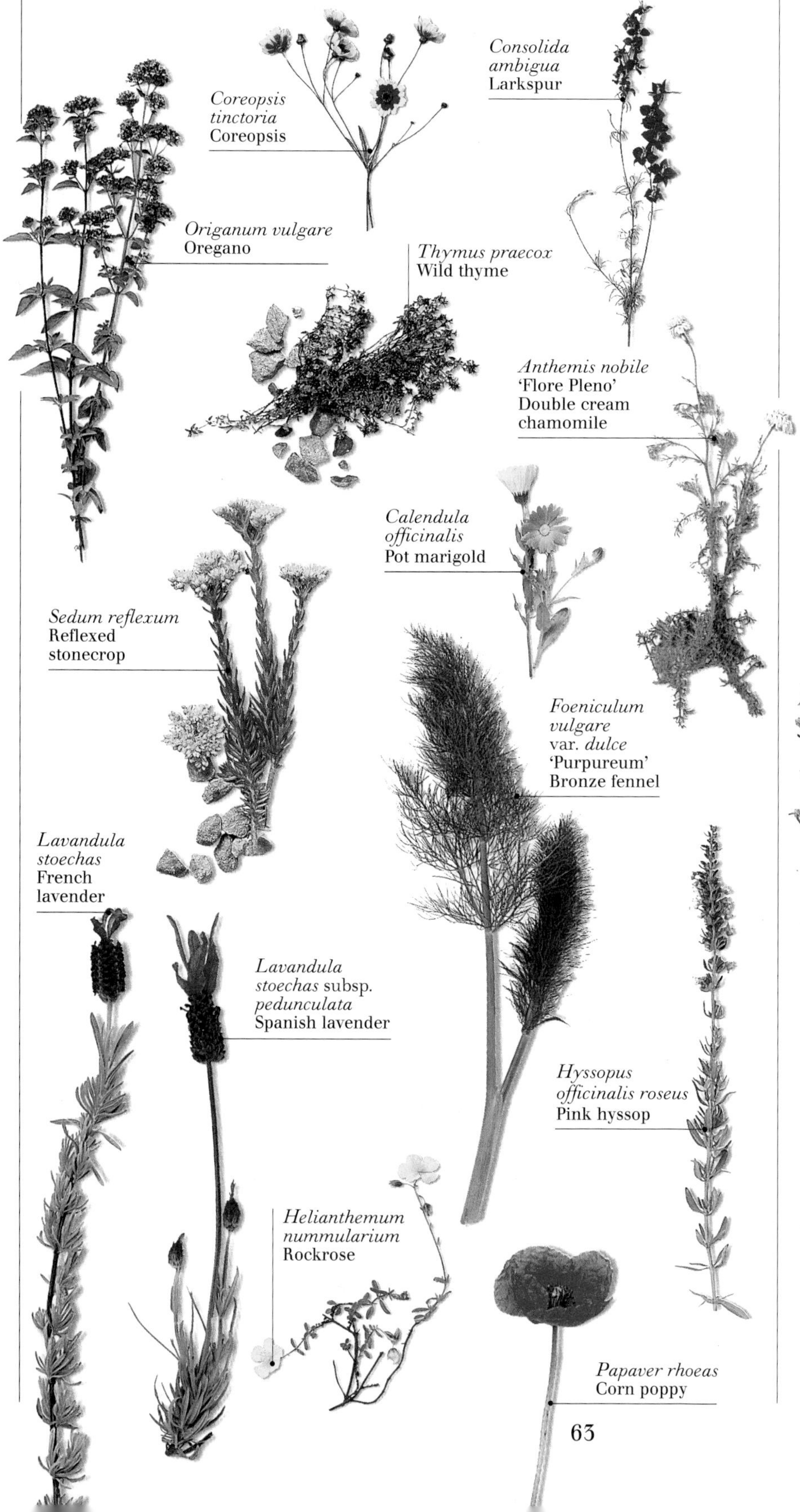

Coreopsis tinctoria
Coreopsis

Consolida ambigua
Larkspur

Origanum vulgare
Oregano

Thymus praecox
Wild thyme

Anthemis nobile 'Flore Pleno'
Double cream chamomile

Calendula officinalis
Pot marigold

Sedum reflexum
Reflexed stonecrop

Foeniculum vulgare var. *dulce* 'Purpureum'
Bronze fennel

Lavandula stoechas
French lavender

Lavandula stoechas subsp. *pedunculata*
Spanish lavender

Hyssopus officinalis roseus
Pink hyssop

Helianthemum nummularium
Rockrose

Papaver rhoeas
Corn poppy

FALL

Many culinary herbs from dry habitats flower late in the year, and evergreens, such as santolinas and artemisias, with their gray-green foliage, are often still in bloom. Decorative seed heads supplement the flowers and leaves.

Amaranthus cruentus
Amaranth

Artemisia absinthium
Wormwood

Linaria vulgaris
Toadflax

Satureja montana
Winter savory

Origanum hirtum
Greek marjoram

Even if your soil is not free-draining, you can create the open, dry, stony habitats described here to enable herbs that enjoy these conditions to flourish. In a garden site that is well drained, these habitats can be used to provide additional decorative features. When planning any of the following habitats, remember to relate them to others in the garden, rather than considering each in isolation. This is especially important for encouraging wildlife, which may need to move from one habitat to another.

Rock gardens and gravel

A rock garden makes a focal point or feature in a garden of any size and is a useful solution to the problem of poorly drained soil. At its most basic, it can consist of a few well-placed rocks, set into an existing bank to form an outcrop.

Gravel is an attractive material that sets off the herbs well, keeps their foliage clean, and acts as an effective mulch (see page 23), keeping down weeds and preserving moisture during hot summers. Coarse soils consisting of sand and gravel, or sandy loam, produce well-drained conditions, and gravel gardens can easily be constructed on them. Many chalky soils are also suitable. The soil should be well prepared by forking in natural fertilizer and then finished with a surface layer of gravel 1–2 inches (2.5–5 cm) deep.

A scree offers a more authentic alternative to gravel. Natural screes are formed at the base of glaciers by fallen rock debris, sand, and soil.

Raised beds, walls, and paths

Where soil drainage is poor, a raised bed creates ideal conditions for a range of useful herbs, and can incorporate a simple rock garden, gravel bed, or area of scree. Raised beds are also useful for creating conditions that are different from the rest of your garden – for example, in an area of naturally alkaline soil, you can make a raised bed with peat for acid-loving plants.

Walls and paths are ideal dry habitats. Brick and stone walls provide good drainage and shelter; plant or sow seeds in the gaps between the stones or bricks (see page 41). Brick, gravel, or paved paths, constructed on light soil or given well-drained foundations, are excellent for many of the lower growing herbs; such as creeping thyme.

Maintenance

Keep rock-garden plants free of dead leaves, which encourage rot. Regularly maintain the levels of grit and gravel mulches and use foliar feed, such as seaweed, as required. Trim back plants in walls and on paths; weed out any surplus self-seeded plants. Remove dead foliage from paths to prevent them from becoming slippery.

A rock garden and raised bed BELOW
These herbs naturally grow on rocky coasts or stony hillsides where summers are long, hot, and dry. Most are hardy but they will not survive wet winters in waterlogged soil. A sunny, open site with sharp drainage is the key to their survival.

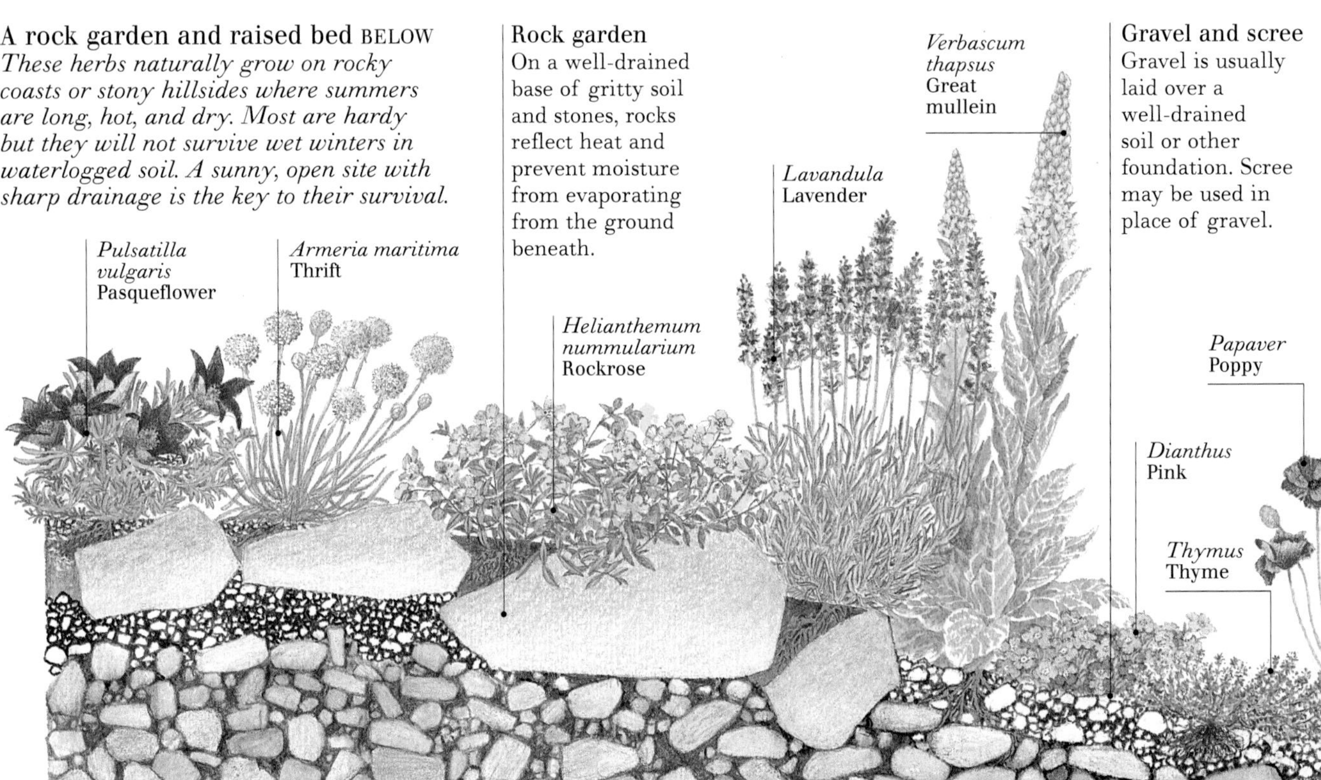
Pulsatilla vulgaris
Pasqueflower
Armeria maritima
Thrift
Rock garden
On a well-drained base of gritty soil and stones, rocks reflect heat and prevent moisture from evaporating from the ground beneath.
Helianthemum nummularium
Rockrose
Lavandula
Lavender
Verbascum thapsus
Great mullein
Gravel and scree
Gravel is usually laid over a well-drained soil or other foundation. Scree may be used in place of gravel.
Papaver
Poppy
Dianthus
Pink
Thymus
Thyme

GARDEN WILDLIFE

The shelter afforded by the rocks in a dry garden attracts wildlife, including lizards. Flowers encourage a wide range of insects, which in turn attract birds.

Attracting bees RIGHT
Flowering herbs, such as this artichoke, are a magnet for honeybees and bumblebees. Butterflies and other insects also feed from the flowers of fragrant herbs.

The gravel garden LEFT
A few inches of gravel or small stones over a well-drained soil provide the ideal habitat for these sun-loving carpeting thymes. The stones and gravel retain moisture, keep the soil cool, and suppress weeds, as well as looking decorative.

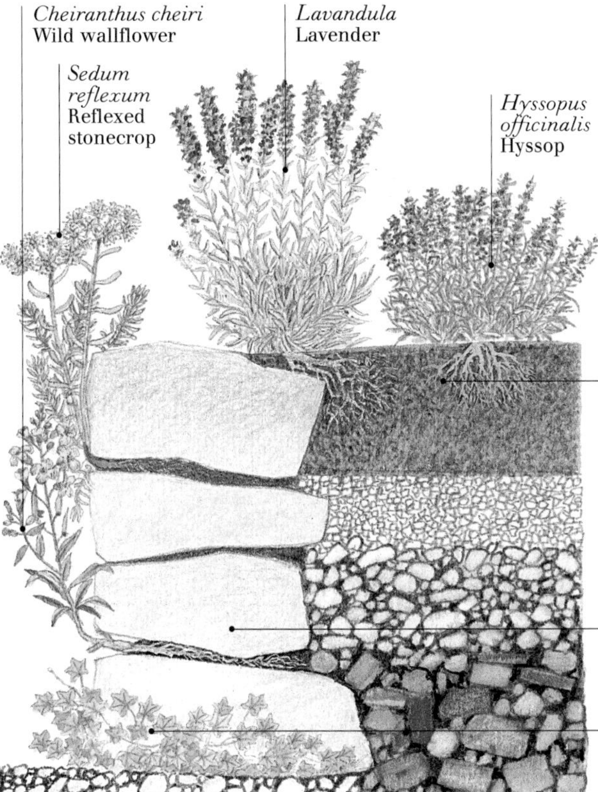

Raised beds

Raised beds are comparatively easy to construct and allow the gardener to provide well-drained conditions on a heavy or badly drained soil.

Walls

Old walls are full of gaps and crevices where suitable plants will thrive for many years. A minimal amount of soil is required.

SUITABLE HERBS

Pages 62–5 illustrate some of the most suitable and attractive plants for open, dry habitats. They are summarized below for quick reference. See the "Herb Directory" for more suggestions.

Amaranthus cruentus
Amaranth

Anthemis nobile
Roman chamomile

Armeria maritima
Thrift

Artemisia
Artemisia

Calendula officinalis
Pot marigold

Centranthus ruber
Red valerian

Cheiranthus cheiri
Wild wallflower

Consolida ambigua
Larkspur

Coreopsis tinctoria
Coreopsis

Cymbalaria muralis
Ivy-leaved toadflax

Dianthus
Pink

Foeniculum vulgare
Fennel

Helianthemum nummularium
Rockrose

Hyssopus officinalis
Hyssop

Lavandula
Lavender

Linaria vulgaris
Toadflax

Origanum vulgare 'Aureum'
Golden marjoram

Papaver
Poppy

Pulsatilla vulgaris
Pasqueflower

Rosmarinus
Rosemary

Salvia
Sage

Santolina chamaecyparissus
Cotton lavender

Satureja montana
Winter savory

Sedum reflexum
Reflexed stonecrop

Thymus
Thyme

Verbascum thapsus
Great mullein

Viola tricolor
Heartsease

Open, Moisture-retaining Habitats

In nature, an open, moist habitat consists of mainly lowland and upland flowering grassland, usually on fertile clay and loam soils. These meadows, which are all humanmade, have been managed for grazing and hay over many decades or even centuries and seem perfect in their harmony of flowers, grasses, and wildlife. In the garden, these habitats typically take the form of borders, island beds, wildflower lawns, or meadows.

The character of a natural grassland habitat is determined by the way it is managed and the type of soil. Rainfall is also important, since many meadow plants will not survive extended dry periods or waterlogged winter conditions. In hay meadows, wildflowers grow with the grasses and form a dense mat that leaves little room for weeds to establish. Grazed grassland has fine turf, and here flowers are low growing and form ground-hugging rosettes that can survive close cropping. Many of these plants either spread by their roots or flower and produce seed near the ground.

A wide range of perennial herbs from meadows and grasslands thrive in gardens and without the competition of grasses, they normally grow larger. Plants from other moist habitats, including wet meadows, will also grow well in an open, moisture-retaining site in the garden. Those from open woodland, like daylily, black cohosh, and peony, are also suitable, although in areas with long, hot summers they require some shade.

WINTER

In moist areas during the winter foliage of self-seeded plants such as chervil and golden feverfew give texture and fresh color, and evergreens such as sweet bay provide structure.

SPRING

Foliage plants now enrich this habitat: variegated herbs, such as golden variegated lemon balm, look their best in spring. Flowering plants such as the yellow cowslip (ideally grown in drifts) appear with ground-covering species, such as Greek valerian and lady's mantle, which have exceptional foliage; lady's mantle may start to bloom early.

Chrysanthemum parthenium 'Aureum' Golden feverfew

Laurus nobilis Sweet bay

Anthriscus cerefolium Chervil

Melissa officinalis 'Aurea' Golden lemon balm

Alchemilla vulgaris Lady's mantle

Primula veris Cowslip

Leucanthemum vulgare Ox-eye daisy

Polemonium reptans Greek valerian

SUMMER

When many herbs in drier habitats have already flowered and are setting seed, those with a good supply of moisture still look green and decorative. Brilliant flower color is provided by such plants as nasturtium, balloon flower, and purple coneflower. Some herbs, like the feathery-leaved dill and the architectural teasel, produce ornamental flower heads, which dry well.

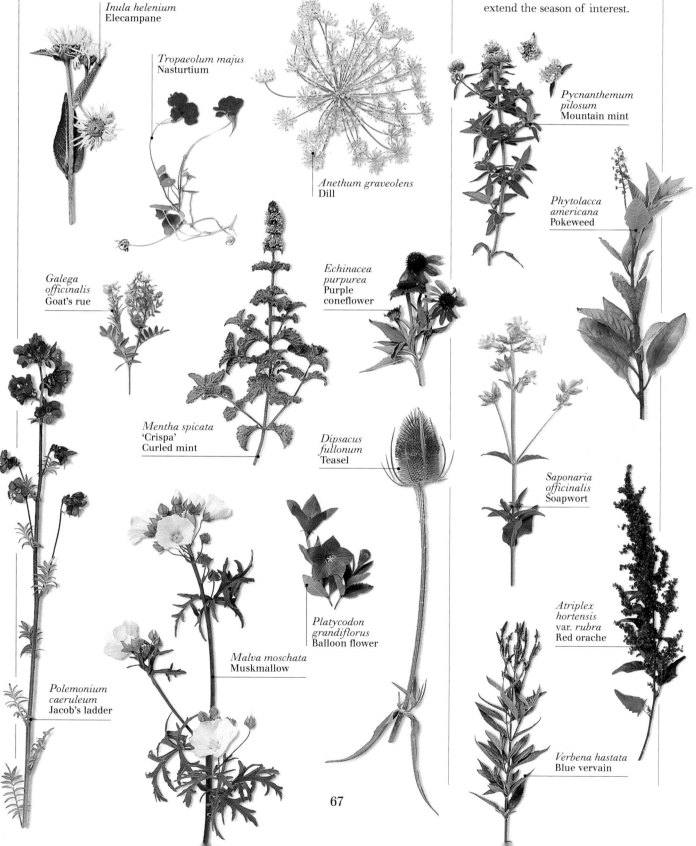

Inula helenium
Elecampane

Tropaeolum majus
Nasturtium

Anethum graveolens
Dill

Galega officinalis
Goat's rue

Echinacea purpurea
Purple coneflower

Mentha spicata 'Crispa'
Curled mint

Dipsacus fullonum
Teasel

Platycodon grandiflorus
Balloon flower

Malva moschata
Muskmallow

Polemonium caeruleum
Jacob's ladder

FALL

Some herbs flower late in the season and are often valuable for bees and butterflies: mountain mint is a favorite. Red orache, with its richly colored foliage, provides decorative seed heads. The dried flower heads of many herbs extend the season of interest.

In the garden, open areas away from trees and shrubs are normally turned into lawn. Given their moisture-retaining soil, they have plenty of potential to be made into attractive borders or island beds. In a wild garden design, you can create flowering lawns or miniature meadows.

An ecological border

The beauty of an ecological border is that it is planted with herbs that are all from the same, or similar, habitats in the wild. The plants are then left to develop naturally and to self-seed, so that the border requires minimal maintenance.

An informal planting LEFT *Moist soil enables deep-rooting Russian comfrey to thrive and annual salad rocket will produce a good crop of hot, spicy leaves and decorative flowers for salads.*

A formal border

A huge range of attractive flowering herbs can be grown in a moisture-retaining formal border, including shade-loving plants. Herbs from dry habitats also thrive, provided they are given good winter drainage and maximum sun.

Island beds

Island beds can also be planted with a wide range of herbs, either naturally or formally. They are viewed from all sides, and this needs to be taken into account when planting them (see pages 76–7). Island beds are usually cut into a lawn but may be set in a paved, bricked, or gravel area.

Flowering meadows and lawns

Flowering meadows are excellent wildlife habitats that re-create natural conditions. You can grow a flowering meadow either by seeding a special mixture of wildflowers and grasses into weed-free soil or by planting wildflowers into existing (and suitable) grasses. An established lawn can be left unmown in spring and early summer, allowing a range of low-growing plants to flower. The lawn can be cut short for the remainder of the year.

An open, moist habitat RIGHT *An open, moist habitat is home to a wide range of herbs. In the garden, these mix well with wild and simple flowers.*

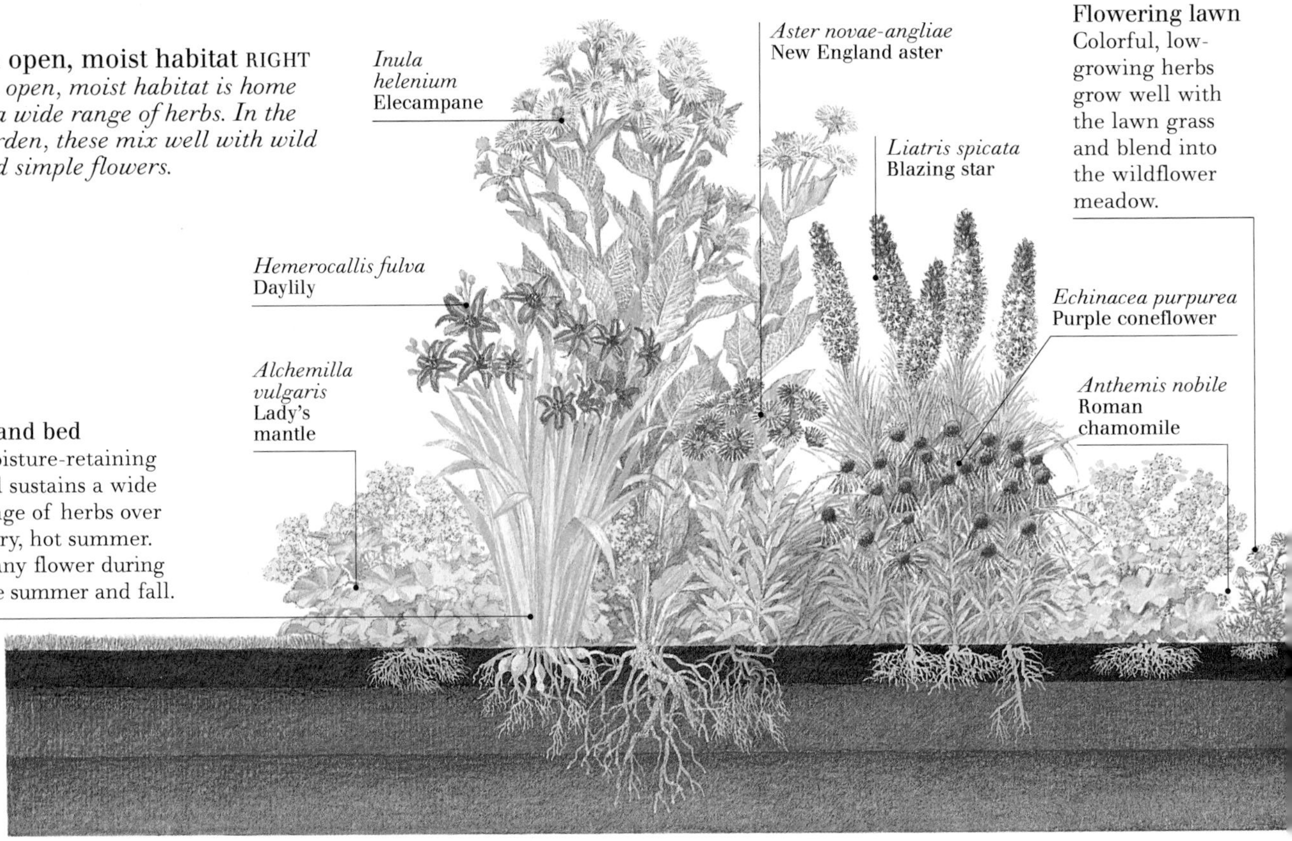

Inula helenium Elecampane

Aster novae-angliae New England aster

Liatris spicata Blazing star

Flowering lawn Colorful, low-growing herbs grow well with the lawn grass and blend into the wildflower meadow.

Hemerocallis fulva Daylily

Echinacea purpurea Purple coneflower

Alchemilla vulgaris Lady's mantle

Anthemis nobile Roman chamomile

Island bed Moisture-retaining soil sustains a wide range of herbs over a dry, hot summer. Many flower during late summer and fall.

A spring meadow LEFT *Drifts of cowslip in grassland are a wonderful sight during late spring. They naturalize well, especially in chalky or alkaline soils.*

Meadows are most effective leading into or from another habitat, as they would in the wild.

Maintenance

In the garden, most open, moist habitats require little in the way of maintenance, especially if they are carefully planted with complementary herbs and other perennials. Mulch the ground and add garden compost as needed.

Formal plantings can be labor-intensive and need regular trimming, weeding, and deadheading. Meadows should be cut on a seasonal basis.

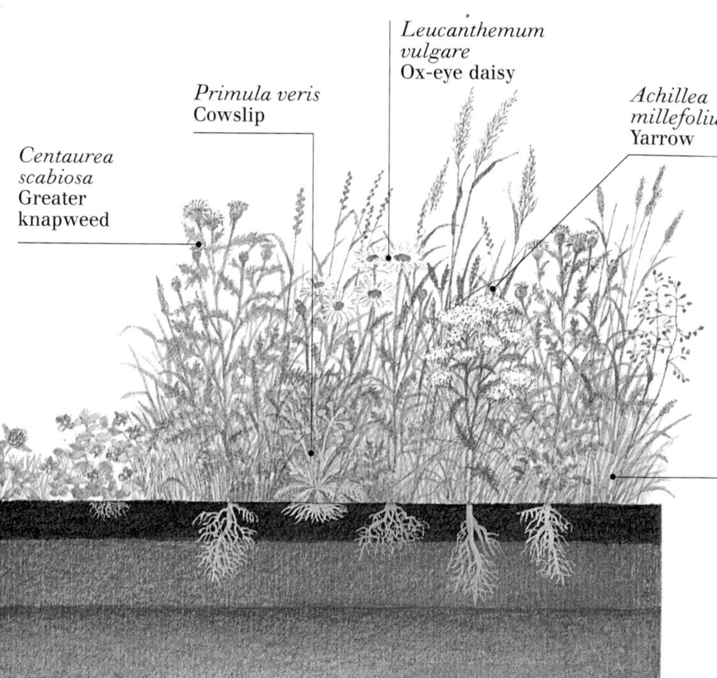

Meadow
A flowering meadow encourages a wide variety of wildlife. Once established, the dense ground cover discourages weeds and helps the soil to retain moisture.

SUITABLE HERBS

Pages 66–9 illustrate some of the most suitable and attractive plants for open, moisture-retaining habitats. They are summarized below for quick reference. See the "Herb Directory" for more suggestions.

Achillea millefolium
Yarrow

Alchemilla vulgaris
Lady's mantle

Anethum graveolens
Dill

Aster novae-angliae
New England aster

Atriplex hortensis var. *rubra*
Red orache

Centaurea scabiosa
Greater knapweed

Chrysanthemum parthenium 'Aureum'
Golden feverfew

Dipsacus fullonum
Teasel

Echinacea purpurea
Purple coneflower

Galega officinalis
Goat's rue

Hemerocallis fulva
Daylily

Inula helenium
Elecampane

Laurus nobilis
Sweet bay

Leucanthemum vulgare
Ox-eye daisy

Liatris spicata
Blazing star

Malva moschata
Muskmallow

Melissa officinalis 'Aurea'
Golden lemon balm

Mentha
Mint

Phytolacca americana
Pokeweed

Platycodon grandiflorus
Balloon flower

Polemonium caeruleum
Jacob's ladder

Polemonium reptans
Greek valerian

Primula veris
Cowslip

Pycnanthemum pilosum
Mountain mint

Saponaria officinalis
Soapwort

Tropaeolum majus
Nasturtium

Verbena hastata
Blue vervain

Artificial Habitats

ARTIFICIAL HABITATS ARE created in the sheltered environment provided by any covered growing area (see also pages 38–9). With control over humidity, temperature, light, and shade, greenhouses and conservatories produce the perfect environment for growing tender plants from tropical and subtropical regions. Extra heat encourages plants, such as lemon verbena, to come into leaf earlier in the spring.

Other covered areas, such as protective tunnels or cloches, provide shelter from the worst frost, wind, and rain, enabling plants to make an early start or survive in colder areas than they would otherwise. Lavender and rosemary benefit from the shelter of a tunnel; although this will also protect lemon verbena and pineapple sage, they will not survive if there is severe or very hard frost.

Inside the house, herbs may also be grown on a sunny windowsill (preferably double-glazed to avoid temperature fluctuation). Turn the pot plants regularly to prevent uneven growth.

Maintenance

Remove any dead leaves and flowers regularly, checking for pests when you do so. Trim back as required. Do not overwater; allow soil to dry out between watering. Provide slow-release fertilizer or foliar feed throughout the growing season.

The kitchen windowsill ABOVE
This is an ideal place to grow culinary herbs, where there is ample light and warmth to promote growth.

Pot plants RIGHT
The house or conservatory provides an ideal climate for fragrant and attractive pot plants, such as scented-leaved pelargoniums.

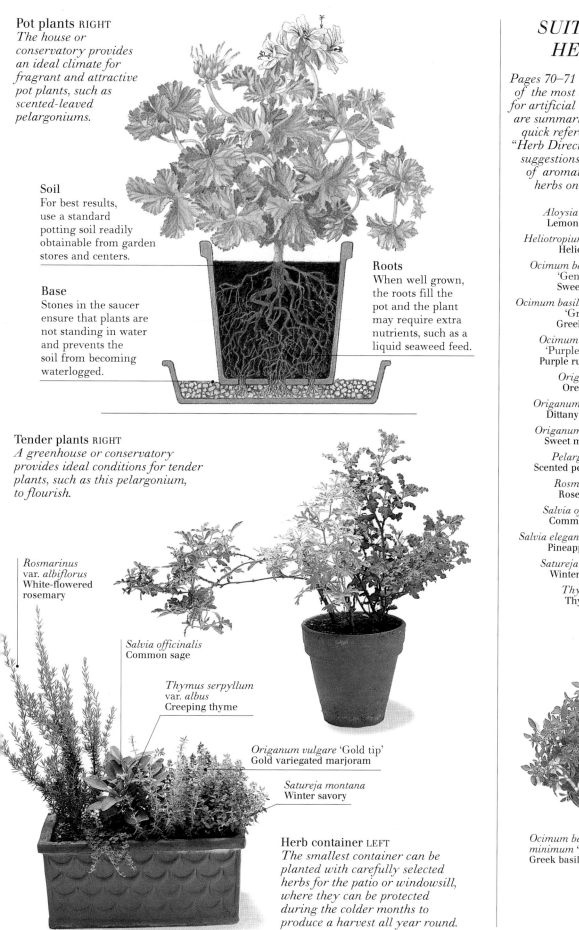

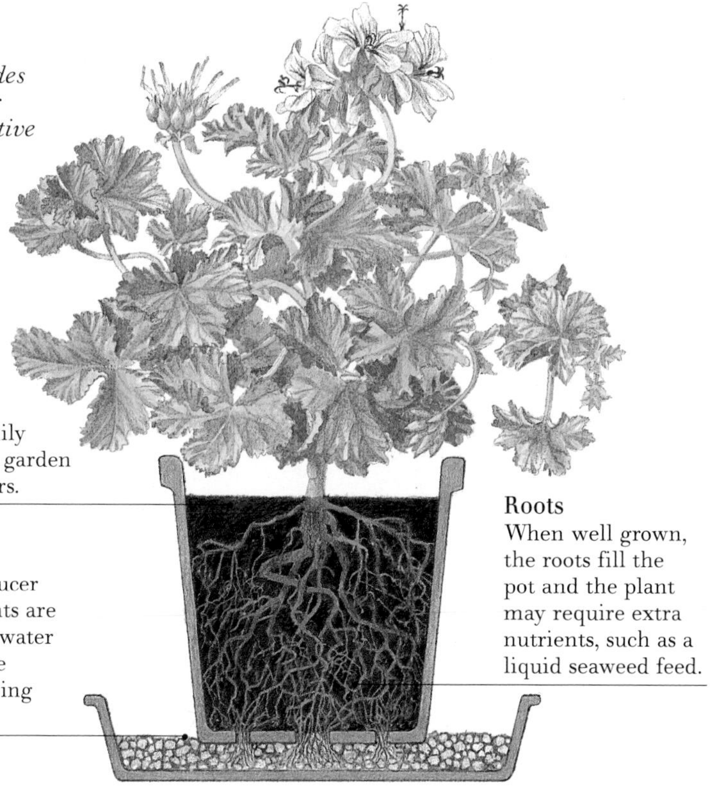

Soil
For best results, use a standard potting soil readily obtainable from garden stores and centers.

Base
Stones in the saucer ensure that plants are not standing in water and prevents the soil from becoming waterlogged.

Roots
When well grown, the roots fill the pot and the plant may require extra nutrients, such as a liquid seaweed feed.

Tender plants RIGHT
A greenhouse or conservatory provides ideal conditions for tender plants, such as this pelargonium, to flourish.

Rosmarinus var. *albiflorus*
White-flowered rosemary

Salvia officinalis
Common sage

Thymus serpyllum var. *albus*
Creeping thyme

Origanum vulgare 'Gold tip'
Gold variegated marjoram

Satureja montana
Winter savory

Herb container LEFT
The smallest container can be planted with carefully selected herbs for the patio or windowsill, where they can be protected during the colder months to produce a harvest all year round.

SUITABLE HERBS

Pages 70–71 illustrate some of the most suitable herbs for artificial habitats. They are summarized below for quick reference. See the "Herb Directory" for more suggestions, and the list of aromatic culinary herbs on page 183.

Aloysia triphylla
Lemon verbena

Heliotropium arborescens
Heliotrope

Ocimum basilicum var. 'Genovese'
Sweet basil

Ocimum basilicum minimum 'Greek'
Greek basil

Ocimum basilicum 'Purple Ruffles'
Purple ruffles basil

Origanum
Oregano

Origanum dictamnus
Dittany of Crete

Origanum majorana
Sweet marjoram

Pelargonium
Scented pelargonium

Rosmarinus
Rosemary

Salvia officinalis
Common sage

Salvia elegans syn. *rutilans*
Pineapple sage

Satureja montana
Winter savory

Thymus
Thyme

Ocimum basilicum var. *minimum* 'Greek'
Greek basil

Designing with Herbs

HERBS CAN PLAY A KEY role in the overall impact of any size garden. This chapter shows you how to select suitable herbs and gives ideas for making full use of the wide range of flowers and the marvelous foliage that herbal plants provide. Subtle combinations of color, height, and texture can create contrast and structure in formal and informal designs. Herbs also lend themselves to natural plantings reflecting their wild habitats, which look most successful in the garden.

Designs for traditional, formal herb gardens are included along with suggestions for planting in the kitchen garden or potager. Even small gardens and patios can benefit from an overall design and imaginative use of windowsills, containers, and walls. You can create a beautiful garden with herbs that provides color and interest throughout the year.

Visual Qualities

HERBS ARE INVALUABLE for using throughout the garden, whether on their own or in conjunction with other plants. There are herbs in all shapes, sizes, textures, and colors and usually with wonderful fragrances. Any garden can be enhanced by the addition of a few herbs, and they can be used almost anywhere – in beds or borders, by water, in walls or on paths, in sun or shade, in natural plantings or more formal designs.

Herbs may be chosen for their flowers, foliage, or fragrance alone. Make full use of their different visual qualities to achieve a varied and interesting planting scheme; keep in mind structure, color, and texture (see box opposite). Low-growing, ground-cover plants make decorative features, especially where they spill over the edges of a path to break up hard lines. In contrast, tall architectural herbs provide dramatic vertical accents and can be used on their own or interplanted with other herbs to provide a focal point of interest.

Structure is provided by shrubby herbs and evergreens. They are the backbone of the garden; without them it lacks substance and looks bare in the winter. Color creates atmosphere. Soft blues, whites, and creams are soothing and gentle; they glow in shade. Oranges and reds are revitalizing and often at their best in bright sun. Foliage comes in many shades of green, but can also be gray, purple, red, gold, or variegated. You can make visual contrasts or create harmony and movement through your garden by careful use of foliage and flower color in mixed plantings.

A shady backdrop LEFT *Dappled shade shows many flowers off to best advantage when out of bright sunlight; white flowers especially are enhanced in shady situations where they glow against the darker background. Decorative foliage, such as the gold variegated lemon balm shown here, is also suited to partial shade.*

Foliage also provides texture. Large leaves with well-defined shapes, such as acanthus, make strong statements. Small, finely cut or feathery leaves, like those of fennel, produce softer and denser forms. Experiment with contrasting textures and colors.

Planning your garden

Careful advance planning is always worthwhile before you begin to plant your garden. Keep in mind how you plan to use the garden and how it will look in winter. Sketch a plan of your garden with any new and existing features. Use books, magazines, and other gardens for additional inspiration; the planting suggestions in this chapter are also good starting points. Refer to the "Herb Directory" (pages 100–77) to help you plot heights, spreads, colors, and so on. Make sure the garden works as a whole, each area merging with the next. Select plants for each season so that your garden contains flowers and foliage year-round.

Plant in groups or singly, depending on the type of habitat and the size of the herbs being used. For example, in borders, use smaller herbs in groups of three or five and larger ones on their own; in shady areas, plant in drifts; in wet areas, groups of plants of one species are most effective.

A patio corner ABOVE
The complementary colors of the sweet-scented, vibrant pinks and the softer mauves of catmint and lavender make an eye-catching arrangement for the patio.

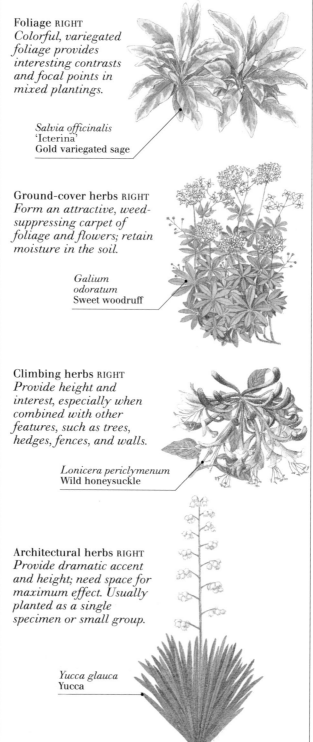

FEATURES TO CONSIDER

Accents are features that lead the eye to different parts of the garden and make focal points in subtle plantings. They can be provided by foliage and flowers of contrasting colors and textures, climbing herbs, tall, architectural plants, and those that provide soft, spreading ground cover.

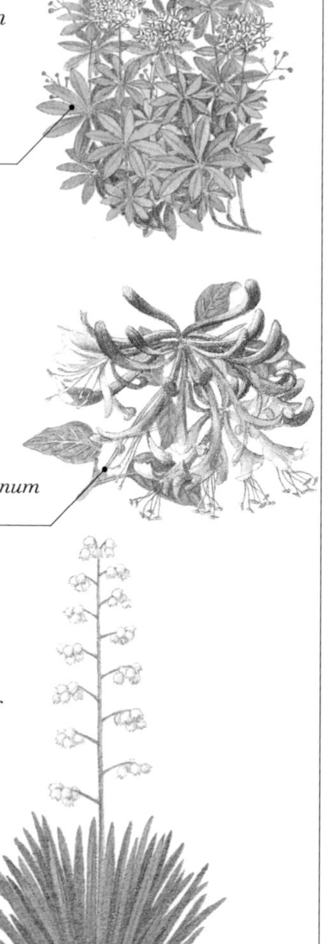

Foliage RIGHT
Colorful, variegated foliage provides interesting contrasts and focal points in mixed plantings.

Salvia officinalis 'Icterina'
Gold variegated sage

Ground-cover herbs RIGHT
Form an attractive, weed-suppressing carpet of foliage and flowers; retain moisture in the soil.

Galium odoratum
Sweet woodruff

Climbing herbs RIGHT
Provide height and interest, especially when combined with other features, such as trees, hedges, fences, and walls.

Lonicera periclymenum
Wild honeysuckle

Architectural herbs RIGHT
Provide dramatic accent and height; need space for maximum effect. Usually planted as a single specimen or small group.

Yucca glauca
Yucca

Borders and Island Beds

NOTHING IS MORE BEAUTIFUL than a mixed planting of decorative herbs with old-fashioned flowers in a border or island bed. Here you can make good use of herbs from several different habitats, such as those from woodland edges or wetlands. To accommodate the maximum variety of herbs, your bed needs to have moisture-retentive soil with good drainage and without risk of waterlogging in winter. This will suit a wide range of species, even many of those that grow naturally in hot, dry conditions.

Plant selection

Traditional borders have low-growing plants at the front and taller ones at the back. This is a safe but dull approach to take. By using a more imaginative planting design that involves varying height across the depth as well as along the length of the border, you can create rhythmic contours to give interest and surprise at each step. Allow some low-growing herbs, such as marjoram, spiny restharrow, and lady's mantle to extend to the middle or rear of the border, and place a few taller species, such as red orache, mullein, and angelica, toward the front to provide dramatic accents through shorter plants. Island beds need a similar approach, but remember to make your planting interesting on all sides.

Always consider seasonal implications. Plant early flowers and bulbs in the middle or back of the border, where they will be clearly visible in spring before other plants have produced much growth. They will be conveniently hidden by other plants later in the year, when their foliage is dying down. Position some late-flowering plants at the front or middle of the border.

Foliage color and texture

Using varied foliage is an excellent way of ensuring year-round interest in your garden. Acanthus and elecampane produce bold leaves with strong shapes, whereas artemisia gives a softer effect, as does lavender. Many members of the carrot family (Umbelliferae) have lacelike leaves. Fennel, with its soft feathery green or bronze foliage, is stunning.

Planting

First, set out the basic structure of the border or island bed using shrubby and evergreen plants; choose herbs such as santolina, rosemary, winter savory, and curry plant. Next, decide on the position

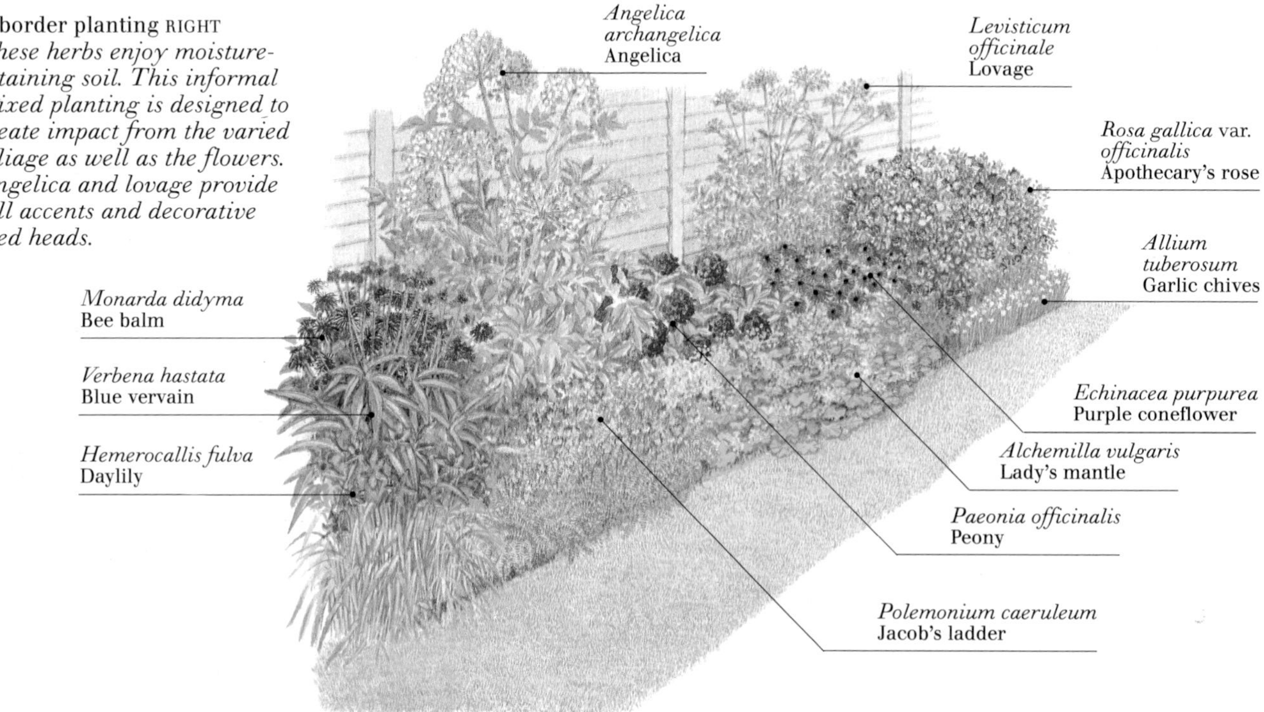

A border planting RIGHT *These herbs enjoy moisture-retaining soil. This informal mixed planting is designed to create impact from the varied foliage as well as the flowers. Angelica and lovage provide tall accents and decorative seed heads.*

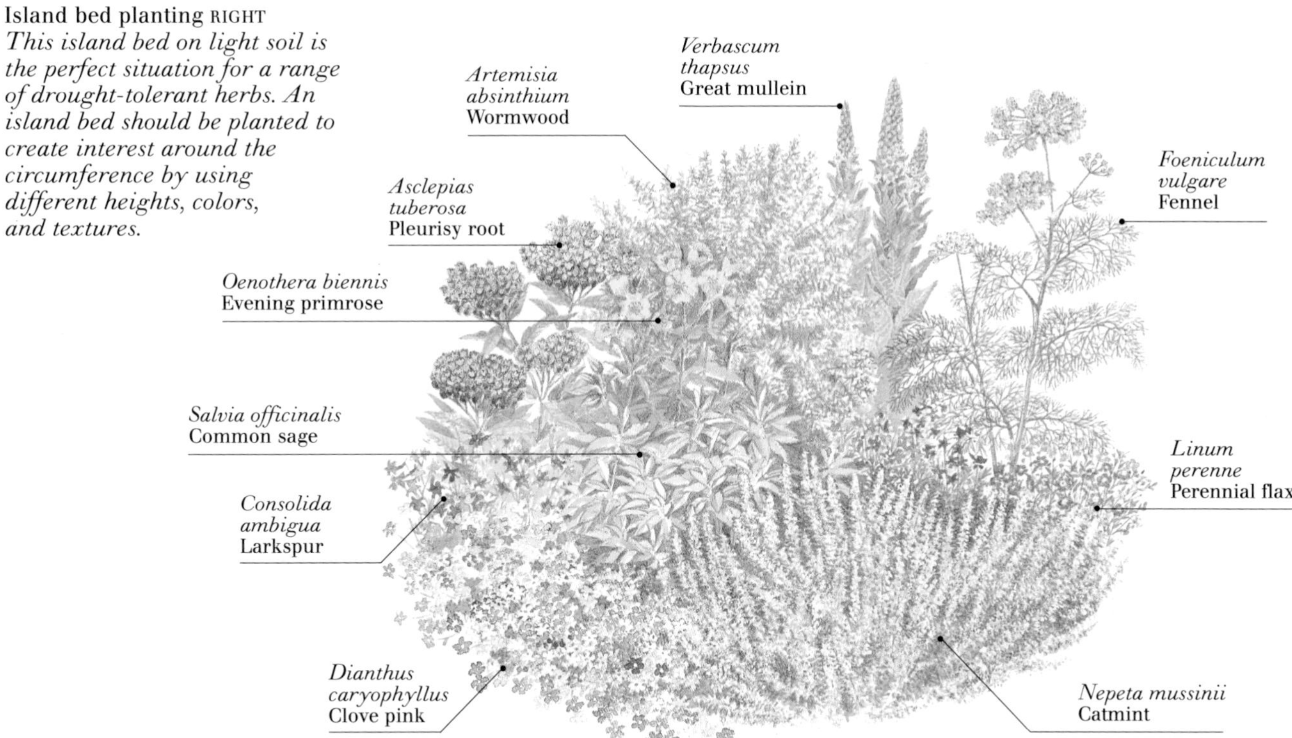

Island bed planting RIGHT
This island bed on light soil is the perfect situation for a range of drought-tolerant herbs. An island bed should be planted to create interest around the circumference by using different heights, colors, and textures.

of the dramatic accents and architectural plants, such as mullein, fennel, and angelica. Once these are in place, begin the in-fill planting. Unless space is restricted, repeat some of the groups of herbs and plant in threes or fives, according to their size and color. Remember that some herbs, such as evening primrose and larkspur, will self-seed, filling in gaps and adding to the informality of the design.

Many decorative and useful annuals, such as dill, fennel flower, coriander, and pot marigold, can be seeded in spring. Leave space in the planting to accommodate these or seed into existing gaps.

Gray and Silver Herbs

Borders and island beds lend themselves to mixed plantings. Gray- and silver-leaved herbs are restful to the eye and can be used to stabilize the brightest planting scheme with their soft foliage.

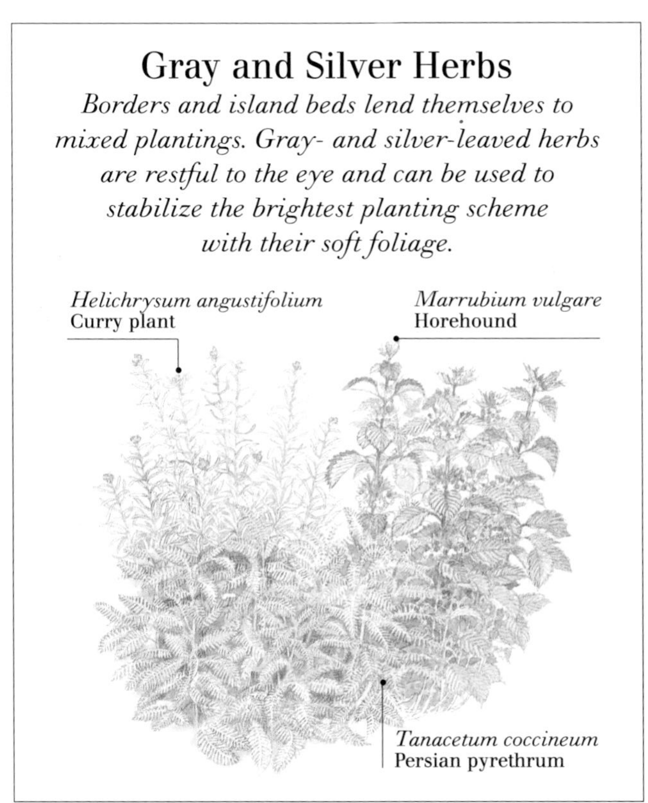

A natural border ABOVE
Here the flowers and foliage create a variety of soft-colored textures that spill onto the path.

Walls, Lawns, and Paths

As in any other part of the garden, walls, lawns, and paths are ideal for planting with herbs for ornament and interest. Paths and walls are dry habitats and best planted with herbs that can survive fairly poor but well-drained conditions (see pages 62–5). Lawns are usually planted on moisture-retaining soils. For a colorful and fragrant lawn on drier well-drained soils, plant carpeting herbs, such as chamomile and creeping thyme.

Walls

If you have an old wall bordering your garden, the likelihood is that it is already colonized by small plants. If you plan to build a wall use lime mortar, not cement, in its construction. Newly built walls, however, often take a long time to weather and become hospitable to plants. There are plenty of herbs that can be used to enhance them. Loosen the mortar between the bricks and squeeze in some soil containing a few seeds of wall germander or wild wallflower, for example, or if there is more space, plant a small rock plant, such as stonecrop, or clove pink. At the base of a wall where the soil is poor and dry, try a few of the Mediterranean herbs, such as rosemary and lavender, which will revel in this sunny, protected site with good drainage.

A wall planting BELOW
Many drought-resistant herbs will thrive in the dry conditions of a wall. Here, the spreading toadflax and stonecrop soften hard lines, wild wallflower and wall germander add a splash of color and height.

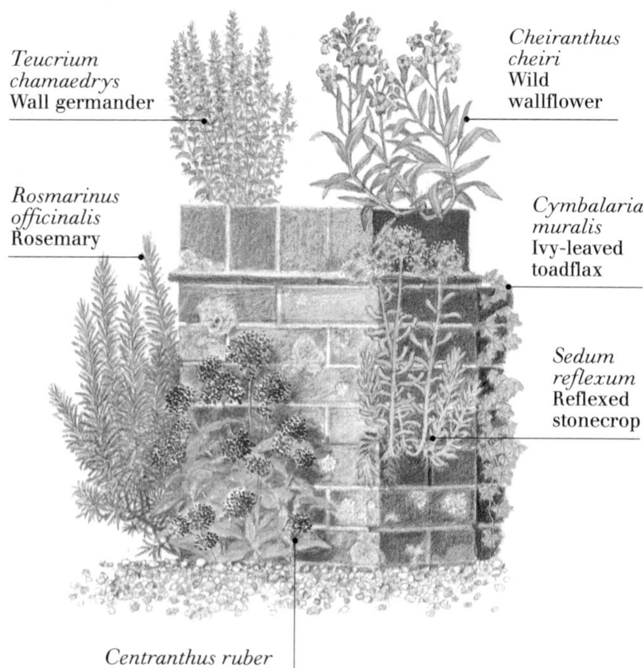

Herbal lawns

There are two main types of herbal lawn: one is made entirely from herbs, such as chamomile or thyme, and is planted for its fragrance; the other

FRAGRANT LAWNS

Instead of grass, grow a small area of herbal lawn, which will be delightfully fragrant to walk on and requires no mowing. Allow the plants space to spread.

Anthemis nobile
Roman chamomile

Anthemis nobile 'Treneague'
Roman chamomile 'Treneague'

Thymus herba-barona
Caraway thyme

Thymus praecox
Wild thyme

Thymus pseudolanuginosus
Woolly thyme

Thymus serpyllum var. *albus*
White-flowered creeping thyme

Thymus serpyllum 'Pink chintz'
Pink-flowered creeping thyme

Thymus serpyllum var. *coccineus*
Red-flowered creeping thyme

Thymus serpyllum 'Russetings'
Creeping thyme 'Russetings'

A stone wall ABOVE
This old stone wall is the perfect site for the delicate, spreading, ivy-leaved toadflax. It flowers for many weeks and readily self-seeds into any cracks.

is mainly composed of grass but is interplanted with herbs for their flowers and foliage.

Fragrant herb lawns can be as large or as small as you like. Start with a small patch and increase the size once you have assessed the amount of upkeep it needs and the time you can devote to it. You can use either seeds or small plants, positioned to allow them to spread. Do not walk on the lawn until the plants are well established.

For a less labor-intensive lawn, simply plant a few low-growing herbs within your existing grassy area. Choose tough plants, such as clovers, daisy, and yarrow, that can survive being walked on, being mowed, and being crowded by grass.

Paths

On gravel, paved, or brick paths, herbs can be used as decorative edging or carefully planted into the path itself to soften its impact.

Although an edging can be informal, with plants spilling out onto the path and disguising hard lines, it is often more successful if it is neat. Smaller, upright plants, such as parsley or chives, form impressive tidy rows, emphasizing the path.

Plantings into the path should look informal. Choose plants that spread and are ground-hugging, such as chamomile and the carpeting thymes. Plant sparsely so that they can spread and so that the path is complemented, not lost.

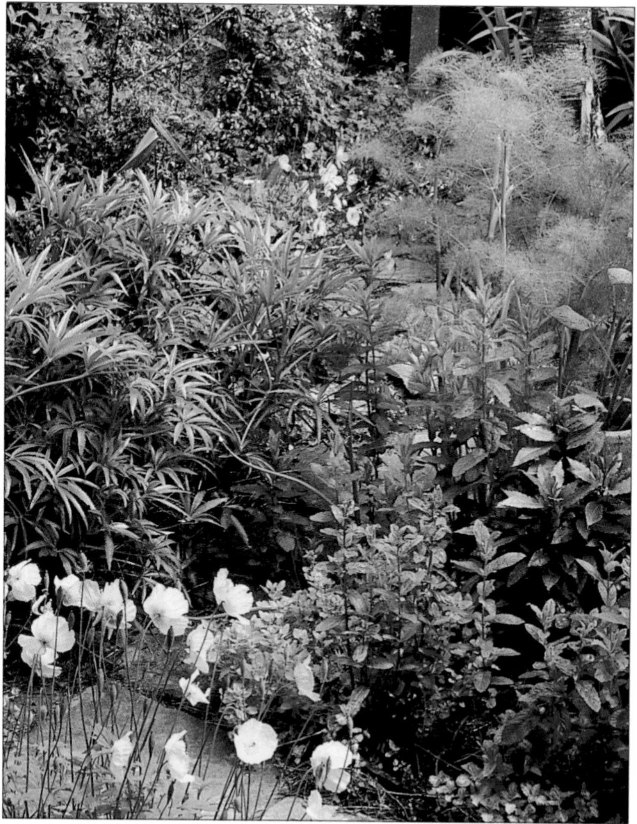

A winding path ABOVE
In early summer the edging to this path is composed of green foliage of different shades and textures of herbs such as mint, fennel, and peony. The yellow poppies add a cheerful note of color.

Edging plants BELOW
Some herbs, such as lavender, can be clipped to make a formal hedge along a border or path, while others tumble over hard edges to create a softer effect.

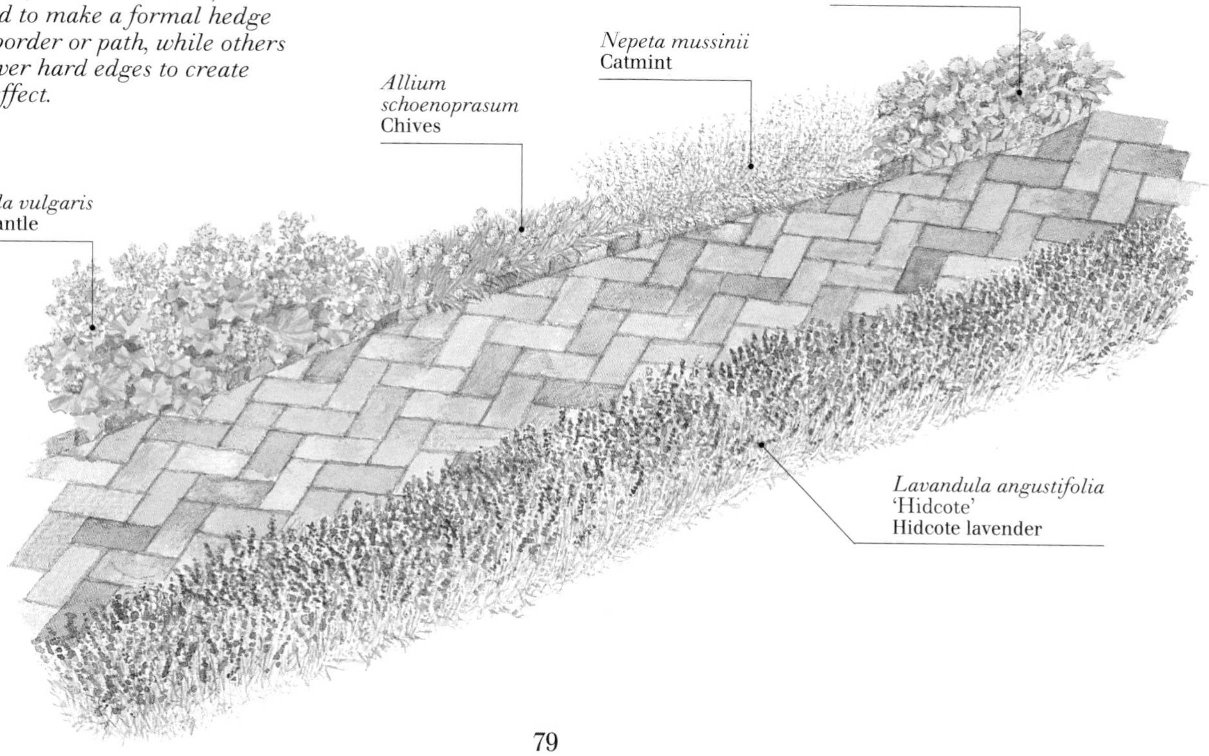

Calendula officinalis
Pot marigold

Nepeta mussinii
Catmint

Allium schoenoprasum
Chives

Alchemilla vulgaris
Lady's mantle

Lavandula angustifolia 'Hidcote'
Hidcote lavender

Woodland and Hedges

For a successful shaded or partially shaded habitat, aim for a natural effect, producing a low-maintenance area that is self-sustaining. Choose plants that are happy in low light levels, and select for the type of soil you have – dry or moist; there are plenty of choices (see also lists on pages 53 and 57). Keep your selection simple.

Shade from a single tree

Under the tree, plant a selection of low-growing, early-flowering bulbs and herbs, such as lungwort and sweet woodruff. Further away taller herbs that flower later, such as foxglove, daylily, and wild cranesbill will flourish in the partial shade, which enhances the colors of their flowers. Consider how the plants you choose grow in the wild – bluebells in drifts and primroses in groups, for example – and imitate this in your garden.

Wider areas of shade

If the shade is widespread, plant fewer species to produce a more dramatic effect. For areas of deep summer shade, make sure you choose herbs that flower early, such as lesser celandine and sweet violet. Bulbs such as snowdrops are ideal in this type of shady situation. Plant them in drifts, again aiming for a natural effect. Near the edge of the shade, where there are higher light levels, include a wider variety of plants, especially if the area is large. Aim to have flowers over a long season – for example, plant February daphne for late winter and early spring flowers, foxgloves for midspring, yarrow for summer to fall, black cohosh for

Bluebells ABOVE
In the garden a small patch of bluebells planted in woodland soil increase naturally to form drifts, as they do in the wild.

A woodland planting RIGHT
For a successful woodland planting in spring keep your selection simple. Grow bluebells and lily of the valley in drifts. Allow space for ground-cover plants, such as lungwort and lesser celandine, to spread. Plant foxgloves in areas with more light. Most woodland species flower in spring.

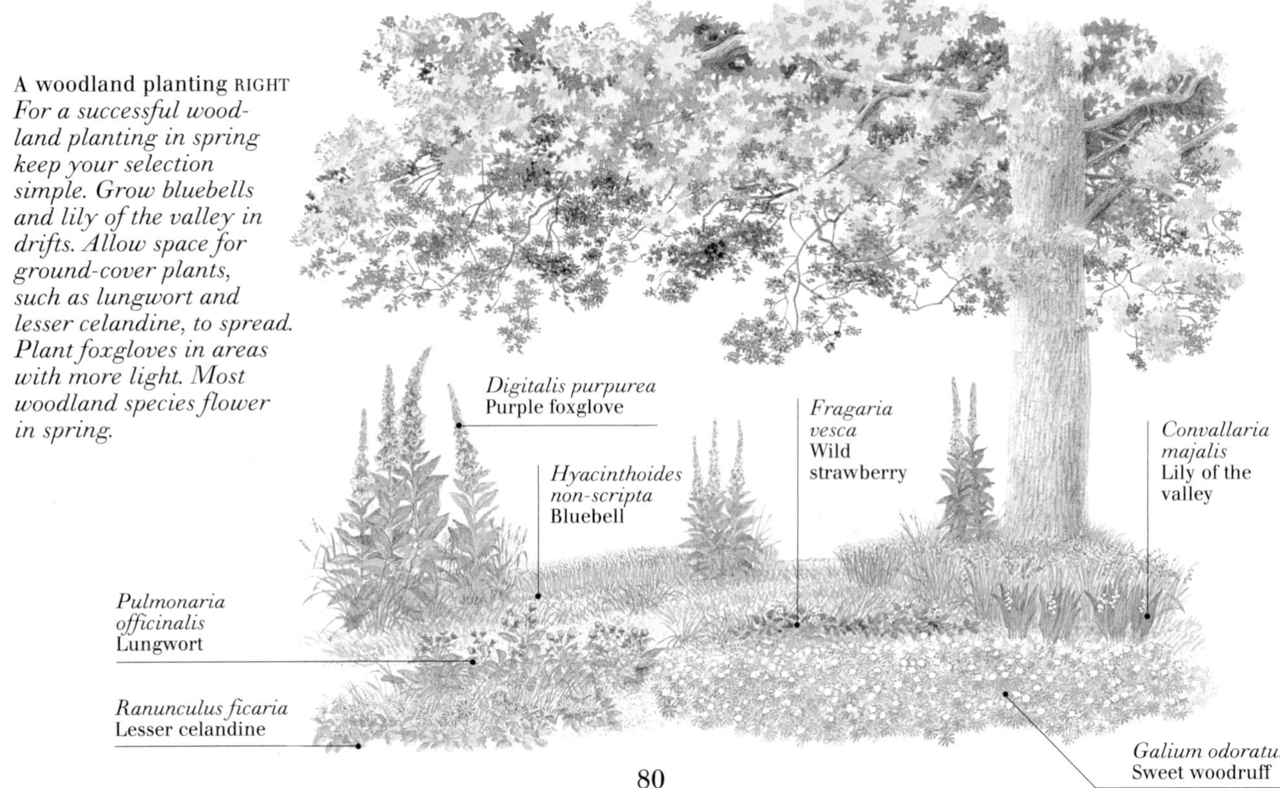

midsummer, and barberry for spring flowers, fall berries, and leaf color. Include a few decorative ground-cover plants to fill in between.

Hedges

The ideal hedge for wildlife and climbing herbs is a re-creation of a natural hedgerow, with a wide selection of shrubs. If you need to plant a hedge (see page 37), it is important that the hedging plants are given plenty of time to establish before you add the more rampant shade-loving climbers, such as hop, dog rose, or honeysuckle.

Formal hedges, such as those grown from beech or conifers, can be made less formal by planting a variety of herbs at their base (see pages 53 and 57 for lists of shade lovers).

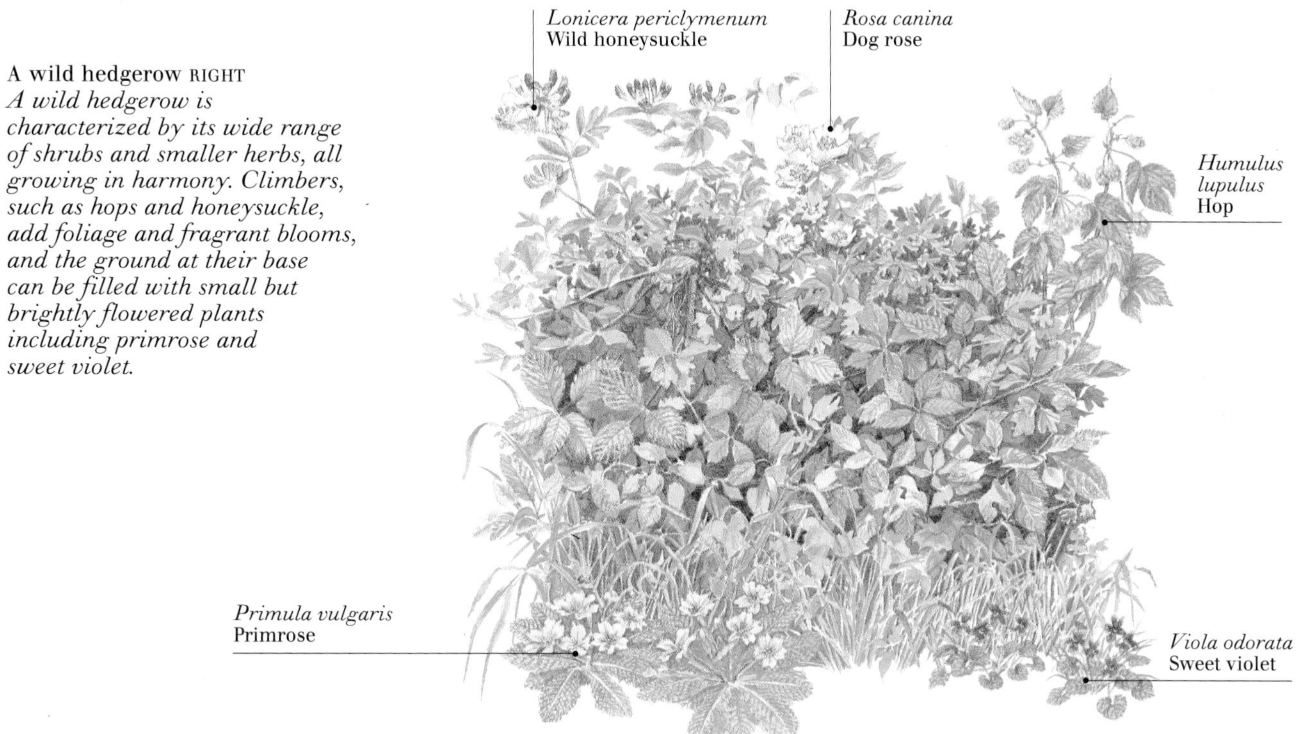

A wild hedgerow RIGHT
A wild hedgerow is characterized by its wide range of shrubs and smaller herbs, all growing in harmony. Climbers, such as hops and honeysuckle, add foliage and fragrant blooms, and the ground at their base can be filled with small but brightly flowered plants including primrose and sweet violet.

GROUND-COVER PLANTS

Ground-cover plants are ideal for planting in shaded places where they form carpets of color, reducing weed growth and providing year-round interest. Rich, moist woodland soil encourages them to spread and form large drifts providing foliage when the early spring flowering of most woodland species is over.

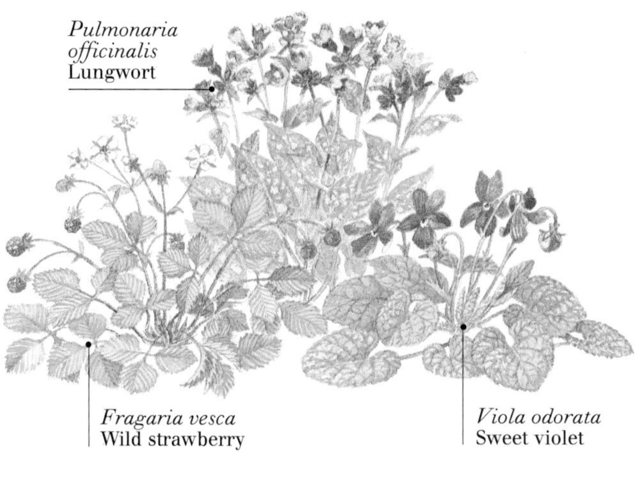

Lungwort ABOVE
There are many decorative varieties of lungwort. Pulmonaria rubra *is particularly ornamental, with bright pink flowers and plain green leaves.*

The Water Garden

A POND IS ALWAYS a focal point in any garden and provides the perfect habitat for a colorful range of herbs that thrive in the water or at the pond edge. When carefully and imaginatively planted, an area of boggy ground in association with a pond or small stream can be one of the most beautiful places in the garden, and is especially favored by many kinds of wildlife, so adding an extra dimension of interest. You need only a tiny pool to create a successful water garden.

The pond and pond edge

When planting a pond, remember to include an oxygenating plant (see box), without which no fish or water-dwelling insects can survive; they also prevent the water from becoming stagnant. Include

A pond planting RIGHT
In a pond, surface-leaved herbs such as bogbean and water lily flourish. Plant tall herbs in groups at the pond edge; lower-growing plants, such as water mint, form a contrast to the spearlike foliage of the flags.

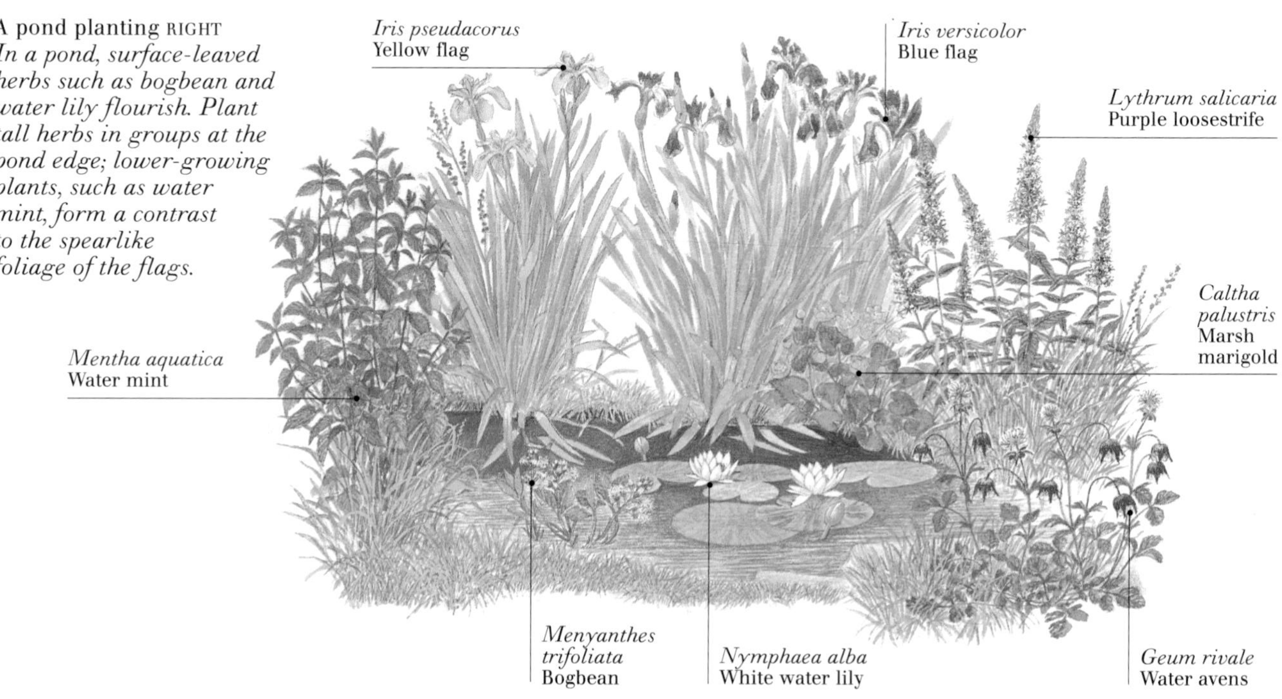

Water lilies LEFT
This natural-looking pond was created from a small stream. Frogs, birds, and insects use the large leaves of the water lilies as resting platforms; pond snails lay their eggs underneath. Ponds attract a variety of wildlife into the garden, an additional benefit of any water feature.

plants with surface-floating leaves, such as water lily and bogbean. Depending on the size of your pond, use only one or two of these, as they spread and need space to look their best. Wild water lily and bogbean are unsuitable for very small ponds.

There are many plants that thrive in the shallow water by the banks of a pond. Choose a variety of heights, shapes, and colors to be sure that you have something of interest throughout the year and plenty to attract wildlife. When planting, take into account the characteristics of each plant. For example, flag irises have narrow, upright leaves that give a vertical emphasis. They contrast well with less erect, wider-spreading plants, such as water mint or marsh marigold.

The bog garden

This area of the garden is considered valuable, as it is permanently damp with rich soil in which a wide variety of herbs can be grown. Unless your pond is in a formal part of your garden or sited within a paved area, plant boggy areas to merge with the pond edge in a natural way.

Positioning and planting

Plant herbs for pond and wetland in groups of the same species to make a mass of color, as often occurs naturally in the wild. Many of the moisture-loving species are tall, including purple and yellow loosestrife and hemp agrimony; contrast them with lower-growing herbs, such as water avens and Greek valerian. The golden-flowered creeping Jenny makes excellent ground cover for moist, shaded ground, as does the spring-flowering bugle.

Plant between spring and fall. First, position water plants that have surface-floating leaves, such as bogbean and water lily, and add a selection of oxygenating plants (see box). It is best to use plastic baskets for any vigorous plants (see page 35); water plants are often sold in these. Next, plant shallow-water plants around the pond's margin. These can also be planted in baskets to restrict their spread. Finally, plant the boggy area with suitable herbs.

OXYGENATING PLANTS

Oxygenating plants are essential for a healthy pond. They float on or below the water surface, and with surface-floating herbs, such as water lily, they provide shade and decorative foliage.

Callitriche autumnalis
Water starwort

Ceratophyllum demersum
Hornwort

Elodea canadensis
Canadian waterweed

Fontinalis antipyretica
Willow moss

Myriophyllum verticillatum
Water milfoil

Ranunculus aquatilis
Water crowfoot

A bog garden RIGHT
In high summer with plenty of moisture, the plants in a bog garden thrive. Some of the most handsome herbs enjoy these conditions and produce a wealth of foliage and flower color. In the shade beneath the taller herbs, bugle and creeping Jenny form attractive ground cover.

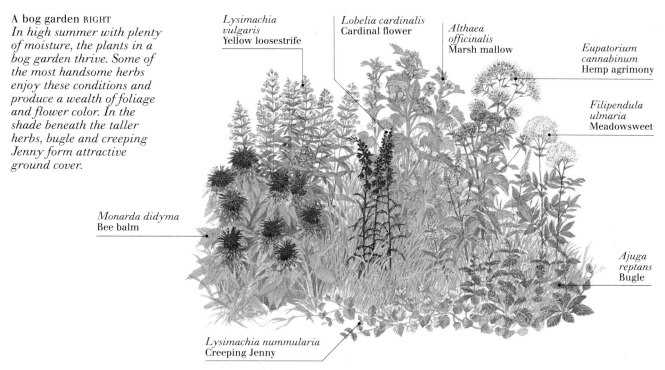

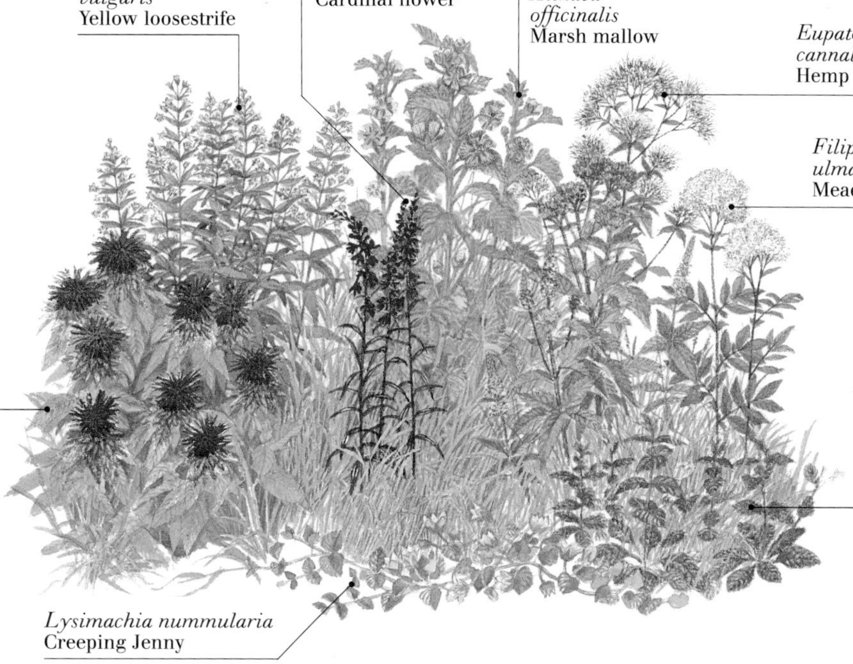

Lysimachia vulgaris Yellow loosestrife
Lobelia cardinalis Cardinal flower
Althaea officinalis Marsh mallow
Eupatorium cannabinum Hemp agrimony
Filipendula ulmaria Meadowsweet
Monarda didyma Bee balm
Ajuga reptans Bugle
Lysimachia nummularia Creeping Jenny

The Dry Garden

HERBS NATIVE TO DRY stony or rocky steppes and Mediterranean hillsides can be grown in parts of the garden where the open, sunny conditions and well-drained soil in which they thrive are present. These natural conditions can be re-created in rock gardens, scree, and raised or gravel beds. Many fragrant and culinary herbs originate from these habitats and there is a wide range of suitable herbs from which to make a selection (see pages 62–5).

Plant selection

Plants suitable for a rock garden are mostly low growing and not too invasive: rock gardens look more natural with areas of bare rock. In the gravel garden (see box) intersperse taller, upright plants with shorter, spreading ones. Never structure planting rigidly by height, which looks unnatural.

Both carpeting and bushy thymes are ideal for dry gardens. The pasqueflower in various forms is also completely at home, and the common rockrose cascades beautifully over rocks or gravel. Many pinks, including the fragrant clove pink, also look lovely here. Other herbs that thrive in the rock garden are saffron crocus, stonecrop, and thrift. When making your choice, ensure that foliage and flowers will be in evidence throughout the year.

Not all plants from rocky areas enjoy a hot, dry site; some require moisture and partial or light shade. Good examples of herbs for the shady areas of a dry garden are the dwarf columbine species, some of the ferns, bearberry, dwarf balloon flower, and garden calamint. Plant these in areas where some moisture is available and shade is provided by overhanging rocks or other plants.

Raised beds

A raised bed makes a decorative garden feature near the house or patio. It provides good drainage for herbs that enjoy hot, dry summer conditions. Include plants that will cascade over the walls, such as wall germander, rockrose, and creeping thymes. Use shrubby herbs, such as purple sage and lavender, to give structure and height, with lower-growing herbs, such as decorative marjorams and winter savory, to fill in around them.

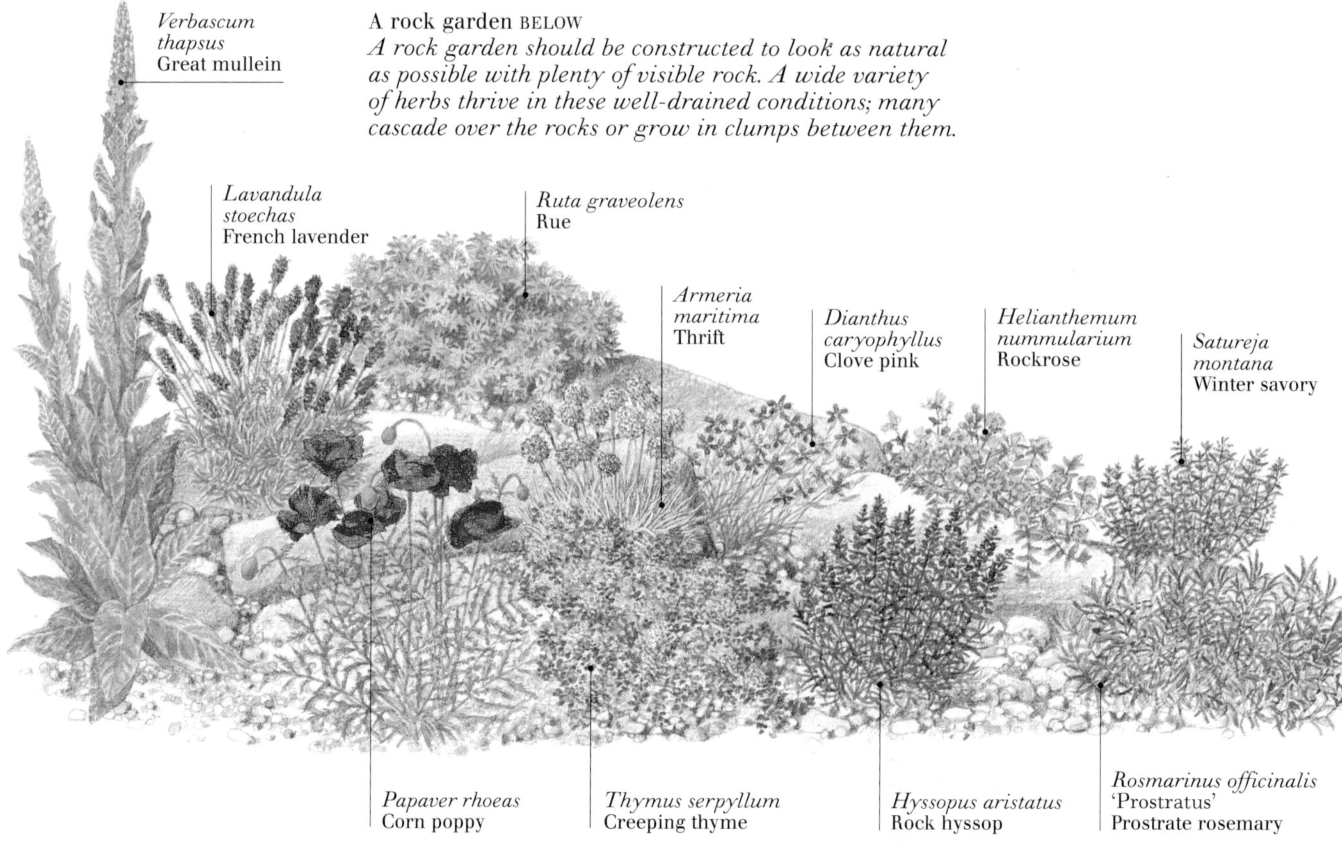

A rock garden BELOW
A rock garden should be constructed to look as natural as possible with plenty of visible rock. A wide variety of herbs thrive in these well-drained conditions; many cascade over the rocks or grow in clumps between them.

Planting

When planting, keep in mind that many rock plants do not like competition. Saffron crocus, for example, needs some space, as does pasqueflower, and chives look their best when left to form a clump. Interplant upright herbs, such as lavender and southernwood, with spreading ones. In a rock garden, begin planting from the top and work downward, positioning some taller species at the base. In a gravel garden, plant taller species first, leaving plenty of space around them for smaller herbs and for seeding annuals.

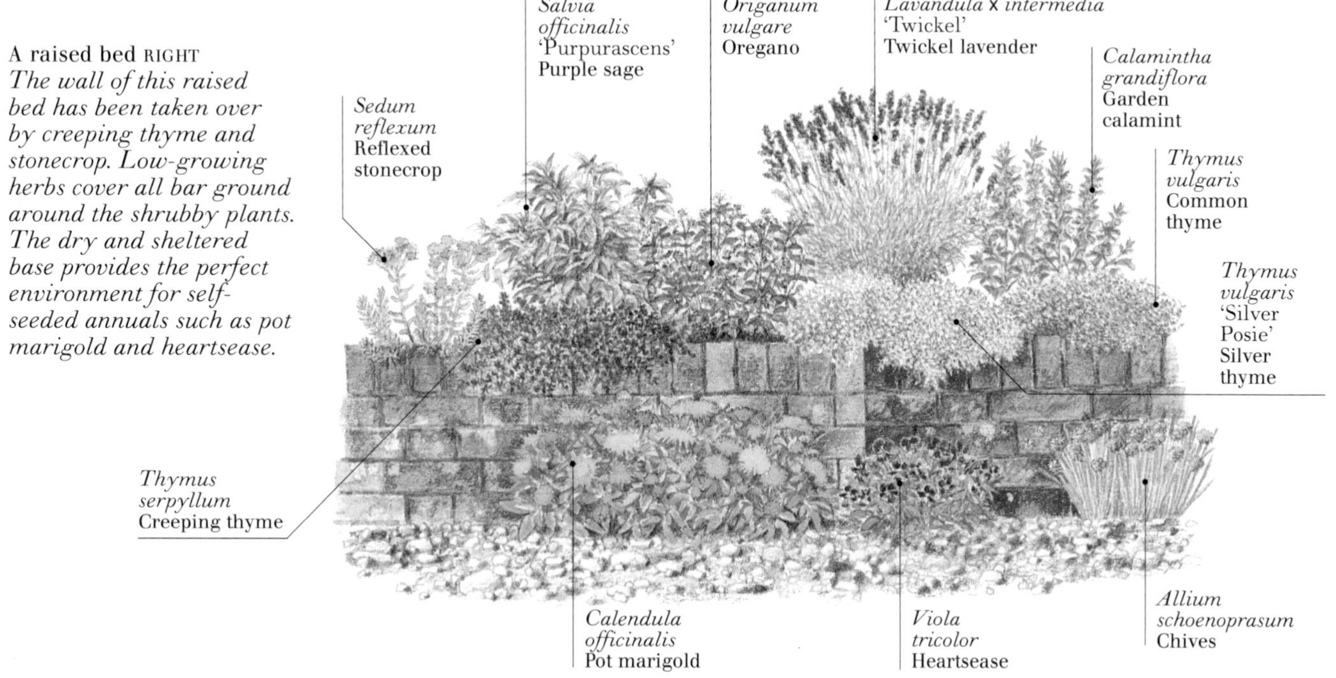

A raised bed RIGHT
The wall of this raised bed has been taken over by creeping thyme and stonecrop. Low-growing herbs cover all bar ground around the shrubby plants. The dry and sheltered base provides the perfect environment for self-seeded annuals such as pot marigold and heartsease.

Colorful thymes ABOVE
The dry garden is a perfect habitat for those herbs, mostly low growing, that love a hot, well-drained site. The varied colors and textures of creeping thymes form soft carpets over the stones and rocks.

GRAVEL GARDENS

This is a simple way to grow rock plants that need good drainage. Plants will readily self-seed to achieve a natural informality. Tall herbs, such as mullein, yucca, and acanthus, will thrive here with colorful annual flowers and carpeting herbs.

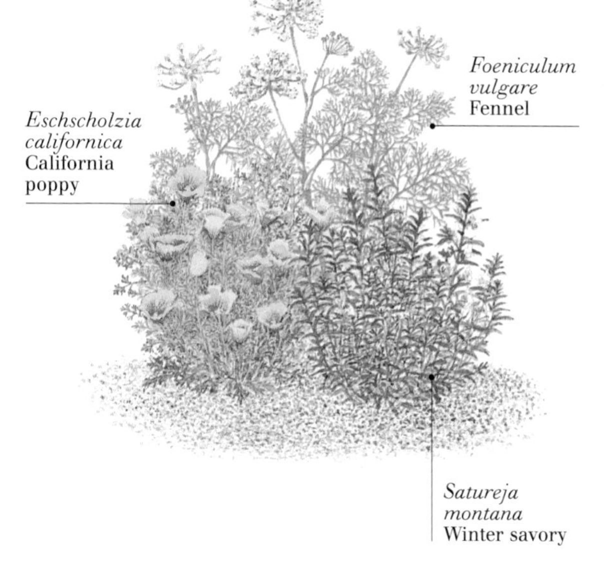

The Container Garden

CONTAINER GARDENS may consist of a single container or many; tubs, pots, troughs, sinks, and hanging baskets can either be used on their own or to highlight part of a larger planting scheme. Temporary container displays are ideal for brightening a corner of the garden that is past its prime or for adding interest to a new garden while you are waiting for other plants to establish. Tender herbs that cannot survive winter temperatures outside are ideal for growing in containers; they can be put outside in late spring, and brought inside at the first sign of frost.

Plant selection

Almost any herb can be grown in a container, although those that are more vigorous will need regular feeding and may require more frequent repotting. Some herbs are in fact far better grown in containers, especially where conditions, such as moisture and sun or shade, need to be regulated. Vigorous plants that become invasive in a small garden, such as mint, can be grown in a container to restrict their growth.

For a large trough or window box scheme, choose a variety of plants, including some for structure and foliage as well as for flowers. If your selection is mainly foliage based, include a few bright annual flowers, such as nasturtium, heartsease, or pot marigold, or use bulbs to add extra color. You can

MINIATURE GARDENS

Many smaller-growing herbs can be planted in a trough as shown here, to create a garden in miniature. The tiny leaves of creeping thymes are particularly suitable.

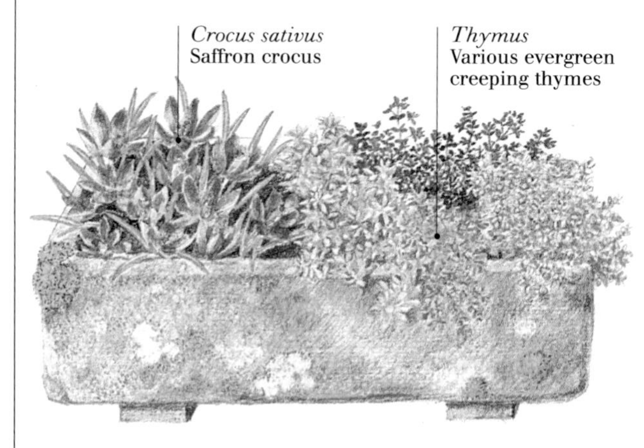

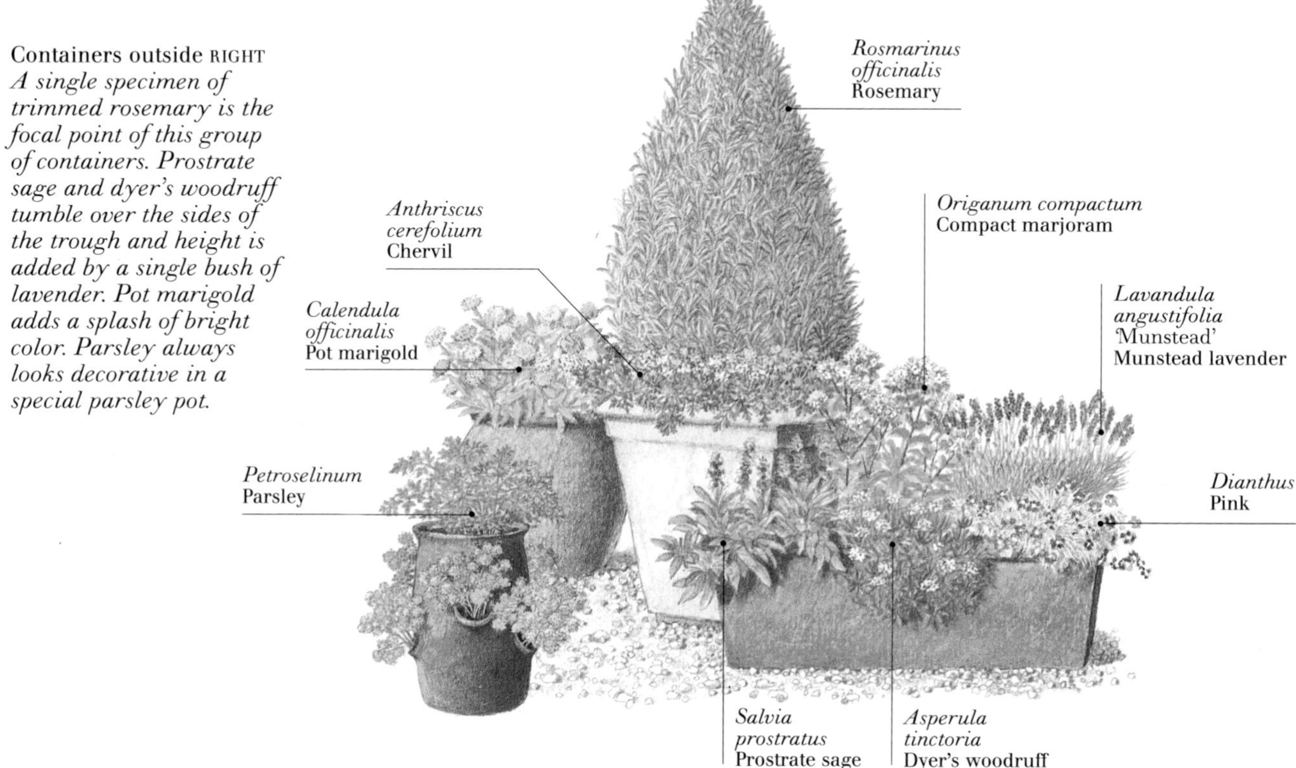

Containers outside RIGHT
A single specimen of trimmed rosemary is the focal point of this group of containers. Prostrate sage and dyer's woodruff tumble over the sides of the trough and height is added by a single bush of lavender. Pot marigold adds a splash of bright color. Parsley always looks decorative in a special parsley pot.

also plant annual flowers around a single specimen herb, such as a bay tree or a clipped rosemary, both of which tend to be rather bare at their bases.

Short-lived herbs, such as basil and parsley, are very well suited to containers. Plant a parsley pot, or pocketed planter, with small clumps of parsley seedlings. Use different varieties to provide visual contrast and interest. The added advantage of putting culinary herbs in containers is that they can be positioned conveniently close to the kitchen and brought inside in winter or when required.

Planting

Choose the size of the container with care: not too small for vigorous plants. Potted plants must be well drained, so put a layer of stones or pieces of broken clay pot at the bottom of the container. Always fill the container with potting soil that is appropriate for the type of herb you are planting; for example, use a gritty mix for plants that require extra drainage and an ericaceous compost for those that need acid conditions. When repotting a plant position it at the same depth that it was in the previous container. Firm in the compost, leaving approximately ½ inch (1.5 cm) at the top to facilitate watering. The same principles apply to planting troughs and window boxes. Hanging baskets should be planted around the edge first and then built up in layers toward the center.

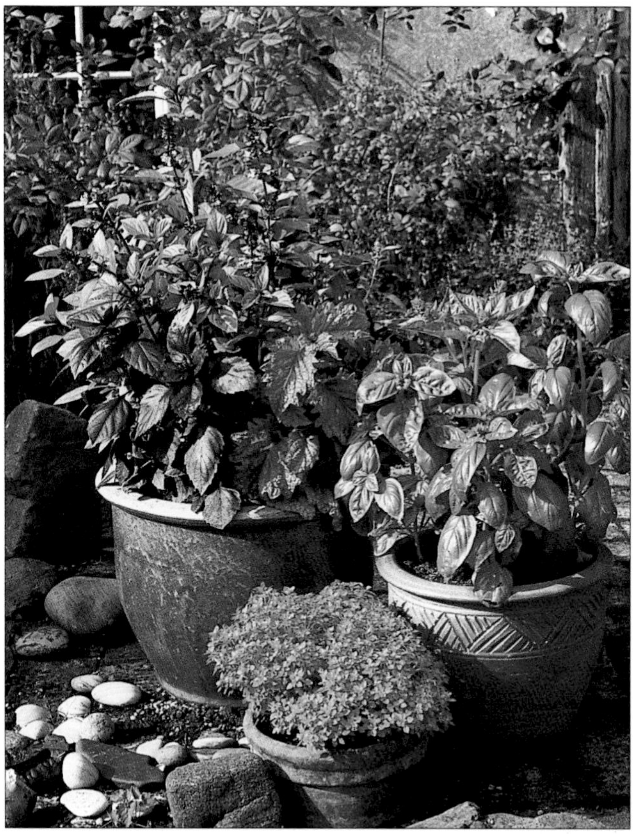

Pots of basil ABOVE
Basil in its many varieties is often best grown in containers. Here a selection of decorative pots has been used and different basils planted for ornamental effect. In colder weather the pots can be brought inside to keep tender basil protected.

Windowsill BELOW
Grow some of the most often used culinary herbs on a kitchen windowsill for easy access. The varied foliage makes them an attractive feature. Turn the pots frequently to grow the herbs in an even shape.

The Patio Herb Garden

EVEN IF YOU HAVE only a tiny yard, barely deserving of the term "patio," you can make it into a marvelous garden area in its own right. If it is constructed of attractive flagstones or well-laid bricks and bordered with narrow beds so much the better, but even this is not essential because tubs and containers (see pages 86–7) of herbs planted and grouped imaginatively make a wonderful, adaptable display. Trellises and window boxes add extra dimension, planting space, and height to a small area. Raised beds also extend the range of plants that you can grow (see page 85).

Patio herbs ABOVE
In this small patio bronze fennel gives a soft, dark backdrop to colorful pinks, thymes, and catmint.

Plant selection

Any herb or shrub that can be grown in a container, raised bed, or narrow border is ideal for the patio. In the limited space available, it might be best to choose a theme, such as a collection of fragrant or culinary herbs. It is most important to make use of all the space available: clothe the house walls with passionflower, jasmine, or honeysuckle trained up a trellis, suspend window boxes from windowsills, plant trailing and spreading herbs, such as creeping thymes, in the gaps between paving stones, and position tubs and troughs in the sun or shade, as appropriate for the plants.

Because the patio is so close to the house, it is important to select herbs for the area with care. Always keep in mind how you use the patio. If you usually sit out there midmorning, make sure that your seat is going to be beside scented herbs that have soothing and refreshing properties, such as lavender and basil; for a relaxing fragrance in the evening, choose from jasmine, lemon verbena, chamomile, and roses. A variety of culinary herbs

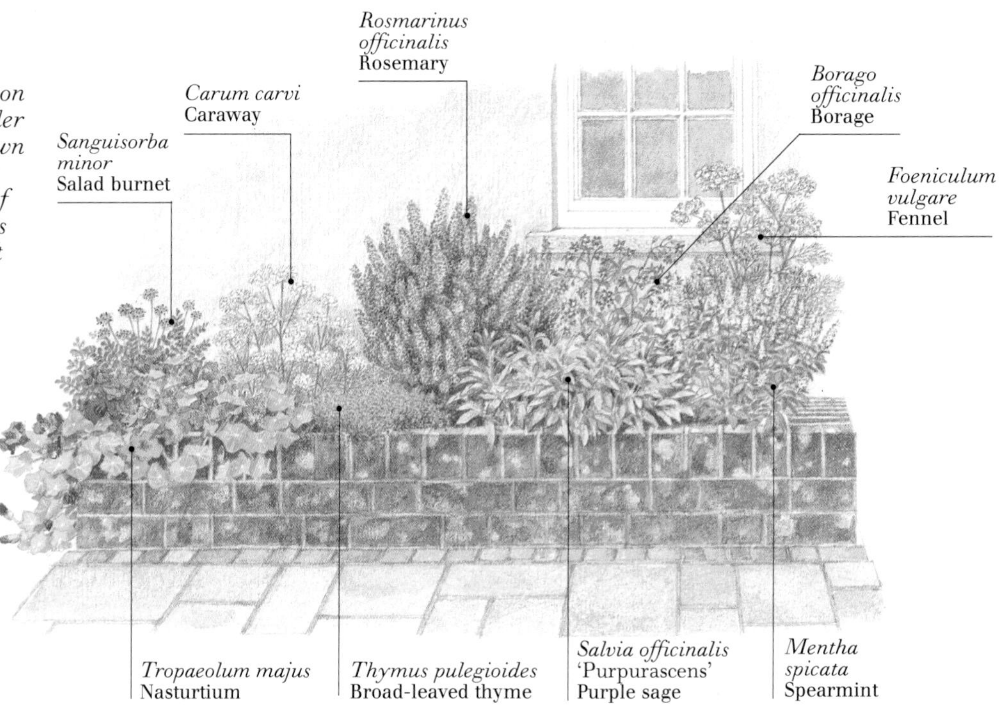

A patio border RIGHT
Make a narrow raised bed on the patio for planting a wider variety of herbs. Those shown here all have culinary uses but also provide a variety of flower and foliage colors, as well as scents that will waft into the kitchen through an open window.

Vertical patio garden RIGHT
An exuberant planting of fragrant and decorative herbs in an area that catches the sun makes an ideal place to sit in. Decorative climbers like honeysuckle will clothe a wall or fence; other herbs give a selection of color, foliage, and scent through the flowering season.

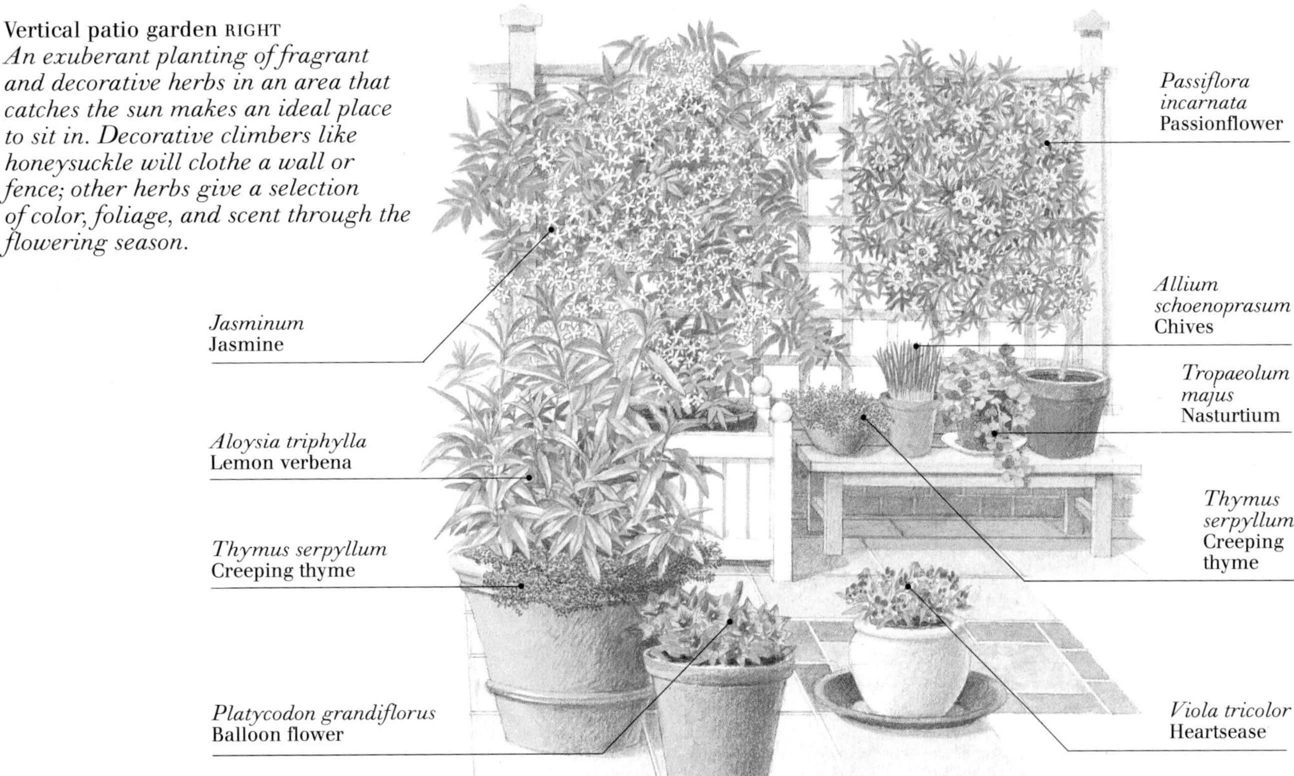

should also be grown on the patio for easy access from the kitchen.

If your patio is bordered by walls or fences, the likelihood is that one side will be sunny and dry and the other more shady and possibly damp. Refer to those sections in chapter 2, "Habitats in the Garden," for suitable plants for these conditions.

Practical considerations

The patio lends itself to growing a wide range of herbs but avoid any that are too vigorous and likely to grow quickly beyond their allotted space. Also try to avoid small pots or containers, which, when positioned in sun traps, will need to be watered daily (sometimes twice a day). This is inconvenient if you spend much time away from home.

Planting

Plant your patio beds in much the same way that you would a border (see pages 76–7), and plant containers following the advice on pages 86–7. Make sure that existing beds have been dug and composted before they are planted (see page 32). Once planted, the soil will be very hard working, so it needs a good start. Direct sow annual culinary herbs, such as dill, pot marigold, and heartsease, for aromatic foliage and flowers.

FRAGRANT HERBS

Many herbs have wonderful scents. Grow them on the patio or climbing the walls, as shown here, and you can enjoy their fragrance at all times of the day and into the evening, both inside and outside the house.

Aloysia triphylla
Lemon verbena

Daphne mezereum
February daphne

Heliotropium arborescens
Heliotrope

Jasminum
Jasmine (various)

Lilium candidum
Madonna lily

Lonicera periclymenum
Wild honeysuckle

Ocimum basilicum
Sweet basil

Pelargonium
Scented pelargonium

Rosa
Rose (various)

Salvia elegans syn. *rutilans*
Pineapple sage

Viola odorata
Sweet violet

The Formal Garden

THE FORMAL GARDEN is characterized by a geometric layout and divisions into smaller beds or compartments, often separated by brick, gravel, or stone paths. A formal herb garden can be designed in any size and shape, and most gardens can accommodate one in their planting scheme. They are normally closely associated with the house, where the herbs are convenient for harvesting and their scent can be appreciated.

Designs

A simple design suitable for a very small area is the cartwheel, which can be made from an old wagon wheel set into the ground but is more usually constructed from bricks, edging tiles, or lumber. The spokes divide the miniature garden, and each section is planted with herbs of the same variety.

Another simple design is the checkerboard, in which square paving slabs alternate with squares of soil. Others are based on divided circles or squares.

Knot gardens are probably the best known of the formal designs. The most intricate designs often require a lot of maintenance, but it is possible to make simpler patterns. The outline is traditionally formed by clipped box, cotton lavender, or dwarf lavender, which should be trimmed regularly as necessary. The small compartments within the knot are either mulched with gravel or planted with low-growing herbs of similar heights. These are mostly perennial plants, but some annuals may also be used in the design.

HEDGING PLANTS

Many herbs suitable for edging can be clipped to make neat hedges for formal gardens or dwarf hedges for a knot garden. Box is a traditional hedging plant, but herbs such as lavender and santolina also provide scent and flowers.

Buxus sempervirens 'Suffruticosa'
Dwarf box

Lavandula angustifolia 'Hidcote'
Hidcote lavender

Lavandula x *intermedia* 'Twickel Purple'
Twickel lavender

Santolina chamaecyparissus
Cotton lavender

Santolina chamaecyparissus 'Lemon Queen'
Cotton lavender 'Lemon Queen'

Teucrium chamaedrys
Wall germander

A cartwheel bed BELOW
The traditional cartwheel is easy to construct and is ideal for a small garden or for positioning near the kitchen. The theme can be culinary, medicinal, or purely decorative, with each compartment containing one type of herb.

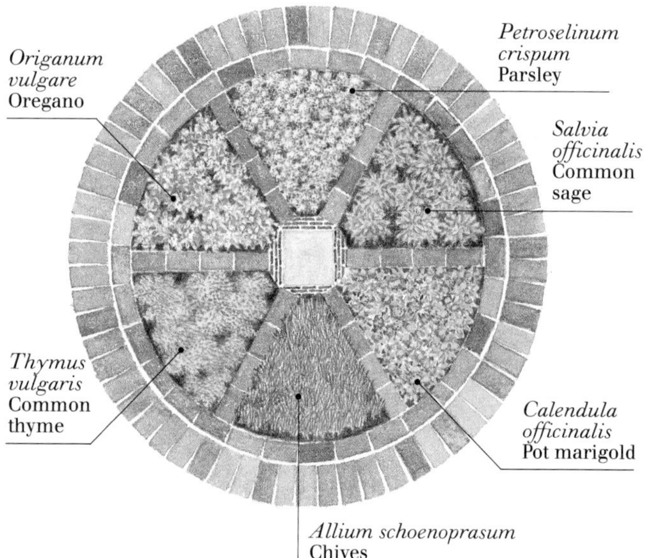

A checkerboard BELOW
Checkerboards are effective when each compartment is planted with a single type of herb. Here, a variety of leaf shapes and flower colors are used, with herbs of different heights providing further interest.

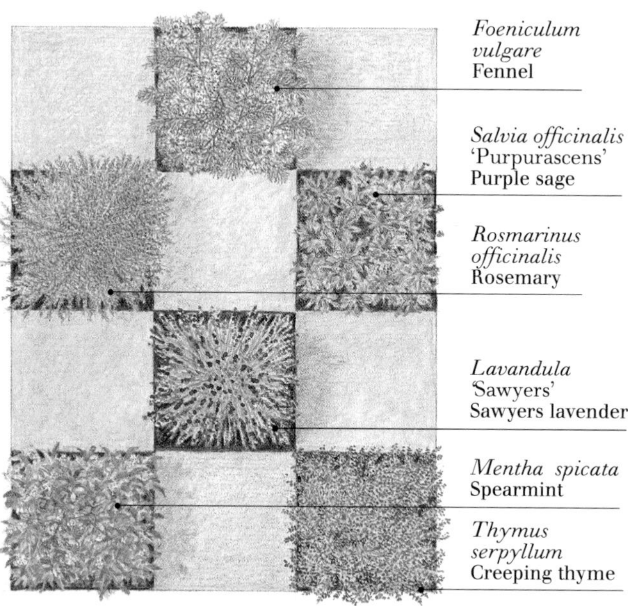

The material for paths and paving is an important consideration in formal gardens. Brick is ideal and can be laid in various decorative patterns. Stone slabs are attractive but expensive; imitation stone slabs, made from concrete, are a cheaper, effective alternative. Grass and gravel paths need regular maintenance by mowing and weeding.

Planning and planting

Plan your garden design over the winter months, beginning by laying out paths and preparing the soil. Decide on a centerpiece, if appropriate, such as a large evergreen herb like rosemary, a clipped bay tree, a stone birdbath, sundial, or sculpture.

Start planting in spring. Except for the larger shrubby herbs, such as rosemary, use a minimum of three plants of each variety; with smaller, less vigorous herbs, plant as many as five or more. In a knot garden or checkerboard, each compartment should be filled with only one type of herb.

Unlike knot gardens, some formal designs are often most interesting when they feature herbs of differing heights. One section might contain low-growing thymes, another by contrast tall herbs, such as fennel, lovage, or angelica. Other suitable low-growing herbs include chives, oregano, parsley, catmint, and flowers like pot marigold, feverfew, chamomile, and pinks.

A formal garden ABOVE
This is a simple formal design, with decorative brick paths and a sculptural centerpiece that acts as a focal point. There is foliage and flower interest over a long season and sufficient structure provided by shrubby herbs to remain appealing over winter.

A formal design BELOW
This simple design can be adapted to a garden of almost any size. Use edgings of dwarf lavender and creeping thymes with a few taller accents in the beds among lower-growing herbs. Planting within the geometric beds can be informal.

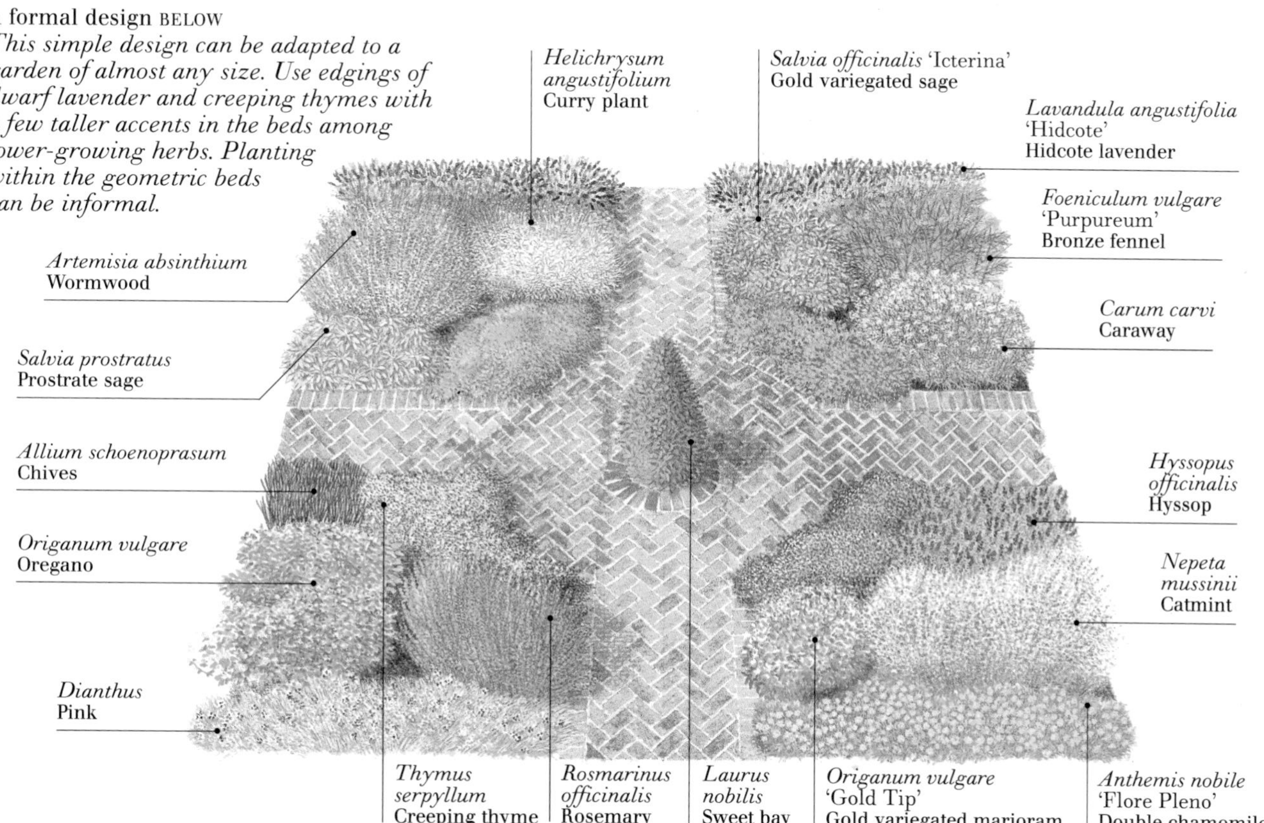

Theme Gardens

HERBS ARE LOOSELY categorized into various groups by their traditional and current uses. Culinary, cosmetic, fragrant, medicinal, and dye herbs, and those that attract bees and butterflies are typical categories. Making a collection of herbs from one particular group can be engrossing and is a challenging way to develop a garden with a purpose. Another idea is to gather herbs from one genus, such as mints, sages, or thymes to make an attractive display. The traditional herb garden was very much a theme garden, when herbs were a necessity of everyday life, and were grown for their uses in medicine, magic, dyeing, and as strewing herbs. Like formal gardens, theme gardens are constructed regardless of habitat, so they will require extra maintenance.

Traditional medicinal bed RIGHT
Here herbs with important medicinal properties are planted together for historic interest and a pleasing effect. Some of these herbs are poisonous and are not for home use.

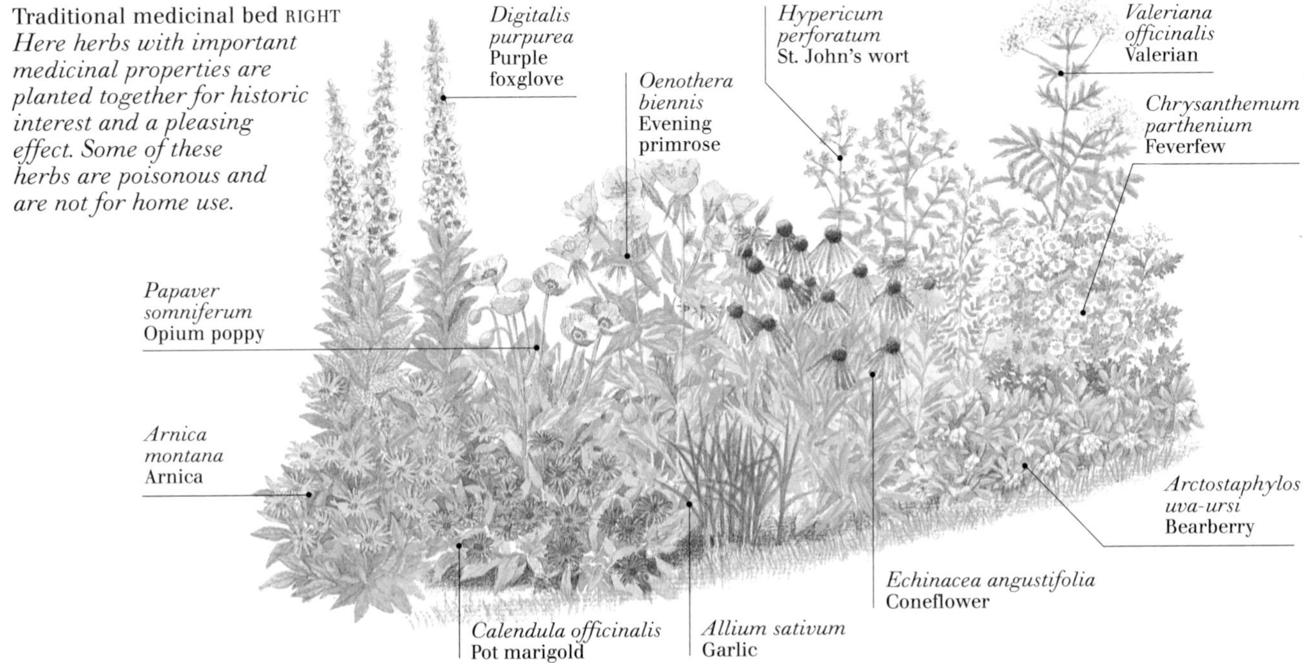

A medicinal garden LEFT
This bed of medicinal plants brings together herbs from all habitats that have medicinal value and interest. Here dramatic elecampane, delicate vervain, and fragrant lavender form part of the luxuriant planting design.

Designs

Theme gardens can be formal or informal; they can be rock gardens, borders, or island beds. Try to make your design appropriate to the theme you have chosen. For a collection of medicinal herbs, for example, it would be interesting to re-create a traditional apothecary's garden or tincture garden, which would have been laid out in beds grouping together herbs for ailments of different sorts – perhaps a bed for digestive problems or one for treating respiratory disorders.

A bee and butterfly garden is best laid out informally, along the lines of an old cottage garden, in which vegetables and flowers were grown together (see also "Companion Planting," page 40). If you plan to make honey, site the hive in a quiet, protected spot facing away from the house but with easy access for collection.

Planting

Because plants from different habitats are grown together in a specialized theme garden, it makes sense to provide optimum conditions for them. Do not put herbs from dry areas into boggy soils or vice versa. An open, well-drained, but moisture-retaining site is best for most herbs. There is plenty of scope for achieving different features. Access to the herbs is an important consideration; paths are practical for reaching herbs for harvesting, but in a bee and butterfly garden, for example, you will need access only for maintenance.

BEE AND BUTTERFLY PLANTS

Flowering herbs are a magnet for honeybees, bumblebees, and colorful butterflies searching for pollen and nectar.

Agastache foeniculum
Anise hyssop

Borago officinalis
Borage

Eupatorium purpureum
Joe-pye weed

Hyssopus officinalis
Hyssop

Origanum
Oregano or marjoram

Pycnanthemum pilosum
Mountain mint

Succisa pratensis
Devil's-bit scabious

Thymus
Thyme (various)

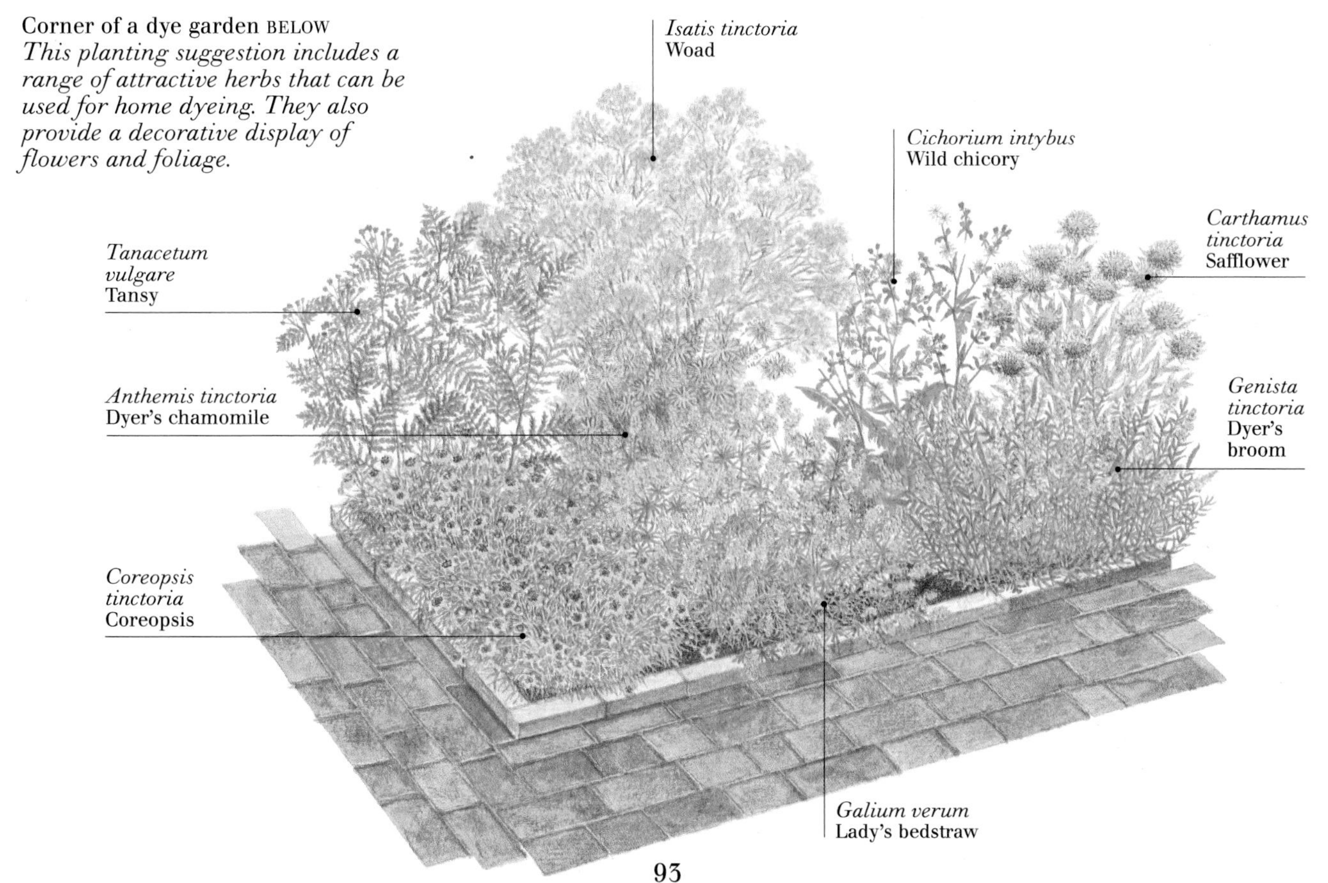

Corner of a dye garden BELOW
This planting suggestion includes a range of attractive herbs that can be used for home dyeing. They also provide a decorative display of flowers and foliage.

Kitchen Garden and Potager

THE KITCHEN GARDEN and its more decorative counterpart, the potager (from the French *potager orné*), are closely associated with herbs. Indeed, aside from their value in cooking, herbs have many uses in the kitchen garden. They are good companion plants (see page 40), attracting pests away from vegetables and encouraging pest predators to come into the garden.

Plant selection

If you are an avid vegetable gardener, there are plenty of herbs that can be planted in your existing beds to complement your annual vegetables and also supplement your food supply. If you have an informal vegetable garden or grow only a few vegetables, simply interplant a selection of annual herbs wherever there is space left either between rows or after a harvested crop. Perennial herbs can be given their own section in the kitchen garden.

A traditional potager consists of small beds and neat paths, often in geometric shapes, including squares, diamonds, and triangles. Parsley, salad burnet, and chives make excellent edging plants along paths, as do flowers like pot marigold, double daisy, and heartsease and vegetables, such as the colored leaf and frizzy lettuces. Dividing hedges can be made by planting hyssop, santolina, or bushy thyme that are kept neatly clipped.

You can create a simple and effective design by planting in blocks across beds, making use of the various leaf colors of vegetables and annual herbs. Seedling crops can be sown to form a tapestry of different colors and textures in a bed, perhaps outlined with one or more types of edging plants. Suitable varieties for the tapestry include coriander (cilantro), alfalfa, chervil, dill, and cut-and-come-again salad crops. Sweet bay trees grown in pots can be used as focal points at the end of paths or in the center of a plot divided into square beds. Where you have climbing beans or peas trained up a trellis or teepee, decorate the base with French marigolds or nasturtiums, which are also companion plants.

Planting

Annual herbs can be seeded with the vegetables in spring. Tender herbs, such as basil, are best started off in pots inside and planted after all danger of frost has passed. Perennial herbs should be planted

Culinary and salad herbs RIGHT *The kitchen garden should be planted to look decorative as well as be productive. Use herbs to interplant between rows of vegetables, making full use of flower and leaf color to relieve the predominant greens.*

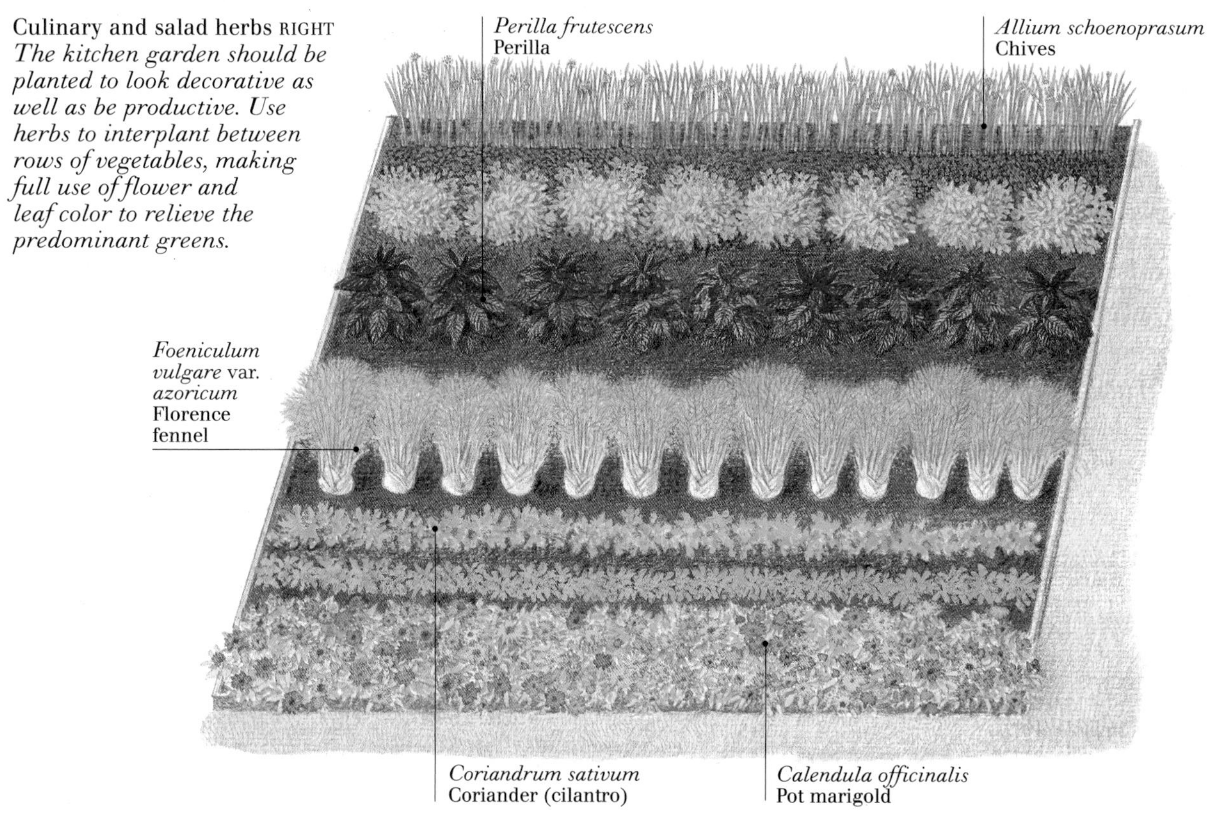

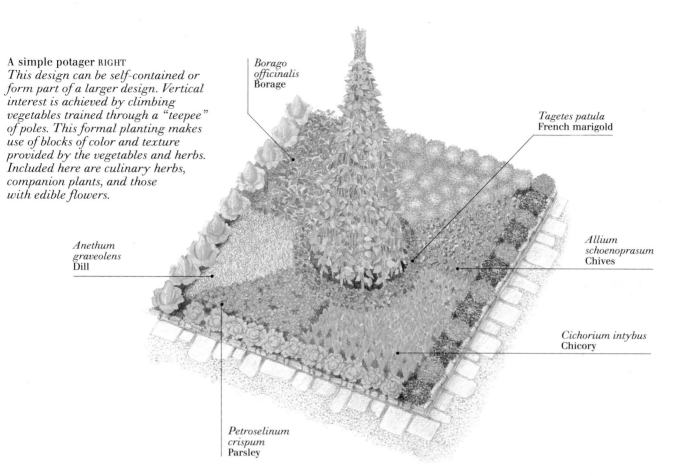

A simple potager RIGHT
This design can be self-contained or form part of a larger design. Vertical interest is achieved by climbing vegetables trained through a "teepee" of poles. This formal planting makes use of blocks of color and texture provided by the vegetables and herbs. Included here are culinary herbs, companion plants, and those with edible flowers.

Borago officinalis
Borage

Tagetes patula
French marigold

Anethum graveolens
Dill

Allium schoenoprasum
Chives

Cichorium intybus
Chicory

Petroselinum crispum
Parsley

as part of the permanent structure of the garden. They can be used effectively as sectional divisions in the beds or as decorative edgings around them, as well as being planted for their culinary use alone. Ensure perennial herbs are given adequate space and time to establish.

COMPANION PLANTING

There are a number of herbs that can be planted as beneficial "companions" to vegetables (see page 40). Planted alongside cabbages, nasturtium will deter whitefly and attract blackfly to itself.

A formal potager ABOVE
This potager is laid out in a traditional formal design with dwarf box and herb hedges of santolina and winter savory. The edging plants are kept neatly clipped, and each compartment is planted with a variety of vegetables or herbs.

The Nature Garden

A NATURE GARDEN can include a patch of annual wildflowers or an area of flowering meadow, and even corners of the smallest gardens can be used. Nature gardens require little traditional gardening maintenance, such as weeding and feeding, and they will quickly attract butterflies, birds, and other wildlife. The most appropriate site is in a less formal part of the garden where there are trees and natural hedges or perhaps near a pond and wetland area. Annual wildflowers become quickly established and can be used to provide color and interest in areas that are eventually destined for longer-term projects.

Annual wildflowers ABOVE
Any patch of ground that can easily be cultivated is ideal for annual and cornfield flowers. Here a simple mixture of cornflowers and chamomile makes a cool summer display.

Plant selection

In most wild situations, grasses and wildflowers grow together, so a grassy area of meadow looks the most natural. Meadows are normally created from seed. Meadow grass seed mixtures and wildflower combinations can be readily obtained from good garden centers or speciality mail-order companies. It is very important to select seed mixes that are suitable for your soil (see page 20); ideally they should be natives to your area. Another method of introducing wildflowers into a grassy area is with small plants. As with seed, choose the species that is appropriate to your soil and location, and plant randomly in groups of five or more. Grasses and flowers compete for space in meadows, and any unsuitable flowers will be unlikely to survive for

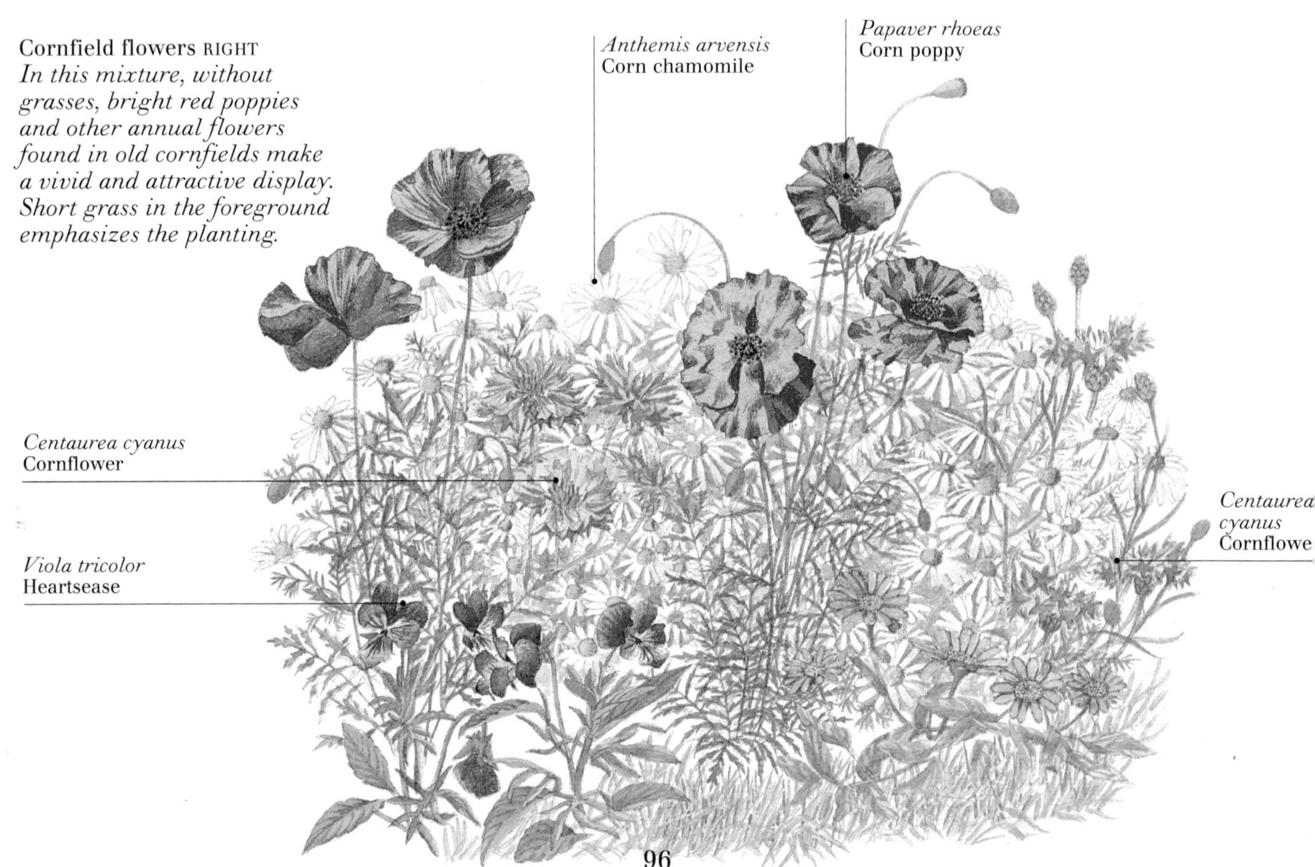

Cornfield flowers RIGHT
In this mixture, without grasses, bright red poppies and other annual flowers found in old cornfields make a vivid and attractive display. Short grass in the foreground emphasizes the planting.

Wildflower meadow BELOW
Wild grasses and native flowers grow naturally together, reminiscent of an old hay meadow. Leave a strip of grass on the edge of the meadow longer than the main lawn so that the two areas merge together.

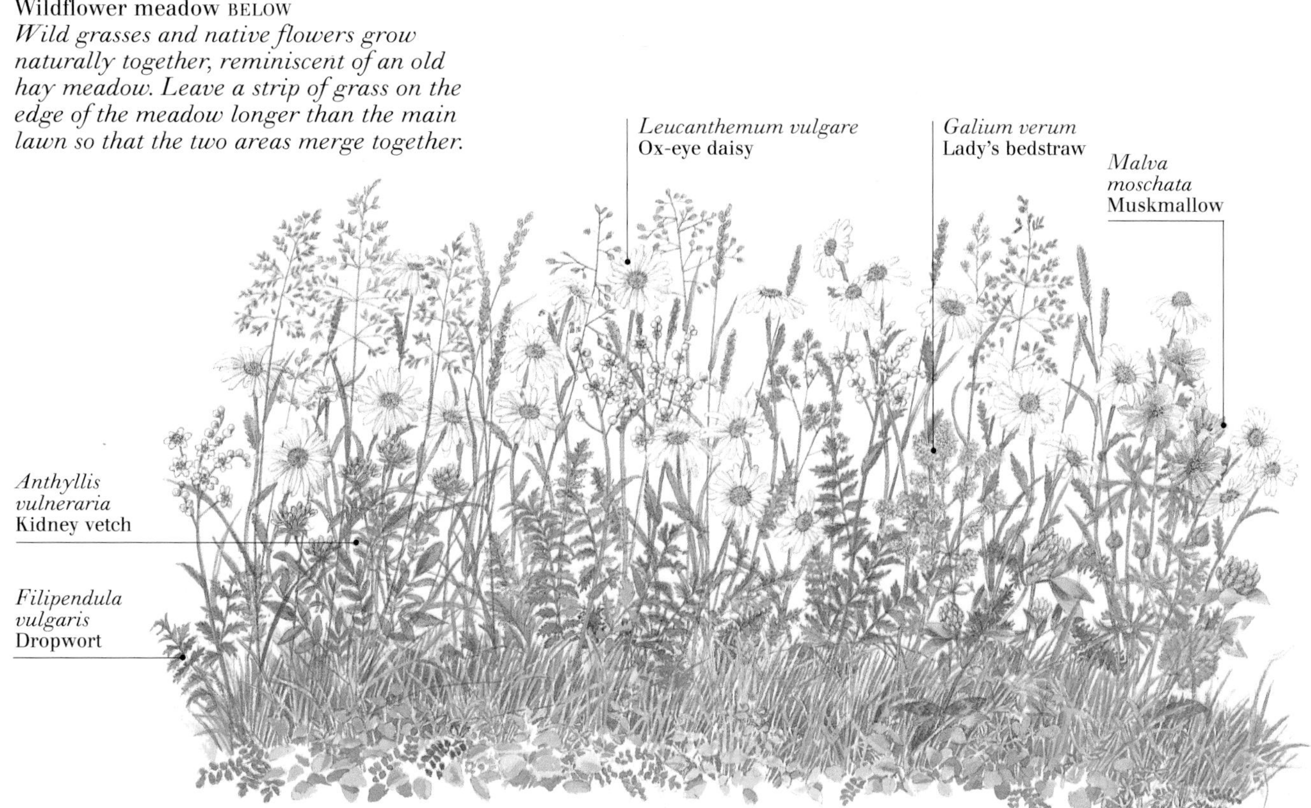

very long. If you have a very small garden or wish to achieve a more colorful effect, then a wildflower-only garden is a good alternative.

Planting

A well-drained site with low fertility is ideal for a meadow. The soil should be carefully prepared to remove all vigorous weeds (see page 43); otherwise these will take over before your meadow has a chance to grow. Once established, the high-density ground cover suppresses weed growth. Do not add compost or any fertilizer to the soil before seeding.

Nature gardens or meadows are best sown in early fall or early to midspring. Sow the grass seed first. Distribute it thinly over the area, then rake in. Broadcast the wildflower mixture; roll it in if the soil is dry, but do not rake because the seed should not be buried. Protect from birds with netting.

Small plants can be introduced into existing grass areas. This should be done in fall or winter, when the grass is short and not growing.

Maintenance

Mow or cut a meadow in mid- to late summer. If growth is vigorous, you may need to cut again in late fall and/or early spring. Remove the cuttings to keep fertility low. With a flower-only garden, simply cut down the dead stems in fall, after the seed has dropped. If one or two varieties seem to be taking hold, remove unripened seed heads to limit their spread. Annual wildflowers need to be cut down and the soil cultivated each year in the fall to ensure continued growth and flowering.

MEADOW FLOWERS

For a successful flower meadow, it is important to choose native flowers and herbs. The following list is a selection of plants that will make an attractive display on most soils. There are many other suitable herbs and wildflowers.

Achillea millefolium
Yarrow

Anthyllis vulneraria
Kidney vetch

Centaurea scabiosa
Greater knapweed

Daucus carota
Wild carrot

Leucanthemum vulgare
Ox-eye daisy

Malva moschata
Muskmallow

Primula veris
Cowslip

The Winter Herb Garden

DURING THE WINTER, snow and frost create a wonderful new landscape. Low winter sun casting long shadows or winter mists can add a mystic beauty to the garden. Cold weather and shorter daylight hours mean conditions are not favorable for new growth or flowering. However, if you take a little care in your selection of plants, you can have a garden that is both decorative and full of interest over the winter season.

Plant selection

In the winter garden, color and form are provided by evergreen herbs such as rosemary, santolina, sage, and lavender. An evergreen hedge following a geometric pattern provides a solid outline, as does a meandering path. Other shrubs give definition and structural interest with branches of different shapes and heights, their stems retaining a stark beauty when stripped of leaves. Any decorative foliage is also of prime importance. Grow golden feverfew for its bright foliage, or try periwinkle, which makes good ground cover with its wiry stems and shiny dark leaves.

Seed heads on tall, upright stems play an important part in giving architectural impact and height. Suitable plants include knapweed, opium

A winter garden RIGHT
February daphne provides a bright focal point in this winter garden, the early flowers of Christmas rose often bloom at the same time as those of snowdrops. Low-growing dwarf comfrey ensures a decorative ground cover. This is an ideal planting for a protected corner.

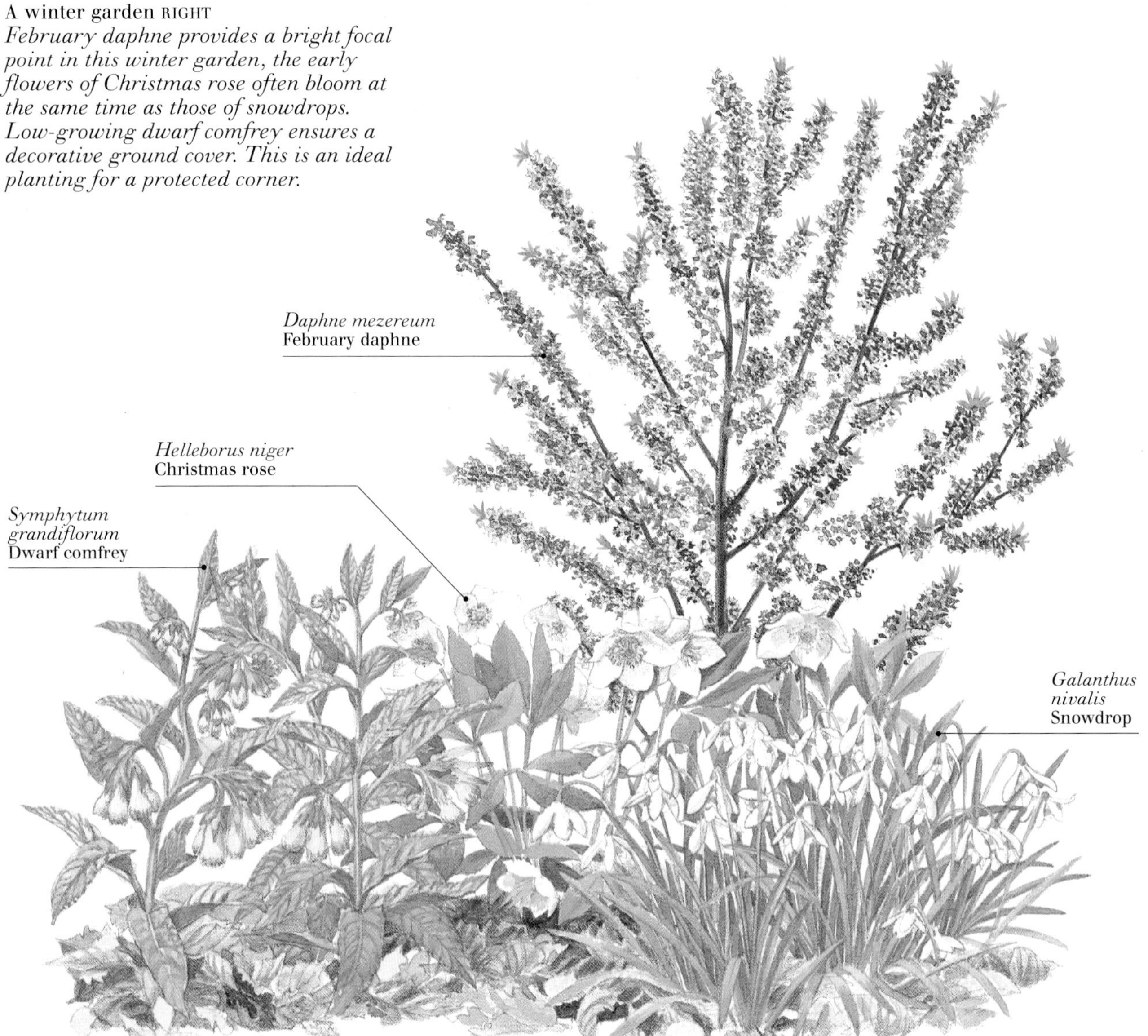

poppy, teasel, wild carrot, and yarrow. A delightful climbing plant is the wild clematis (travelers' joy), which decorates the walls and hedgerows where it grows, its cottony seed heads changing hue with the light over much of the winter.

In a sheltered situation, plant woodland flowers, such as snowdrops and primroses, to bloom early. Christmas rose will flower in midwinter, followed by February daphne, a superb winter shrub.

Planting

Plan for the winter at the same time as you are planning the whole garden, carefully considering what will remain in winter to give interest. It is now clear why the basic structure of the garden is so important. The only special preparation for the winter garden is the summer sowing of hardy annuals and biennials, such as caraway, chervil, fennel flower, and parsley, which will give fresh green growth during the cold months.

Trimming back in the fall or after flowering gives the garden a tidy appearance over the winter and encourages new growth in spring.

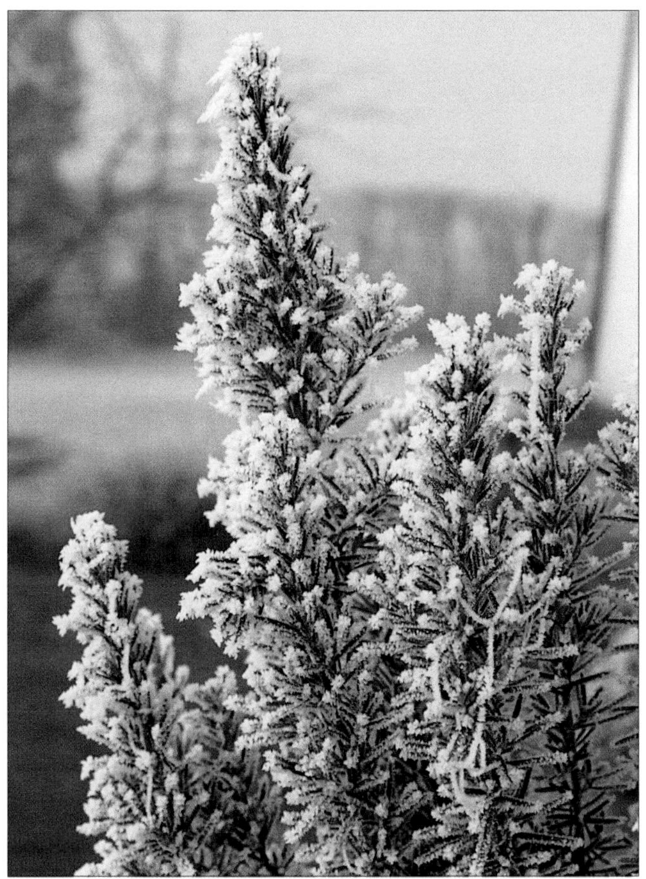

Rosemary in snow ABOVE
A light fall of snow brings a touch of magic to the winter garden and enhances the architectural form of shrubby evergreen herbs like this rosemary.

Dried seed heads BELOW
Herb seed heads should be left on the plants to give extra interest to the winter herb garden. Ornamental seed heads look beautiful when covered with frost or light snow.

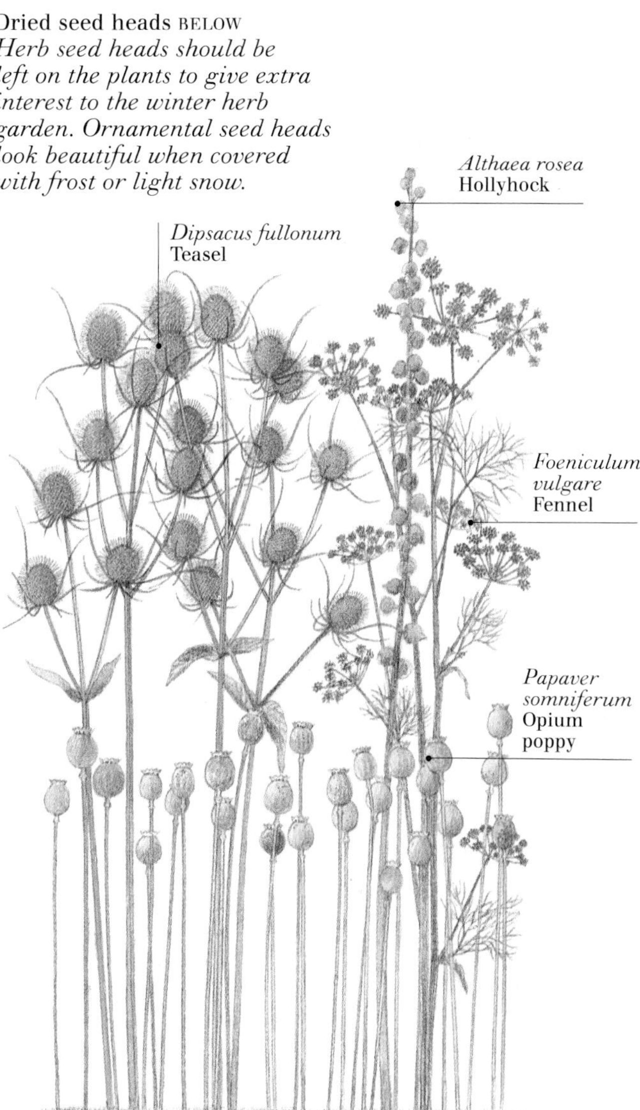

DECORATIVE SEED HEADS

Many herbs produce decorative seed heads that can be cut and dried for winter arrangements in the home.

Althaea rosea
Hollyhock

Anethum graveolens
Dill

Atriplex hortensis var. *rubra*
Red orache

Clematis vitalba
Travelers' joy

Daucus carota
Wild carrot

Dipsacus fullonum
Teasel

Foeniculum vulgare
Fennel

Gentiana lutea
Yellow gentian

Papaver somniferum
Opium poppy

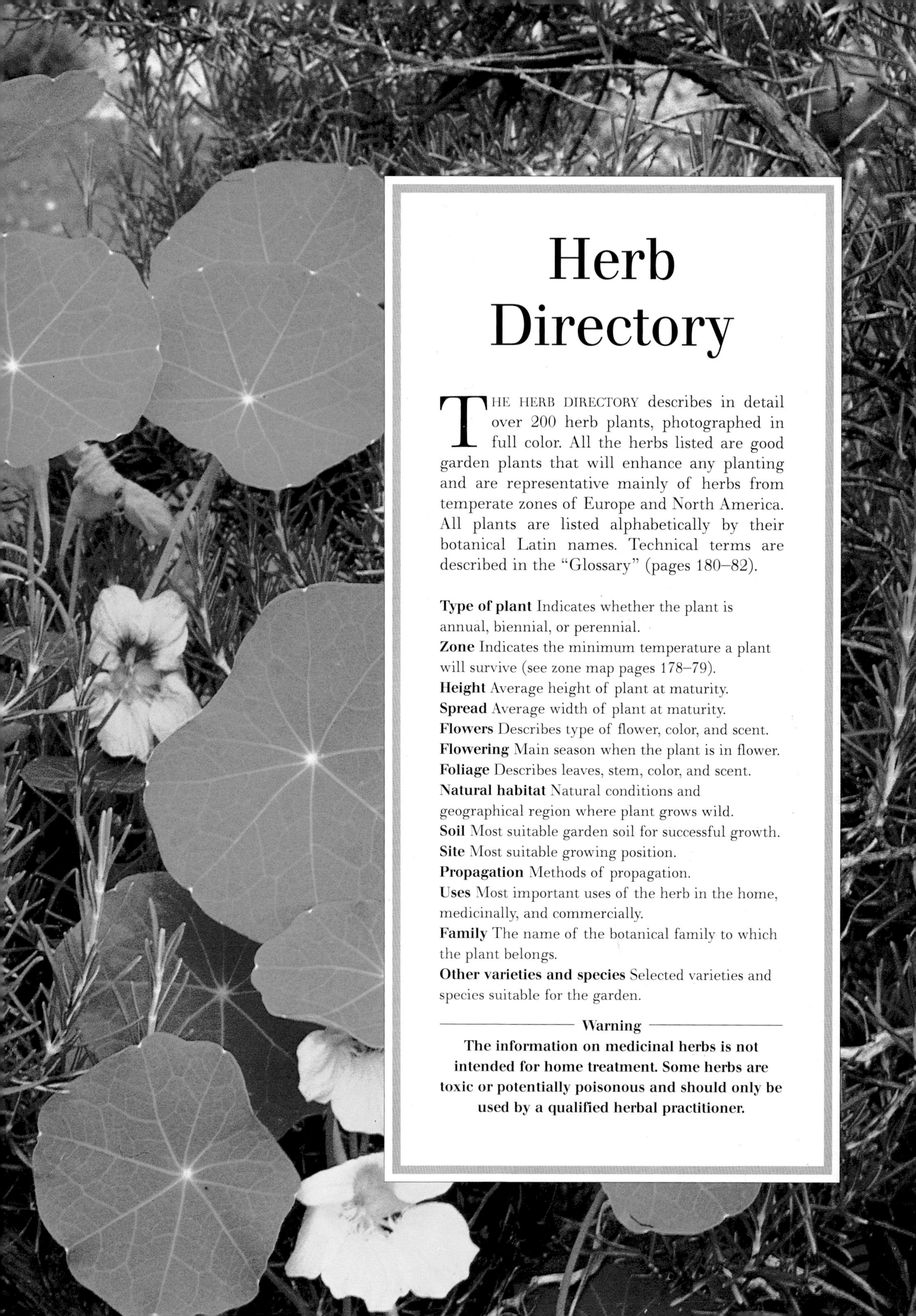

Herb Directory

THE HERB DIRECTORY describes in detail over 200 herb plants, photographed in full color. All the herbs listed are good garden plants that will enhance any planting and are representative mainly of herbs from temperate zones of Europe and North America. All plants are listed alphabetically by their botanical Latin names. Technical terms are described in the "Glossary" (pages 180–82).

Type of plant Indicates whether the plant is annual, biennial, or perennial.
Zone Indicates the minimum temperature a plant will survive (see zone map pages 178–79).
Height Average height of plant at maturity.
Spread Average width of plant at maturity.
Flowers Describes type of flower, color, and scent.
Flowering Main season when the plant is in flower.
Foliage Describes leaves, stem, color, and scent.
Natural habitat Natural conditions and geographical region where plant grows wild.
Soil Most suitable garden soil for successful growth.
Site Most suitable growing position.
Propagation Methods of propagation.
Uses Most important uses of the herb in the home, medicinally, and commercially.
Family The name of the botanical family to which the plant belongs.
Other varieties and species Selected varieties and species suitable for the garden.

Warning

The information on medicinal herbs is not intended for home treatment. Some herbs are toxic or potentially poisonous and should only be used by a qualified herbal practitioner.

Acanthus mollis

Acanthus

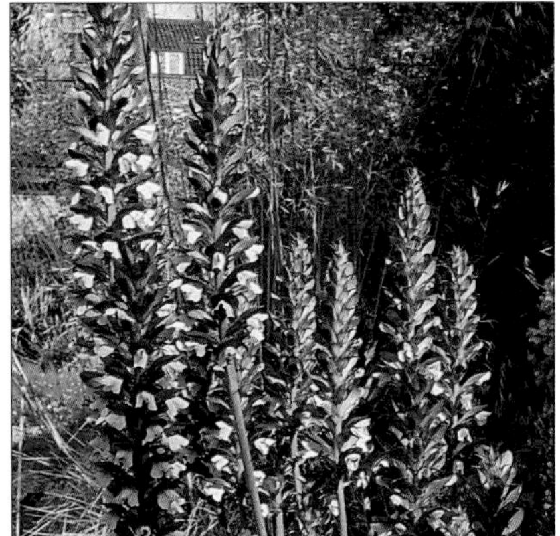

SOMETIMES KNOWN as bear's breech, acanthus is a stately plant. Its tall spikes of mauve-and-white flowers make a stunning sight in summer, and the dark green, glossy, deeply divided leaves are highly decorative – in fact, they inspired ancient Greek architectural embellishment. The plant was also used medicinally by the ancient Greeks.

Acanthus is a specimen plant. Grow it so that the fine foliage and the magnificent flower spikes can be seen to best advantage. It looks wonderful in an island bed or border, where the surrounding plants should be much lower growing.

In regions where acanthus will not survive the winter, it can be grown successfully in a large container. In the first winter especially, it is necessary to give the plant a deep mulch, from 6 in (15 cm), of leaves, bracken, straw, or similar material to protect it from freezing temperatures.

Perennial Zone 6
Height To 4 ft (1.2 m).
Spread 18 in (45 cm).
Flowers Mauve-purple and white, funnel shaped, with purple bracts.
Flowering Late summer.
Foliage Dark glossy green, deeply cut, broad, upper leaves spiny toothed.
Natural habitat Scrub, woodland, stony hillsides. Native of western Mediterranean.
Soil Well drained, loamy.
Site Full sun or partial shade.
Propagation Sow seeds in spring; divide in fall or spring; take root cuttings in winter.
Uses Formerly medicinal.
Family Acanthaceae (acanthus family).
Other varieties and species *A. dioscoridis*; *A. hungaricus longifolius*; *A. spinosus.*

Achillea millefolium

Yarrow

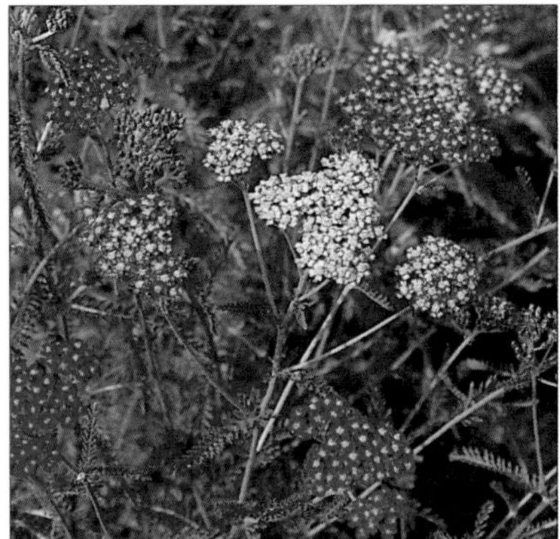

YARROW IS AN aromatic perennial. The variety illustrated here is the very ornamental 'Cerise Queen,' with flower shades of soft pink to deep cerise. The attractive foliage is made up of thousands of tiny leaves (hence the name *millefolium*).

Since it seeds profusely, yarrow must be kept within bounds. Seed heads should be cut off before they ripen and at this stage can be hung up to dry and used in decorative dried arrangements. This plant is a good subject to naturalize in an area of wild grasses.

Yarrow was once used as a wound poultice in ancient times. Many of its common names refer to its ability to stem the flow of blood. It is also valuable as a remedy for fever and as a digestive tonic. A useful dye plant, it produces browns and greens.

Perennial Zone 3
Height To 2 ft (60 cm). Spreading.
Flowers White or pink, small, forming a flat-topped cluster.
Flowering Midsummer to fall.
Foliage Lance shaped and highly divided, giving a lacy appearance.
Natural habitat Meadows, pastures, and roadsides in Europe. Naturalized in North America, Australia, and New Zealand.
Soil Most soils except the poorest.
Site Full sun or partial shade.
Propagation Sow seeds in spring; divide in spring or fall; take softwood cuttings in early summer.
Uses Medicinal; dye plant; dried flowers.
Family Compositae (daisy family).
Other varieties and species *A. millefolium* 'Fire King'; *A.* 'Coronation Gold'; *A. filipendulina* 'Cloth of Gold'; *A. ptarmica* 'The Pearl.'

Adonis vernalis

Spring Adonis

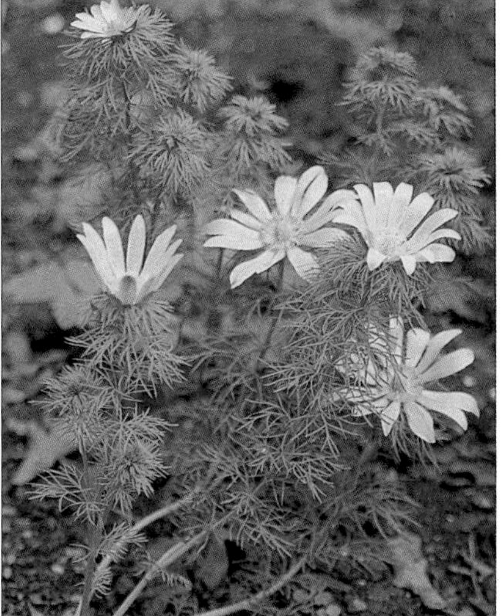

THIS SMALL HERB is named after the Adonis of Greek legend, from whose blood the plant is reputed to have sprung. It is valued today as a heart tonic. The beautiful downy flower buds appear at the top of each stem before much of the leaf unfolds. The greenish yellow flowers have a starlike silky appearance and look brilliant when catching the sun, which they always face.

Spring Adonis makes a beautiful rock garden plant and should be planted in a small group for best effect. It grows from a rhizome, and is therefore easily divided once it has become well established.

Perennial Zone 5
Height 8–10 in (20–25 cm).
Spread 7 in (18 cm).
Flowers Bright greenish yellow, star shaped, with a silky sheen, short stems.
Flowering Early spring.
Foliage Pale green, finely divided, feathery.
Natural habitat Sunny mountain slopes and alkaline grassland in central and southeastern Europe.
Soil Alkaline loam, withstands drought.
Site Full sun or partial shade.
Propagation Sow seeds in fall; divide after flowering.
Uses Medicinal.
Family Ranunculaceae (buttercup family).
Other varieties and species *A. aestivalis*; *A. amurensis*; *A. annua*; *A. brevistyla.*

Warning

The whole plant is poisonous and should not be taken internally.

Agastache foeniculum

Anise Hyssop

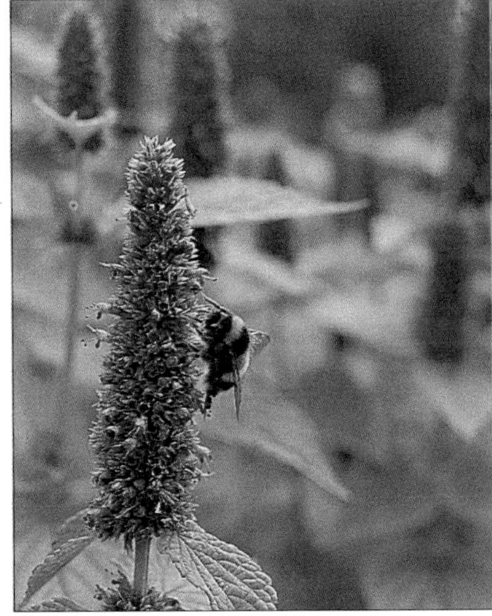

THIS NATIVE of the North American prairies is a beautiful plant with anise-scented leaves and decorative spikes of mauve-purple flowers. It is often known as *A. anethiodora*, or blue giant hyssop.

Anise hyssop is an excellent flower for beekeepers, since it attracts honeybees and bumblebees. It also looks stunning planted in a border or island bed with other herbs and wild plants. Unfortunately, anise hyssop is short lived, and it is best to take a few cuttings every year to ensure that it is not lost over the winter.

The fresh or dried leaves of the plant are used for flavoring and for tea. The dried flowers are a good ingredient for potpourri. The herb also has medicinal properties, and a leaf tea is used for fevers, coughs, and colds.

Perennial Zone 5
Height To 3 ft (90 cm).
Spread 2 ft (60 cm).
Flowers Mauve-purple, in long conical spikes.
Flowering Late summer.
Foliage Short stalked, triangular, sharply toothed, anise scented.
Natural habitat Prairies and dry thickets of North America.
Soil Well-drained loam.
Site Full sun.
Propagation Sow seeds in spring.
Uses Medicinal; culinary; bee plant.
Family Labiatae (mint family).
Other varieties and species *A. cedronella*; *A. mexicana*; *A. rugosa*; *A. verticillata.*

Ajuga reptans

Bugle

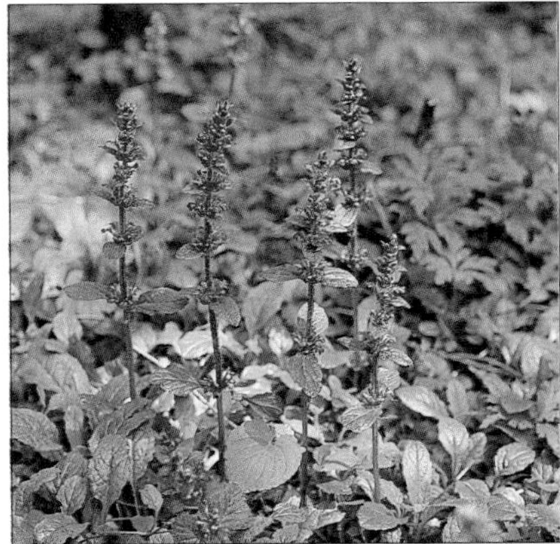

BUGLE HAS SHINY dark green and purple, oval leaves and spikes of purple-blue flowers. It is a densely spreading plant that makes a superb ground cover. There are several extremely decorative forms, such as 'Atropurpurea' (beet-colored leaves), 'Burgundy Glow' (magenta leaves edged with cream), and 'Variegata' (gray-green leaves edged with cream).

In the garden bugle requires a moist and humus-rich soil, and in hot regions some shade from the sun. It will grow well through gravel, provided there is good soil and some moisture underneath, and it thrives in a damp area near a pond, in a hedgerow, or in shade.

Bugle was traditionally known as the carpenter's herb, as it was used to stop bleeding.

Perennial Zone 3
Height To 12 in (30 cm). Spreading.
Flowers Purple-blue; white lines on lower lip formed in whorls on flower spike.
Flowering Late spring to summer.
Foliage Greenish purple, shiny, oval.
Natural habitat Damp woods and pastures. Native of Britain, Europe, and western Asia.
Soil Humus rich, moist to damp.
Site Full sun or partial shade.
Propagation Sow seeds in summer and fall (erratic); plantlets produced by runners.
Uses Formerly medicinal.
Family Labiatae (mint family).
Other varieties and species *A. reptans* 'Atropurpurea'; *A. r.* 'Burgundy Glow'; *A. r.* 'Multicolor'; *A. r.* 'Variegata'; *A. chamaepitys*; *A. pyramidalis.*

Alchemilla vulgaris

Lady's Mantle

SOMETIMES KNOWN as lion's foot or dewcup, lady's mantle makes a dense ground cover. This attractive herb is often used to edge a border, especially to fall over hard paving. Trim the flower heads back after blooming, the plant will then continue to flower through the summer.

The species usually grown in gardens is *A. mollis*, from Asia Minor. It is vigorous and has hairy leaves that give it a softer look. There are also several low-growing alpine species, including *A. alpina*, which are excellent for the rock garden.

An important medicinal herb in the 16th century, lady's mantle is now used to treat menstrual and digestive disorders. The dried flower heads of all species look good in flower arrangements.

Perennial Zone 5
Height 6–18 in (15–45 cm).
Spread To 2 ft (60 cm).
Flowers Greenish yellow, very small, in panicles.
Flowering Mid- to late summer.
Foliage Soft green, distinctive, pleated with strong veins. Kidney shaped, lobed and toothed basal leaves have long stalks.
Natural habitat Loamy pastures and grasslands. Open woodland and mountains, on moist soil. Native of Britain, Europe, northern and western Asia, and northeastern North America.
Soil Deep loam.
Site Full sun or partial shade.
Propagation Sow seeds in spring to early summer. Divide roots in spring or fall; self-seeds.
Uses Medicinal; dried flowers.
Family Rosaceae (rose family).
Other varieties and species *A. alpina*; *A. conjuncta*; *A. mollis.*

Allium schoenoprasum

Chives

Chives have particularly pretty, pink to purple flower heads and make a lovely edging for a border or formal herb garden. Even when not in flower, the clumps of lush green, cylindrical, hollow stems are attractive.

Chives prefer a fertile soil with some moisture, but will grow in surprisingly dry conditions, including gravel or the rock garden. To propagate divide into clumps of half a dozen small bulbs and replant during the spring. Chives die down completely in winter.

Chives have become a popular and indispensable seasoning, imparting a delicate onion flavor. The flowers can be used to decorate and flavor salads and soups.

Perennial bulb Zone 3
Height 8–12 in (20–30 cm).
Spread 12 in (30 cm).
Flowers Pink-mauve to purple. Spherical heads grow on long stems.
Flowering Summer.
Foliage Rich green, long, cylindrical, hollow. Onion flavor.
Natural habitat From damp grassland and stream banks to dry, rocky places. Native of northern Europe and naturalized in North America.
Soil Rich loam.
Site Full sun.
Propagation Divide clumps (bulbs), or sow seeds in spring; self-seeds.
Uses Culinary; dried flowers.
Family Liliaceae (lily family).
Other varieties and species *A. cepa* (onion green); *A. cepa* var. *proliferum* (tree onion); *A. cernuum* (wild onion); *A. fistulosum* (Welsh onion); *A. flavum* (small yellow onion); *A. sativum* (garlic); *A. tuberosum* (garlic chives); *A. ursinum* (ramsons).

Allium tuberosum

Garlic Chives

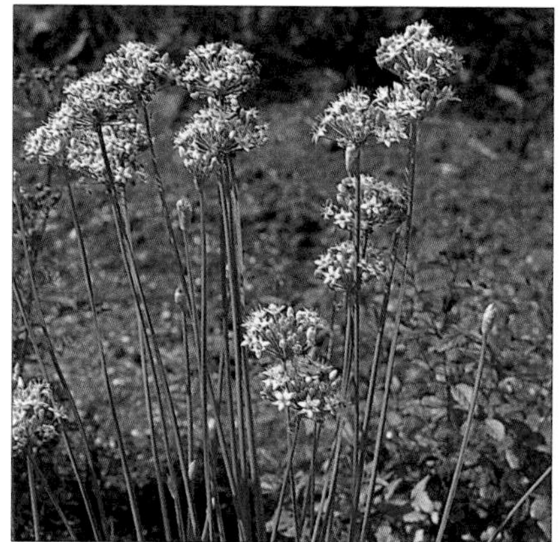

The garlic chive is also called Chinese chive or Chinese leek. If grown in clumps, it will make a wonderful display in late summer when the starlike white flowers bloom. Because of its delicate beauty and culinary value, it deserves a place in both the ornamental and the kitchen garden. Like other decorative alliums, it grows well in rock gardens, but to produce maximum leaf for culinary use it needs a richer, moister soil. In the formal garden garlic chives make an attractive edging, and cutting them regularly for culinary use encourages new growth.

The flat leaves can be used in the same way as chives. The flower buds are delicious dressed with oil and the tiny white flowers look very festive sprinkled on a fresh green salad. Garlic chives also make a charming cut or dried flower.

Perennial Zone 3
Height 12–18 in (30–45 cm).
Spread 12 in (30 cm).
Flowers White, starlike umbels in flat-topped clusters.
Flowering Late summer.
Foliage Flat leaves, garlic flavor.
Natural habitat Dry steppes or prairies. Native of Japan, China, and Nepal.
Soil Fertile, sandy to moist loam.
Site Full sun or light shade.
Propagation Sow seeds in spring; divide clumps in spring or fall; self-seeds.
Uses Culinary; cut and dried flowers.
Family Liliaceae (lily family).
Other varieties and species *A. tuberosum* 'Broadleaf'; *A. t.* 'Tenderpole'; *A. moly*; *A. roseum*; *A. schoenoprasum*; *A. sphaerocephalon*.

Aloysia triphylla

Lemon Verbena

Lemon verbena forms a woody shrub in its natural habitat, and is cultivated chiefly for the amazing lemon scent of its leaves.

In mild climates it can be grown outdoors in sheltered positions, on light, well-drained soil. As it is only half-hardy, it is normally best grown in a container. In winter, before any hard frosts, move the container indoors. The plant will be dormant over the winter and come into leaf in late spring. Cut it back to shape at this stage, and you will have a decorative and highly scented shrub to put out on the patio. Lemon verbena is prone to infestation by red spider mites. Use cold-water sprays or insecticidal soap to control them.

The leaves of lemon verbena make a delicious tea, which is soothing for indigestion, and add a delightful lemon fragrance to many dishes. Always harvest the leaves before the plant flowers.

Half-hardy perennial Zones 7–10
Height To 6 ft (1.8 m).
Spread To 4 ft (1.2 m).
Flowers Pale lavender, tiny, in panicles.
Flowering Late summer.
Foliage Yellow-green, with a shiny surface, dull underneath, lance shaped and strongly lemon scented.
Natural habitat Fields and roadsides. Native of Chile and Argentina.
Soil Rich and moisture retaining but well drained.
Site Full sun.
Propagation Take semiripe cuttings in summer, kept under plastic or mist; seeds rarely obtainable.
Uses Tea; culinary; potpourri; medicinal.
Family Verbenaceae (verbena family).
Other varieties and species None.

Althaea officinalis

Marsh Mallow

As its name suggests, the beautiful herb marsh mallow, also known as mallard, grows in damp places. A tall, stately plant with an abundance of gray-green, soft, velvety leaves, it bears masses of delicate pink flowers in late summer. The seed heads resemble small, flat, round "cheeses," in which each seed forms a segment.

The marsh mallow looks attractive growing near water or in clumps at the back of an island bed or border, where its muted foliage makes a backdrop for other brighter flowers. It is an excellent feature plant, too.

Marsh mallow, in common with most other members of the mallow family, has since earliest times been used for food, and all parts of the plant are edible. The roots were once used to make the sweets known as marshmallows; they can also be cooked as a vegetable, and the young leaves and shoots may be eaten in salads. The Romans considered it to be a delicacy.

Medicinally, this herb has been valued for its soothing properties to treat inflammation, coughs, bronchitis, and hoarseness. Externally, the leaves are used as a poultice and to relieve the pain and swelling of bee stings.

Perennial Zone 3
Height 3–4 ft (90 cm–1.2 m).
Spread 2 ft (60 cm).
Flowers Very pale pink, five petaled, growing in clusters up the stem in leaf axils.
Flowering Late summer.
Foliage Gray-green, very soft and downy, five lobed, folded like fans.
Natural habitat Damp places by streams, tidal rivers and the sea, damp meadows. Native to most of Europe, Asia, Australia, and eastern North America.
Soil Rich, moisture retaining to damp. Thrives in salty seaside conditions.
Site Full sun.
Propagation Sow seeds in spring (erratic); take cuttings in early summer; divide roots when dormant.
Uses Culinary; medicinal.
Family Malvaceae (mallow family).
Other varieties and species *A. rosea*; *Lavatera arborea*; *L. trimestris* 'Mont Blanc'; *Malva moschata*; *M. sylvestris*.

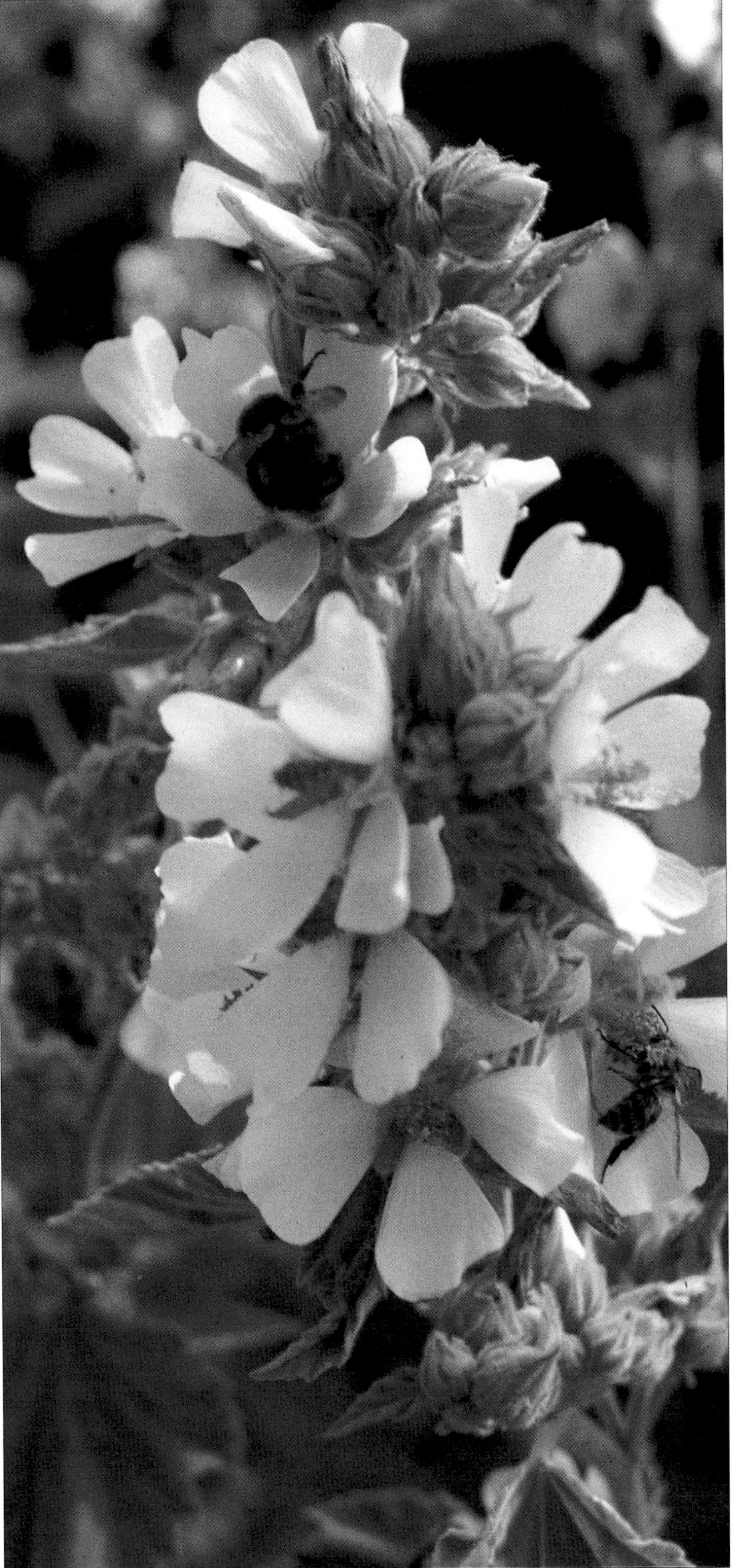

Althaea rosea

Hollyhock

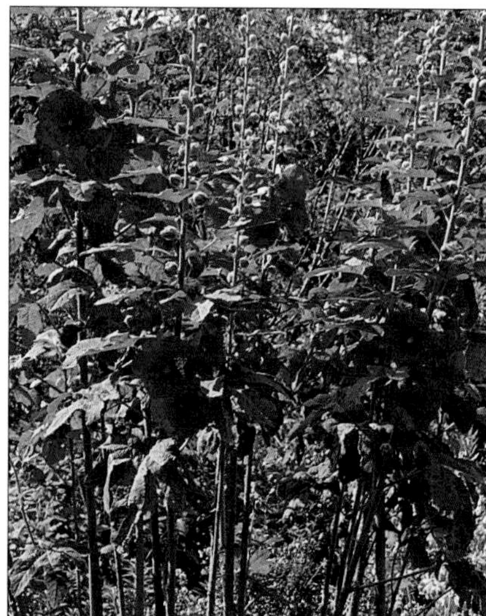

THE HOLLYHOCK was introduced from China in the 16th century. It comes in a diverse range of flower colors, from white and the palest shades to rich reds, pinks, and a deep purple-black. There are also double forms. It is a stately plant that looks good, and grows best, against a wall. Hollyhocks love good drainage and thrive in brick and lime rubble.

In suitable conditions hollyhock self-seeds readily. It is this random seeding that produces the groups of hollyhocks with flowers of different shades that are so appealing.

Hollyhock has similar medicinal properties to *A. officinalis*. The flowers are used as a tisane to treat chest complaints, or as a mouthwash.

Biennial Zone 5
Height To 10ft (3m).
Spread 2ft (60cm).
Flowers White and pastel shades to deepest purple. Large, cuplike around a tall stem.
Flowering Summer.
Foliage Yellow-green, large, heart shaped, on long stalks.
Natural habitat Fields and disturbed ground. Originates from China but naturalized in southern Europe.
Soil Well drained.
Site Full sun.
Propagation Sow seeds in spring or late summer; self-seeds.
Uses Medicinal.
Family Malvaceae (mallow family).
Other varieties and species *A. rosea* 'Chater's Double'; *A. r.* 'Summer Carnival'; *A. holdreichii; A. pallida.*

Amaranthus cruentus

Amaranth

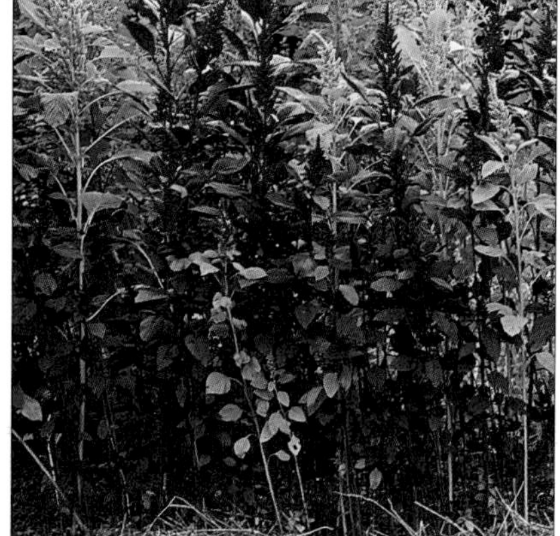

AMARANTH IS A spectacular plant with exotic flowers. The decorative *A. cruentus*, from Mexico, is not only a beautiful and colorful herb but a potentially valuable grain crop, especially in developing countries.

Grow this plant for its decorative value. Its colorful leaves and long, dense, branched flower heads in rich crimson are spectacular in a small group. For best results sow the tiny white seeds when the soil is warm in late spring or early summer and the danger of frost is past. Amaranth requires a moisture-retentive soil to germinate. Once it is growing, it will withstand very dry conditions. The tall plants support each other, but they should be protected from wind.

In ancient Greece the amaranth was sacred to Artemis and was said to have special healing properties.

Half-hardy annual
Height To 6ft (1.8m).
Spread 18in (45cm).
Flowers Crimson or greenish, small, borne on many long dense panicles.
Flowering Late summer to early fall.
Foliage Dull green, bronze, or crimson, large, oval on long stalks.
Natural habitat Wasteland in tropical regions.
Soil Fertile, well drained.
Site Full sun.
Propagation Sow seeds when the soil is over 65°F (18°C), in early summer.
Uses Culinary; fodder crop; formerly medicinal.
Family Amaranthaceae (amaranth family).
Other varieties and species *A. caudatus*; *A. hypochondriacus*; *A. tricolor* 'Joseph's Coat'; *A. t.* 'Molten Fire.'

Anethum graveolens

Dill

ALL FORMS OF DILL are decorative at every stage of growth. With its feathery foliage, dill looks pretty in a border or in a formal herb garden and produces attractive flower and seed heads, which dry well.

Dill should be grown in a clump or mass. Sow it in spring by broadcasting the seeds. In order to obtain a good leaf harvest use the most suitable variety (listed below), and make sure that the plants do not dry out, as they will go straight up to flower.

Dill has always been an essential flavoring in Scandinavian cooking, and the seeds are used extensively for pickling cucumbers and to flavor bread and cakes. The chopped leaves are sprinkled on many dishes. Dill seed is good for the digestion.

Annual
Height To 3ft (90cm).
Spread 12in (30cm).
Flowers Yellow, small, in terminal flat umbels.
Flowering Late summer.
Foliage Blue-green, feathery, composed of linear leaflets. Very aromatic.
Natural habitat Wasteland and cornfields. Native of southern Europe, southern Russia, and western Asia.
Soil Tolerates most soils, resists drought.
Site Full sun.
Propagation Sow seeds in spring, or plant in succession for culinary use.
Uses Culinary; medicinal; dried flowers and seed heads.
Family Umbelliferae (carrot family).
Other varieties and species *A.g.* 'Dukat' (leaf); *A. graveolens* 'Mammoth' (seeds); *A.g.* 'Vierling' (cut flower, leaf).

Angelica archangelica

Angelica

THE STATELY angelica is a striking plant by any standards. It should be grown for its decorative and architectural value as a specimen. Plant either near water or in a mixed border. In the first year angelica normally produces only a large leafy rosette. It will self-seed profusely.

Angelica stem is used as a green candied cake decoration. The herb is also an ingredient of certain liqueurs, such as Benedictine. Medicinally it is used as an infusion to treat bronchitis, flatulence, and colds. Angelica can be mistaken in the wild for water hemlock, which is very poisonous and favors a similar habitat.

Biennial Zone 3
Height To 7 ft (2.1 m).
Spread 3 ft (90 cm).
Flowers Yellow-green, small, in large globular umbels at the top of the stem. Followed by pale cream, oblong seeds.
Flowering Summer.
Foliage Bold bright green, much divided and finely toothed on long hollow stalks clasping the stem.
Natural habitat Damp situations, wet meadows, and streamsides. Probably native of Syria, distributed throughout northern Europe.
Soil Rich, deep and moist.
Site Full sun or light shade (in hot climates).
Propagation Sow fresh seeds in fall, transplant 3 ft (90 cm) apart in spring.
Uses Culinary; medicinal.
Family Umbelliferae (carrot family).
Other varieties and species Many, including *A. atropurpurea*; *A. sylvestris*.

Anthemis

Chamomile

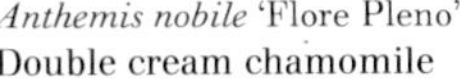

Anthemis nobile 'Flore Pleno'
Double cream chamomile

Anthemis tinctoria
Dyer's chamomile

Anthemis tinctoria
Dyer's chamomile

THE CHAMOMILES were once classified as belonging to the genus *Anthemis*. More recently they have been given a genus of their own, *Chamaemelum*. The full common name of *A. nobile* is Roman chamomile. *Matricaria recutita* (German chamomile) is an annual.

With their small, white, daisylike flowers, all the chamomiles make attractive garden plants and form a decorative, creeping ground cover. The wonderful apple-scented foliage provides fragrant lawns. With a maximum height of 6 in (15 cm), the double cream form illustrated is a lovely low-growing plant for the rock garden, the front of a border, or a formal herb garden. *A. nobile* grows to 12 in (30 cm) high in flower and looks equally good in the border or herb garden. As a lawn herb it needs to be cut regularly, although the nonflowering clone, 'Treneague,' requires no cutting. *A. tinctoria*, with larger, yellow flowers, is known as dyer's chamomile and produces bright yellow dyes. It grows 2 ft (60 cm) high, and the foliage is not apple-scented.

Chamomile, one of the oldest garden herbs, was revered by the ancient Egyptians for its curative powers. For centuries it has been grown in herb gardens both for decoration and for its medicinal properties. Today chamomile flowers are made into a tisane for a general tonic and a sedative. A compress is effective to treat wounds and inflammation. The flowers are also used in hair preparations to lighten hair color and in potpourri. The flowers of both Roman and German chamomile are used to produce valuable essential oil.

Perennial Zones 3–4
Height To 12 in (30 cm). Creeping.
Flowers White ray florets with yellow center, small, borne on a single stem.
Flowering Early to late summer.
Foliage Grass-green, fine threadlike segments with a feathery appearance, apple scented.
Natural habitat Dry grassland in Europe, North Africa, and temperate Asia. Naturalized in North America.
Soil Well drained, sandy. Double form prefers a richer, moist soil.
Site Full sun or partial shade.
Propagation Sow seeds in spring in fine soil; divide in spring.
Uses Cosmetic; medicinal; compost activator; essential oil. *A. tinctoria* is a dye plant.
Family Compositae (daisy family).
Other varieties and species
A. nobile 'Flore Pleno'; *A. n.* 'Treneague'; *A. arvensis*; *A. tinctoria*; *A. t.* 'Alba'; *A. t.* 'E. C. Buxton'; *A. t.* 'Wargrave.'

Anthriscus cerefolium

Chervil

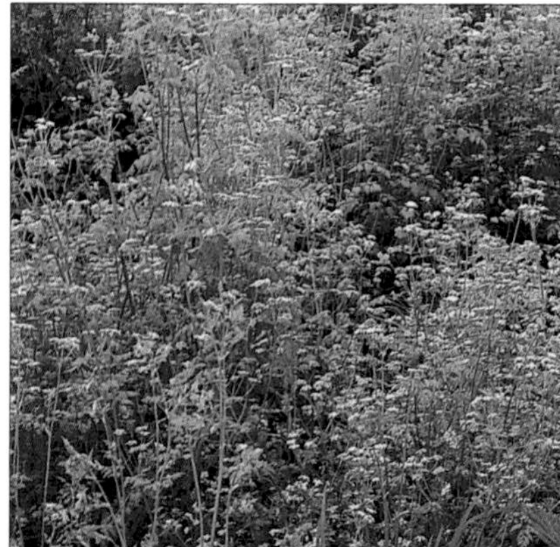

An attractive herb with extremely delicate, fernlike leaves and pretty white flowers, chervil is very short lived in many situations and goes rapidly to seed. However, the seedlings make a fine ground cover.

Chervil does best in cool, slightly moist conditions. Grow it where it will receive sun in winter but will be shaded as the sun heats up. It is best sown in late summer for a winter and spring crop, and again in early spring to produce leaf in early summer.

As a culinary herb chervil should be more widely used. In France it is appreciated as an ingredient of *fines herbes* and *bouquet garni*. The flavor is very delicate, with a hint of aniseed. Add chervil to a dish just before serving, since cooking destroys its subtle flavor.

Annual
Height To 2 ft (60 cm).
Spread 12 in (30 cm).
Flowers White, tiny, in flat compound umbels.
Flowering Spring to summer.
Foliage Pale green, delicate, fernlike, deeply segmented. Aniseed flavor.
Natural habitat Hedge banks and waste ground. Native of southeastern Europe, the Middle East, southern Russia and the Caucasus. Naturalized in North America.
Soil Light with humus, some moisture.
Site Partial shade in summer.
Propagation Sow seeds in late summer, fall, or spring; self-seeds.
Uses Culinary; medicinal.
Family Umbelliferae (carrot family).
Other varieties and species 'Brussels winter,' curled and flat-leaved varieties.

Anthyllis vulneraria

Kidney Vetch

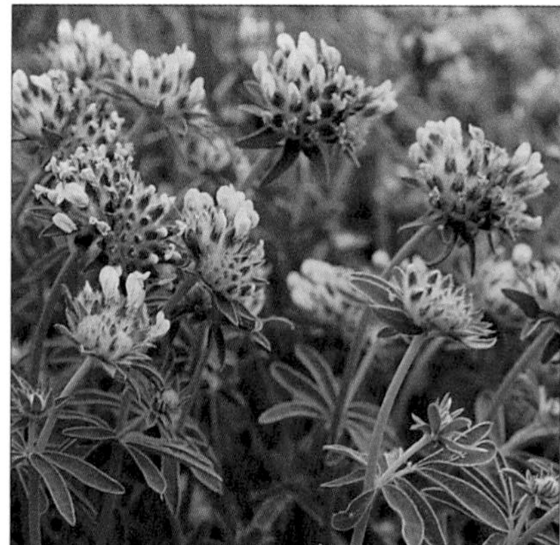

Many of the wild vetches make colorful and useful garden plants. The bright egg-yellow flowers of kidney vetch, often tinged with red, densely smother the plant and act as a magnet for bees and butterflies. Cut back the plant after flowering to encourage more flowers later in the season, but leave some seed heads to mature for use as unusual decorations.

Kidney vetch makes an excellent ground-cover plant and can survive on poor sandy soil in hot conditions, although the flowering period will be shorter and the growth less lush than in a good garden soil.

This herb was used medicinally. The Latin name *vulneraria* indicates its onetime application to heal wounds. Kidney vetch was also favored as a laxative and to relieve coughs.

Perennial Zone 4
Height To 12 in (30 cm).
Spread 18 in (45 cm).
Flowers Egg-yellow with touches of crimson or purple, and distinctive inflated, white, woolly calyx tubes.
Flowering Early to late summer.
Foliage Light green, silky-white below, small, pinnate. Large terminal leaflet.
Natural habitat Chalky grassland, sea cliffs, and dunes. Native of Europe and North Africa, and naturalized in North America.
Soil Well drained, light, sandy or chalky.
Site Full sun.
Propagation Sow seeds in fall; divide in spring; take softwood cuttings in summer; self-seeds.
Uses Formerly medicinal; dried flowers; bee and butterfly plant.
Family Leguminosae (pea family).
Other varieties and species *A. hermanniae*; *A. montana*.

Aquilegia vulgaris

Columbine

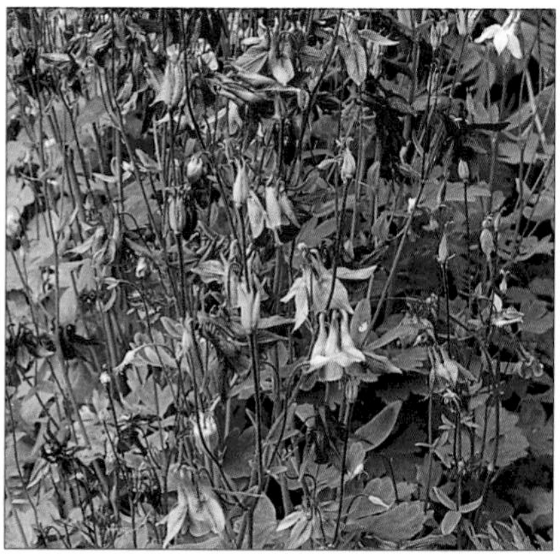

The columbine is a favorite, old-fashioned, cottage-garden flower, now available in a myriad of color combinations. Several grow wild in North America, and the red-and-yellow species *A. canadensis*, once used medicinally by the Indians, is especially dazzling, as is the beautiful state flower of Colorado, *A. caerulea*, with its nodding, mauve-blue-and-white flowers and long spurs.

Columbines should be grown singly or in small groups. Plant them on the edge of woodland, where they can enjoy dappled, light shade. When planted singly in a mixed border, the spectacular blooms look enchanting hovering above other plants.

Perennial Zone 5
Height 1–2 ft (30–60 cm).
Spread 9 in (23 cm).
Flowers Blue or dull purple, sometimes pink or white, nodding, bell-like, with distinctive spurs, on branched stems.
Flowering Late spring to early summer.
Foliage Dark bluish green, lower leaves. Upper leaves smaller, three lobed.
Natural habitat Rich, calcareous, mixed woodland and mountain forests, often damp. Native of Europe, naturalized in eastern North America.
Soil Rich, moisture retaining.
Site Partial shade, light shade, or sun.
Propagation Sow seeds in fall or spring; self-seeds.
Uses Formerly medicinal; dried seed heads.
Family Ranunculaceae (buttercup family).
Other varieties and species Many species and hybrids, including *A. caerulea*; *A. canadensis*; *A. chrysantha*; *A. fragrans*.

Warning

This plant is poisonous in all parts, especially the seeds.

Arctostaphylos uva-ursi

Bearberry

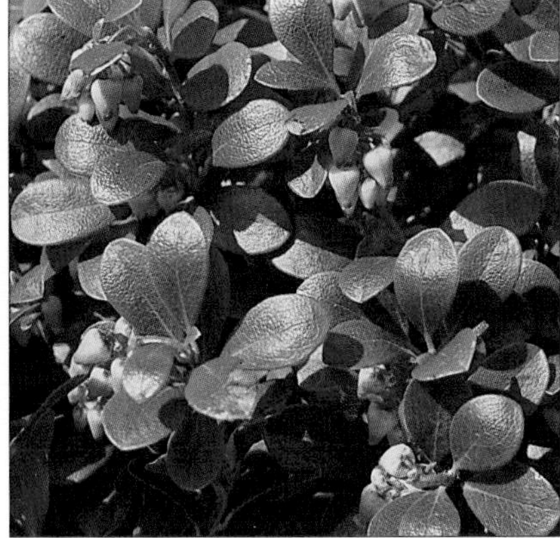

BEARBERRY IS also commonly known by its Latin name of *uva-ursi.* This evergreen herb is an attractive ground-cover plant, with small, shiny, dark green leaves and tiny, pink-tipped, white flowers followed by red berries in the fall.

Bearberry grows best where there is no chalk in the soil and prefers acid conditions. If there are conifers in the garden, it will greatly enjoy the dappled shade beneath them where the tree litter is acidic.

This herb has important medicinal properties which are particularly valued by herbal practitioners in the treatment of urinary, bladder, and kidney infections, but should not be used for home treatment. The berries yield ash-gray and blue dye.

Perennial shrub Zone 2
Height To 6 in (15 cm).
Spread 2 ft (60 cm).
Flowers White with a pink tip, waxy, small, in terminal drooping clusters. Red berries in fall.
Flowering Early summer.
Foliage Dark green, leathery, spatula shaped, long trailing mat-forming shoots.
Natural habitat Acid heaths, conifer woods, and mountains. Distributed widely across the Northern Hemisphere.
Soil Light, humus rich, rather dry to sandy, with some moisture.
Site Partial shade or full sun.
Propagation Sow seeds in fall; layer shoots, and take greenwood cuttings in summer.
Uses Medicinal; dye plant.
Family Ericaceae (heather family).
Other varieties and species
A. uva-ursi 'Point Reyes'; *A. u.* 'Vancouver Jade'; *A. u.* var. *hookeri* 'Monterey Carpet'; *A. alpina.*

Armeria maritima

Thrift

THRIFT, OR SEA-PINK, is a seaside plant that grows in the poorest sandy soils. Thrift now belongs to the genus *Armeria*, but was formerly classified as *Statice.*

In the wild, thrift often forms dense masses, and in a suitably dry, well-drained soil it can be grown in a drift. It is an excellent ground cover, or edging plant, especially in a formal herb garden, and makes a picturesque rock plant. Flowering continues over a long period, and the dried heads are very pretty, but when they become untidy they should be cut down.

Thrift was once valued medicinally for the treatment of obesity, nervous disorders, and urinary infections, but is now little used.

Perennial Zone 4
Height 6–12 in (15–30 cm).
Spread 7 in (18 cm).
Flowers Rose-pink, sometimes white, in dense globular heads on stalks.
Flowering Late spring to fall.
Foliage Dark green, narrow, linear, grasslike.
Natural habitat Cliffs, mountain pastures, and salt marshes. Native of Asia, Europe, and North America.
Soil Well drained, light, slightly acid.
Site Full sun or partial shade.
Propagation Sow seeds in fall; take semiripe cuttings or divide in summer; self-seeds.
Uses Formerly medicinal; dried flowers.
Family Plumbaginaceae (sea lavender family).
Other varieties and species *A. corsica*; *A. juniperifolia*; *A. latifolia*; *A. plantaginea.*

Arnica montana

Arnica

ARNICA, ALSO KNOWN as mountain tobacco and leopard's bane, is a simple, brilliant, daisylike European mountain flower. The plant's small golden-yellow flowers look best in rock gardens or a raised bed. Several arnica species are indigenous to North America. The seeds of arnica do not keep their germinating power and should be sown as soon as possible after harvest. The creeping rhizome can be divided in spring to make new plants.

All arnica species bear similar flowers and seem to possess the same valuable medicinal qualities. Arnica is the bruise herb above all others. Although it was once used internally for various conditions, it is now applied mainly externally as an ointment. It is taken internally only in homeopathic potency for bruising, shock, trauma, and injuries.

Perennial Zone 3
Height 1–2 ft (30–60 cm).
Spread 6 in (15 cm).
Flowers Golden-yellow, daisylike, on a single stem.
Flowering Midsummer to early fall.
Foliage Basal rosette of four to eight downy leaves.
Natural habitat Sandy, acid mountain pastures. Native of central Europe.
Soil Humus rich, acid, sandy.
Site Full sun.
Propagation Sow fresh seeds in fall or early spring; divide in spring.
Uses Medicinal.
Family Compositae (daisy family).
Other varieties and species
A. chamissonis; *A. cordifolia*; *A. fulgens*; *A. sororia*; *A. longifolia.*

Artemisia

Artemisia

Artemisia absinthium
Wormwood

Artemisia pontica
Roman wormwood

Artemisia ludoviciana
Western mugwort

Artemisia abrotanum
Southernwood

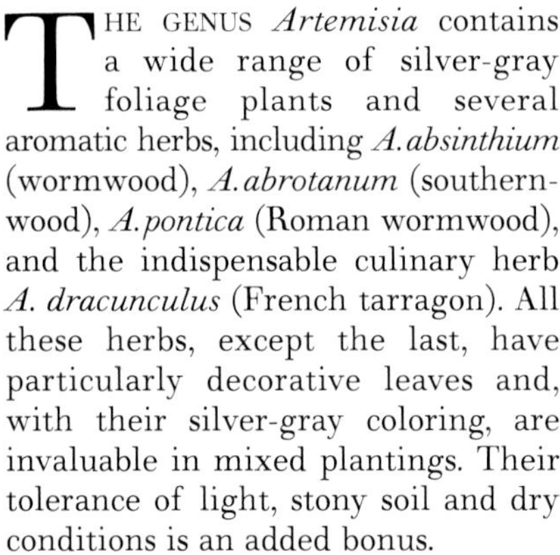

THE GENUS *Artemisia* contains a wide range of silver-gray foliage plants and several aromatic herbs, including *A. absinthium* (wormwood), *A. abrotanum* (southernwood), *A. pontica* (Roman wormwood), and the indispensable culinary herb *A. dracunculus* (French tarragon). All these herbs, except the last, have particularly decorative leaves and, with their silver-gray coloring, are invaluable in mixed plantings. Their tolerance of light, stony soil and dry conditions is an added bonus.

Wormwood, or green ginger as it is also known, is an outstanding foliage herb, especially the variety 'Lambrook Silver,' and is undemanding in its requirements. All varieties seem to thrive in drought conditions, but they do demand good winter drainage as they will not survive with waterlogged soil around their roots. The ground-cover varieties require a covering of grit or gravel, to keep wet soil off their foliage.

Wormwood is a bitter herb and was used to make the lethal drink absinth; it is still used to flavor vermouth and liqueurs. The plant also has valuable medicinal qualities, and is used as a bitter tonic to stimulate appetite and digestion. It should be used with great discretion under medical supervision.

The attractive green-gray foliage of southernwood has a fragrant fruity scent. Plant this herb where it will be brushed against to release its aroma. Roman wormwood has finely divided and fragrant leaves. It has a creeping rootstock that requires plenty of space. *A. ludoviciana* (western mugwort) is an exceptionally decorative plant; it bears aromatic, lance-shaped, woolly, silvery white leaves.

Perennial Zone 4
Height 3–5 ft (90 cm–1.5 m).
Spread 3 ft (90 cm).
Flowers Greenish yellow, minute, globular, grow in erect leafy panicles.
Flowering Summer to fall.
Foliage Gray-green, covered in fine silky hairs, deeply divided into narrow segments, stalked, aromatic.
Natural habitat Dry rocky hillsides and prairies. Found across central Europe, Asia, and North America.
Soil Fertile soil mixed with crushed rocks, sand, and gravel.
Site Full sun. Base must not be shaded.
Propagation Sow seeds in late summer; take semiripe cuttings in summer; divide in fall.
Uses Medicinal; alcoholic drinks; insect repellent; dried flowers.
Family Compositae (daisy family).
Other varieties and species
A. absinthium 'Lambrook Silver'; *A. abrotanum*; *A. arborescens*; *A. dracunculus*; *A. glacialis*; *A. ludoviciana*; *A. maritima*; *A. patillaris*; *A. pontica*; *A.* 'Powis Castle'; *A. schmidtiana*; *A. vulgaris*.

Warning

This plant is potentially toxic. Use under medical supervision only and avoid during pregnancy.

Asclepias tuberosa

Pleurisy Root

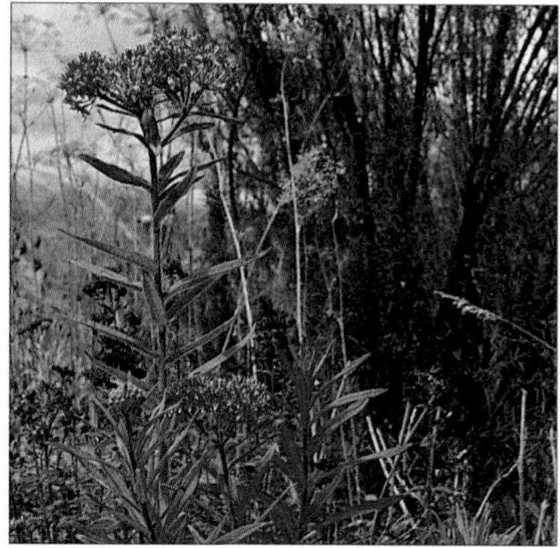

PLEURISY ROOT, also commonly known as butterfly weed, and orange milkweed, is a native of North America in common with several other members of the same genus. All were used medicinally by the Indians.

Pleurisy root is superb when in full flower, and its bright orange blossoms are attractive to butterflies. This plant dislikes wet soil and unless it is given good drainage is likely to die. It is recommended for rock gardens or for positioning against a sunny wall. The vigorous long taproot ensures the plant's survival.

Most milkweeds are distinguished by their acrid milky juice, although pleurisy root actually contains little. The tuberous root is used in medicine, in particular to treat conditions of the respiratory tract, including pleurisy.

Perennial Zone 5
Height To 3ft (90cm).
Spread 18in (45cm).
Flowers Bright orange, in a flat-topped corymb, with several heads branching from the main stem.
Flowering Early summer to early fall.
Foliage Dark green, lance shaped, arranged in a spiral.
Natural habitat Dry roadsides and prairies in the U.S.
Soil Well drained, gravelly or sandy.
Site Full sun.
Propagation Sow seeds in fall or spring; divide in spring; root cuttings.
Uses Medicinal; cut flowers.
Family Asclepiadaceae (milkweed family).
Other varieties and species *A. hallii*; *A. incarnata*; *A. quadrifolia*; *A. syriaca*.

Warning

This plant is potentially poisonous. Do not use for home treatment.

Aster novae-angliae

New England Aster

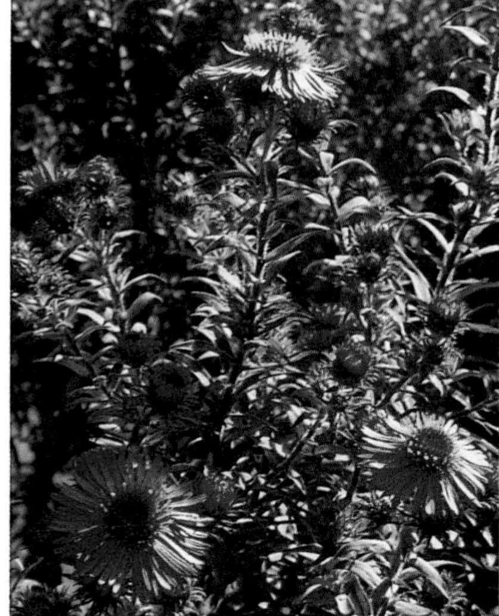

THE ASTER, or Michaelmas daisy, flowers abundantly into late fall when most flowers have finished blooming. Asters come in many forms and varieties, and flower colors range from white through shades of blue, mauve, pink, and deep red to violet.

In its wild form the New England aster can grow very tall, and would require staking in most gardens. However, several garden varieties are lower growing and provide colorful flowers for the border or island bed.

New England aster is a vigorous and healthy species, but allow space around each plant so that it can spread. In areas of summer drought on lighter soils, it may be short lived.

North American Indians once used the root of New England aster as a tea to treat fevers and diarrhea.

Perennial Zone 4
Height 3–7ft (90cm–2.1m).
Spread 18in (45cm).
Flowers Blue-violet, daisylike, with up to 100 rays.
Flowering Late summer to fall.
Foliage Lance shaped without teeth.
Natural habitat Moist meadows and thickets. Native of North America.
Soil Moisture retaining, fertile.
Site Full sun to light shade.
Propagation Sow seeds or take softwood cuttings in spring; divide in spring or fall.
Uses Formerly medicinal.
Family Compositae (daisy family).
Other varieties and species *A.n.* 'Barr's Blue'; *A.n.* 'Harrington's Pink'; *A.n.* 'Herbstschnee'; *A. novi-belgii*.

Atriplex hortensis var. *rubra*

Red Orache

RED ORACHE is an arresting herb with a deep red stem and purple-red leaves. A single plant in rich soil will grow to a substantial size with several stems and will make an impressive architectural feature plant if given space around it. It self-seeds profusely if allowed, and seedlings will appear the following spring. Orache is also available in golden-leaved and green-leaved forms, both of which are very decorative in the garden.

Orache is also known as mountain spinach, which indicates its culinary use. Young leaves may be added to salads, cooked like spinach, or made into a soup. For use as a vegetable, the plant must be given plenty of water when growing or the leaves will be tough. Medicinally orache was used to treat sore throats and jaundice. At the end of the season, dry the seed heads for winter arrangements.

Annual
Height To 5ft (1.5m).
Spread 2ft (60cm).
Flowers Greenish, inconspicuous, in spikes.
Flowering Summer to early fall.
Foliage Reddish purple, large, triangular, on stalks, mealy when young.
Natural habitat Waste ground and coastal regions. Distributed throughout most of Europe.
Soil Moisture-retaining, fertile loam.
Site Full sun.
Propagation Sow seeds in late spring or fall.
Uses Culinary; formerly medicinal; dried seed heads.
Family Chenopodiaceae (goosefoot family).
Other varieties and species *A. hortensis*; *A.h.* 'Green Leaved'; *A.h.* 'Gold Leaved.'

Balsamita major

Alecost

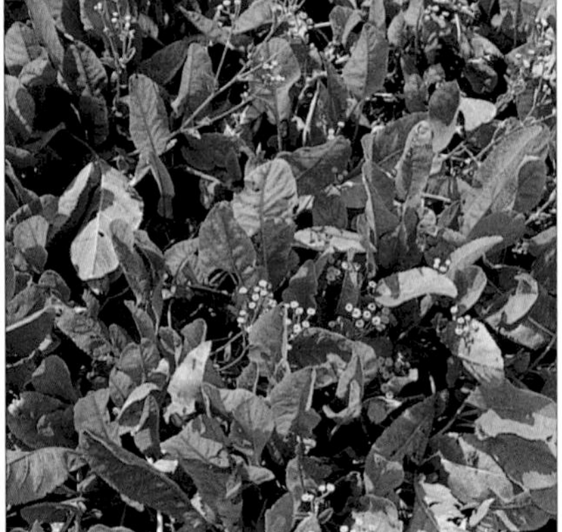

ALECOST, OR costmary, is an excellent foliage plant that bears aromatic gray-green leaves smelling of balsam. It grows into a dense bush which will fit into any planting scheme and act as a superb foil for bright summer flowers. Give this herb plenty of space, since it has a creeping rootstock and will form a good-sized clump after a few seasons. It has recently been reclassified into another genus as *Tanacetum balsamita*.

Alecost was formerly employed to flavor and preserve ale. The herb was once used medicinally to treat burns and stings and made into a tea for colds and catarrh. Alecost has insect-repellent qualities and is utilized on its own or with other insect-repellent herbs of the same family, like tansy, to deter moths and other insects in the home. Use alecost sparingly in the kitchen, since the flavor is intense. The dried leaves are often included as an ingredient of potpourri.

Perennial Zone 4
Height To 3 ft (90 cm).
Spread 2 ft (60 cm) or more.
Flowers Yellow, small, buttonlike, in loose clusters.
Flowering Late summer to early fall.
Foliage Gray-green, long, ovate, finely serrated, aromatic.
Natural habitat Roadsides and riverbanks. Native of Europe and western Asia, naturalized in North America.
Soil Fertile, well drained.
Site Full sun or light shade.
Propagation Divide in fall or early spring.
Uses Insect repellent; potpourri; formerly medicinal; culinary.
Family Compositae (daisy family).
Other varieties and species *B. vulgaris.*

Baptisia australis

Blue False Indigo

THIS NORTH American wild shrub does not produce the true indigo dye, which is obtained from several species of the genus *Indigofera*, a tropical shrub. Its main value is as a decorative herb. The striking, dark green, cloverlike leaves make it a good foliage plant and an excellent backdrop for herbaceous perennials and annuals. It is spectacular when its intense blue, pea flowers are in bloom early in the season.

Members of the genus *Baptisia* are tricky to germinate, and seeds should be soaked overnight in warm water before sowing.

The root was used medicinally by North American Indians, as a tea and an anti-inflammatory poultice.

Perennial shrub Zone 4
Height 3–5 ft (90 cm–1.5 m).
Spread To 4 ft (1.2 m).
Flowers Deep blue to violet, pealike.
Flowering Late spring to early summer.
Foliage Dark green, cloverlike, thrice divided, leaflets wider at the tip.
Natural habitat Open woods and forest edges. Native of North America.
Soil Nutrient rich, moist to dry.
Site Full sun or light shade.
Propagation Sow seeds in early spring; divide in spring or fall.
Uses Formerly medicinal; dye plant.
Family Leguminosae (pea family).
Other varieties and species: *B. alba*; *B. cinerea*; *B. pendula*; *B. tinctoria*; *Indigofera suffruticosa*; *I. tinctoria*.

Warning

This plant is potentially toxic.

Bellis perennis

Daisy

THE DAISY is a familiar lawn weed and although gardeners go to much trouble to eradicate them, there has been a change of heart toward this little plant. In spring and early summer, a lawn covered in flowering daisies and possibly other miniature flowers, like *Veronica* (speedwell) and *Glechoma* (ground ivy), can be a stunning sight. Such an area of lawn could also be planted with spring-flowering bulbs.

There are many decorative forms of the daisy. Some have pink and red flowers, others have double blooms. They make attractive edgings in the herb or vegetable garden.

An old common name for the daisy is bruisewort, indicating one of its many medicinal uses. Today it is rarely employed in medicine except in homeopathy. The leaves can be added to green salad and the flowers sprinkled on top for decoration.

Perennial Zone 3
Height To 3 in (7.5 cm).
Spread 4 in (10 cm).
Flowers White to pink petals with a yellow center, numerous.
Flowering Spring to summer.
Foliage Oval shaped, in a ground-hugging rosette.
Natural habitat Grassland. Native of Europe and western Asia.
Soil Most fertile, well-drained soils.
Site Full sun.
Propagation Sow seeds in spring or summer.
Uses Medicinal; culinary.
Family Compositae (daisy family).
Other varieties and species *B. perennis* Carpet Series; *B. p.* 'Goliath'; *B. p.* 'Pomponette'; and many others.

Berberis vulgaris

Barberry

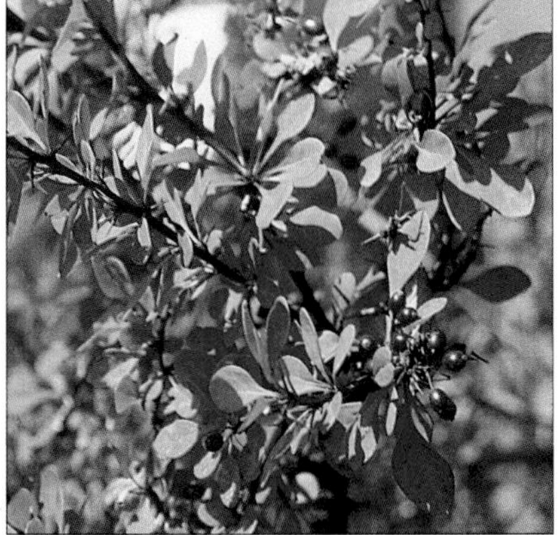

THE WILD EUROPEAN barberry has many practical uses and is well worth growing for its small, shiny, dark green leaves and clusters of yellow flowers in early summer. Because of its suckering rootstock it makes an excellent plant for the natural hedge or the shrub garden.

Barberry produces masses of red-purple berries in the fall, rich in vitamin C, which can be made into jam, jelly, and syrup. The syrup is useful for treating sore throats and as a gargle. The white wood of the barberry is used in the manufacture of toothpicks, and the bark, stem, and roots yield a good dye in various shades of yellow.

Perennial shrub Zones 4–5
Height 8 ft (2.4 m).
Spread To 4 ft (1.2 m).
Flowers Yellow, small, in drooping clusters. Scarlet-purple fruit.
Flowering Late spring to early summer.
Foliage Dark green, tiny, elliptical, shiny, leathery leaves with finely toothed margins.
Natural habitat Edges of woods, hedgerows, waysides, and light deciduous woodland. Native of Europe, eastern Asia, and North Africa. Naturalized in New England.
Soil Light, chalky.
Site Partial shade.
Propagation Sow seeds or plant suckers in fall; take cuttings in early fall.
Uses Culinary; medicinal; wood; dye plant.
Family Berberidaceae (barberry family).
Other varieties and species
B. thunbergii 'Atropurpurea Nana' and many others of garden merit; *B. canadensis.*

Borago officinalis

Borage

BORAGE, OR BURRAGE, has long been grown in herb gardens and is a firm favorite because of its beautiful intense blue, starlike flowers.

Borage self-seeds readily and in good soil forms a substantial plant. If you keep bees, it is worth seeding a large patch, since it will flower for months and bees love it. Borage will grow well in a container of rich soil, but will need frequent watering in hot weather. It self-seeds readily.

Borage leaves impart a fresh cucumber flavor to summer drinks and should be used in fruit cups and wine cups. The young leaves make a delicious addition to a green salad, and the flowers look spectacular sprinkled over the top. The flowers can also be candied. Wonderful honey is produced from the flowers.

Traditionally borage was used to drive away sorrow and melancholy. It has well-tried medicinal properties and an infusion makes a soothing treatment for bronchitis and catarrh.

Annual
Height 18 in (45 cm).
Spread To 18 in (45 cm).
Flowers Bright blue turning pink, with prominent black anthers, star shaped.
Flowering Summer.
Foliage Dull green, large, wrinkled, oval, pointed, very hairy. Cucumber scent.
Natural habitat Waste ground. Native of the Mediterranean.
Soil Fertile, well drained.
Site Full sun.
Propagation Sow seeds in spring or fall.
Uses Culinary; medicinal; bee plant.
Family Boraginaceae (borage family).
Other varieties and species White-flowered forms are not uncommon.

Calamintha grandiflora

Garden Calamint

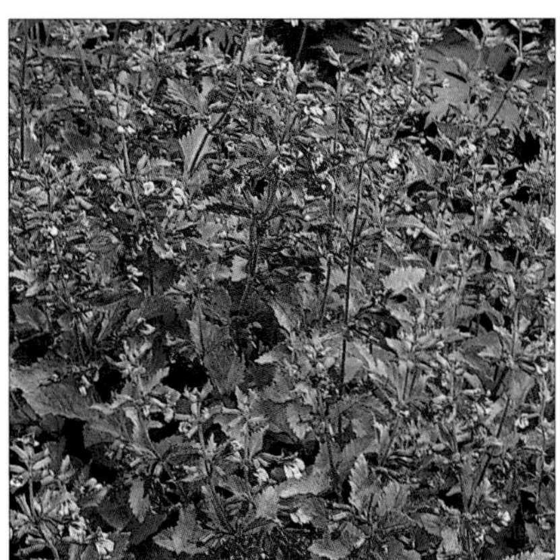

GARDEN CALAMINT, also known as mountain balm, is a small bushy plant with mint-scented leaves. The small, pink, sagelike flowers continue for a long season.

Grow calamint near the edge of the border, where its scent can be appreciated and its attractive flowers enjoyed. It looks good in the rock garden but needs to be out of the hottest sun in light or partial shade and can also be grown in the dappled shade of trees or on a hedge bank.

Garden calamint has some healing properties, although it cannot be considered an important medicinal plant. A tisane made from either fresh or dried leaves is refreshing and a mild tonic. John Gerard, the English herbalist, recommended calamint for the cure of melancholy, so this is a tea that could be a pleasant pick-me-up during the dull days of winter.

Perennial Zones 4–5
Height 1–2 ft (30–60 cm).
Spread 18 in (45 cm).
Flowers Purplish pink, drooping, sagelike.
Flowering Mid- to late summer.
Foliage Broadly ovate, downy, toothed, aromatic, stalked.
Natural habitat Dry banks by hedgerows and open woods. Native of central and southern Europe, Asia Minor, the Caucasus, and North Africa.
Soil Most soils if well drained.
Site Full sun or partial shade.
Propagation Sow seeds in spring; divide in fall or spring; take cuttings in spring.
Uses Culinary; medicinal.
Family Labiatae (mint family).
Other varieties and species
C. ascendens; *C. nepeta*; *C. sylvatica.*

Calendula officinalis

Pot Marigold

THE POT MARIGOLD is one of the most showy of the annual herbal flowers. The wild plant can be seen growing all over the Mediterranean region in Europe, on wastelands and cultivated ground. In the wild it has smaller blooms, but centuries of selection has produced varieties with larger flowers. There are now many varieties of this herb, from dwarf to tall, with single but mostly double flowers in all shades from pale orange to deep red-orange. Each bushy plant bears many dozens of flowers and distinctive seed heads, in which the seeds form a tight circular cluster. You can pull the heads off by hand when they are ripe and dry looking (see pages 45–7); they will break up easily into large individual seeds.

The pot marigold often seeds itself, but seeds can be sown in spring, and the plants will be in full flower during summer. Pot marigold really brightens up the herb garden and can be grown equally well in a flower border or an island bed. It looks much more natural grown as an individual plant rather than *en masse*.

The pot marigold is a valuable medicinal plant. For herbal use the dwarf-growing and single varieties are best. The flowers' antiseptic and healing properties are now utilized in ointments, tinctures, and creams, which are widely available. The flowers are also used in hair and cosmetic preparations, and the petals are sprinkled on salads and used in cooking as a coloring. The young leaves can be added to salads. The flowers yield a yellow dye for cloth.

Do not confuse the pot marigold with the other marigolds, which are listed under *Tagetes*: for example, *T. patula* (French marigold).

Annual
Height 1–2 ft (30–60 cm).
Spread 8 in (20 cm).
Flowers Pale to deep orange, daisylike, with many petals. Aromatic.
Flowering Late spring to early fall.
Foliage Pale green, spatula shaped, becoming narrower higher up the branched stem.
Natural habitat Vineyards, cultivated fields, and wasteland. Native of Asia and central and southern Europe.
Soil Loam and most garden soils. Will tolerate dry conditions.
Site Full sun.
Propagation Sow seeds in spring.
Uses Medicinal; culinary; dye plant.
Family Compositae (daisy family).
Other varieties and species
C. officinalis 'Art Shades' (tall);
C. o. 'Fiesta' (dwarf);
C. o. 'Geisha Girl' (tall);
C. o. 'Kablovus' (tall).

Calluna vulgaris

Heather

HEATHER, ALSO KNOWN as ling, is closely related to the ericas or heaths, popular garden plants that are loved for the color provided by their foliage and flowers in the fall.

All plants of the heath family grow in acid soils, so give them the natural conditions they enjoy by making a peat bed. The foliage turns various shades of red, orange, yellow, or gold; and as heather is a good ground-cover plant it can be planted in drifts to show off its color to best advantage.

Heather has been put to many uses over the centuries. The twisted stems were once used to make brooms, and the roots to make pipes. The flowers are loved by bees and produce a delicious honey. Heather was formerly used medicinally for urinary and kidney infections. Adding heather to a bath is said to help in the relief of rheumatic pain. The flowers dry well if hung in an airy place out of the sun.

Perennial evergreen subshrub Zone 3
Height To 3 ft (90 cm).
Spread To 2 ft (60 cm).
Flowers Pink, small, bell shaped, in terminal, one-sided racemes.
Flowering Late summer to late fall.
Foliage Gray-green turning to red, tiny, stalkless, triangular leaves, in tight rows.
Natural habitat Peat bogs, dry hillsides, and open woodland. Native of Europe and Asia Minor, naturalized in eastern North America.
Soil Acid, well drained.
Site Full sun.
Propagation Take cuttings in summer; layer in spring.
Uses Formerly medicinal; bee plant.
Family Ericaceae (heath family).
Other varieties and species Numerous garden varieties.

Caltha palustris

Marsh Marigold

THE BRIGHT GOLDEN flowers of the marsh marigold, or king cup, are a sure sign that spring is well under way. It resembles a giant buttercup and bears large, glossy, green leaves and some of the stems grow along the ground, rooting as they go.

Wherever there is water or moist soil that does not dry out in summer, the marsh marigold is an easy plant to grow. Site this stunning spring flower by the water's edge or in a few inches of water, and it will quickly spread into a large drift.

The marsh marigold was once used medicinally (it was said to cure warts).

Perennial Zone 2
Height 12 in (30 cm). Spreading.
Flowers Buttercup-yellow, large, with five petallike sepals and yellow stamens.
Flowering Spring.
Foliage Green, large, glossy, kidney shaped, toothed, on long stalks.
Natural habitat Marshes, wet meadows, streamsides, and the edges of ponds and lakes. Native of central and northern Europe, Asia, and North America.
Soil Wet to moisture retaining.
Site Full sun or partial shade.
Propagation Divide in fall or early spring; sow seeds in fall.
Uses Formerly medicinal.
Family Ranunculaceae (buttercup family).
Other varieties and species
C. palustris 'Flore Pleno'; *C. leptosepala.*

Warning

All parts of this plant are irritant. Wear gloves when handling.

Cardamine pratensis

Lady's Smock

THIS DELICATE little, lilac spring flower naturally grows in great drifts in Europe and North America. In Britain it appears with the first cuckoo and is known as cuckooflower. This once-common salad herb is cresslike, with a pleasantly hot flavor.

Lady's smock makes a stunning show in a small clump or planted over a larger area. It looks natural by water and will do best here, though it will grow in grass that becomes waterlogged (preferably flooded) in winter.

When flowering is over, a long seed pod develops, and the plant will readily self-seed. It can also propagate itself from its leaves which, in the summer, root where they fall and touch moist, shaded soil.

To grow the plant for salad, give it a rich, moisture-retaining loam; the pretty flowers can be used to decorate the finished dish.

Perennial Zone 3
Height To 12 in (30 cm).
Spread 9 in (23 cm).
Flowers Rose-pink or lilac to white, in terminal racemes.
Flowering Spring to early summer.
Foliage Lower leaves are round to kidney-shaped, forming a rosette. Upper leaves are narrower.
Natural habitat Moist meadows, open moist woods, and streamsides in Europe and North America.
Soil Fertile, moist loam.
Site Full sun or partial shade.
Propagation Sow seeds in summer or fall; divide in fall; take leaf tip cuttings in summer.
Uses Culinary.
Family Cruciferae (cabbage family).
Other varieties and species
C. pratensis 'Flore Pleno'; *C. trifolia.*

Carthamus tinctoria

Safflower

SAFFLOWER IS ALSO known as false saffron, American saffron, and dyer's saffron. Beyond its practical value it is also a decorative annual, with spiny leaves and lovely, thistle-like, golden-yellow flower heads.

Safflower is often grown as an ornamental in the herb garden and is a good border plant. Before sowing in spring, look closely at the seeds, which are shiny, white and shell-like. Sow a small patch of the plant, or several patches if you have room. Its flowers will brighten up the garden from summer into fall.

The golden flowers of safflower are in great demand as a dye and yield both yellow and a pinkish red; these are used mainly for dyeing silk. The flowers are also blended with talc to make rouge and may be dried for winter decorations. They also provide a saffron substitute for coloring food. However, safflower seeds are most valued today as a source of edible oil. This is rich in linoleic acid, which helps to lower blood cholesterol and is widely sold as a health food product.

Annual
Height 2–3 ft (60–90 cm).
Spread 9 in (23 cm).
Flowers Orange or yellow, in a thistlelike head.
Flowering Summer to fall.
Foliage Stalkless, lance shaped, spiny, distinctly veined.
Natural habitat Dry areas. Native of Africa, widely naturalized.
Soil Well drained.
Site Full sun.
Propagation Sow seeds in spring.
Uses Culinary; dye plant; dried flowers.
Family Compositae (daisy family).
Other varieties and species None.

Carum carvi

Caraway

CARAWAY IS CLOSELY related to dill, fennel, anise, and cumin. The dainty white flower heads are set off well by its finely cut, fernlike foliage which creates a wonderfully soft texture when grown in a clump. Sown in summer, the small plants will establish before the winter and make an attractive ground cover. They will mature the following summer. Gather seeds when they are brown and ripe.

Caraway, mentioned in the Bible and grown by the ancient Egyptians, has been in use for 5,000 years. The young leaves can be added to salads, and the root cooked as a vegetable. The seeds are extensively utilized to flavor cakes and breads, and to season vegetables, cheese, and sausages. The seeds have also long been utilized medicinally, in particular to soothe digestive upsets.

Biennial Zones 3–4
Height 12–30 in (30–75 cm).
Spread 12 in (30 cm).
Flowers White, small, in terminal umbels, followed by aromatic seeds.
Flowering Early to late summer.
Foliage Finely cut, fernlike.
Natural habitat Waste ground. Native of central Europe, the Middle East, and Asia. Naturalized in North America.
Soil Most soils, especially light.
Site Full sun.
Propagation Sow seeds in spring or late summer.
Uses Culinary; medicinal.
Family Umbelliferae (carrot family).
Other varieties and species None.

Ceanothus americanus

New Jersey Tea

THIS WOODY SHRUB, also known as red root, grows wild on dry gravelly banks and in open woods in the eastern U.S. The flowers, borne over a long period, form white puffy clusters. When the heads are fruiting, they are equally decorative, the fruits changing from pink through red to brown, and then to dark brown when ripe. The young stems are a brilliant pink-red color.

New Jersey tea is an attractive and useful garden shrub as it flowers late in the summer and early fall. It grows well on poor, light soil. It should be pruned hard in late winter to keep it from becoming straggly.

As its name indicates, the leaf of this herb was used to replace regular tea during the American Revolution. The root was employed by the Indians for a variety of ailments.

Perennial shrub Zone 5
Height 1–2 ft (30–60 cm).
Spread 2 ft (60 cm).
Flowers White, forming puffy heads. Followed by pink, red, and brown fruits.
Flowering Late summer to early fall.
Foliage Bright green, oval, toothed, short stalked.
Natural habitat Dry banks and woods. Native of North America.
Soil Well drained to gravelly.
Site Full sun to partial shade.
Propagation Sow seeds in fall (stratify); take softwood cuttings in spring or early summer.
Uses Medicinal; tea; dye plant.
Family Rhamnaceae (buckthorn family).
Other varieties and species Many decorative garden species and varieties include *C. arboreus*; *C. dentatus*; *C. impressus*; *C. incanus*; *C. papillosus*; *C. rigidus*.

Cedronella canariensis

False Balm of Gilead

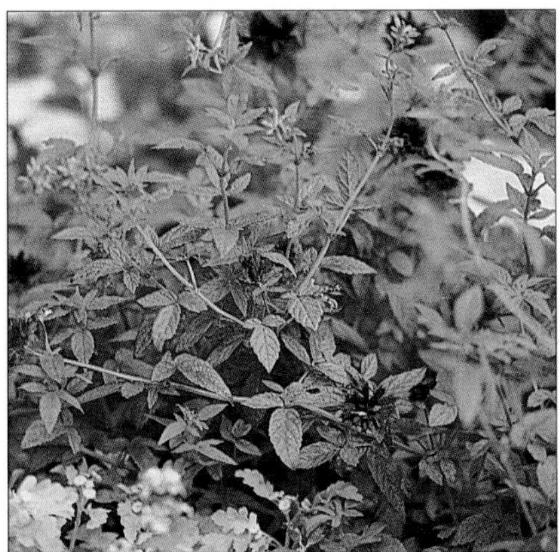

THIS APPEALING herb is something of an imposter, as it is in no way related to balm of Gilead. (The true balm of Gilead mentioned in the Bible, *Balsamodendron opobalsamum*, is a rare, small tree – now a protected species – which grows in countries on both sides of the Red Sea.) False balm of Gilead is nevertheless an attractive plant, with a balsamic scent – hence its common name.

False balm of Gilead is grown for its fragrance and its attractive foliage, and looks best when grown as a single specimen or in a small group in a border or island bed. It is not very hardy; it needs protection in winter and requires a free-draining soil.

The bruised leaves and stems of *Cedronella* are recommended as an effective mosquito repellent. The dried flowers make an attractive addition to potpourri.

Perennial Zones 7–8
Height To 3 ft (90 cm).
Spread 2 ft (60 cm).
Flowers Pink-mauve, small, sagelike, in a terminal spike.
Flowering Summer.
Foliage Light green, three lobed, compound and toothed, stalked. Aromatic.
Natural habitat Native of southern North America and the Canary Islands.
Soil Well-drained, sandy loam.
Site Full sun.
Propagation Sow seeds in spring.
Uses Insect repellent; potpourri.
Family Labiatae (mint family).
Other varieties and species *Agastache mexicana* syn. *Cedronella mexicana.*

Centaurea cyanus

Cornflower

BLUEBOTTLE IS AN old country name for the cornflower, a striking European wild flower that has been grown in gardens for centuries.

Like the poppy, the seeds can be scattered randomly through a border or island bed planting and will give brilliant accents of color, often in unexpected places.

The flower and seed head of the genus *Centaurea* is distinctive. At the base of the flower is a thistlelike head of overlapping bracts, which makes a decorative seed head when ripe and is an attractive addition to dried flower arrangements. Decoctions from the flower heads of both the cornflower and *C. montana* were used as an eyewash to treat inflamed and tired eyes. The juice of the petals provides a blue ink and also a watercolor paint.

Annual
Height 1–3 ft (30–90 cm).
Spread 8 in (20 cm).
Flowers Bright blue ray florets with dark center, solitary, on long stalks.
Flowering Early to late summer.
Foliage Gray-green, downy, alternate, lanceolate.
Natural habitat Cornfields, waste ground. Native of southern and eastern Europe, naturalized in parts of North America.
Soil Fertile loam and alkaline soil.
Site Full sun.
Propagation Sow seeds in fall or spring.
Uses Medicinal; cut and dried flowers; dye plant; potpourri.
Family Compositae (daisy family).
Other varieties and species *C. cyanus* Blue Boy Series; *C. montana*; *C. moschata* 'Sweet Sultan.'

Centaurea scabiosa

Greater Knapweed

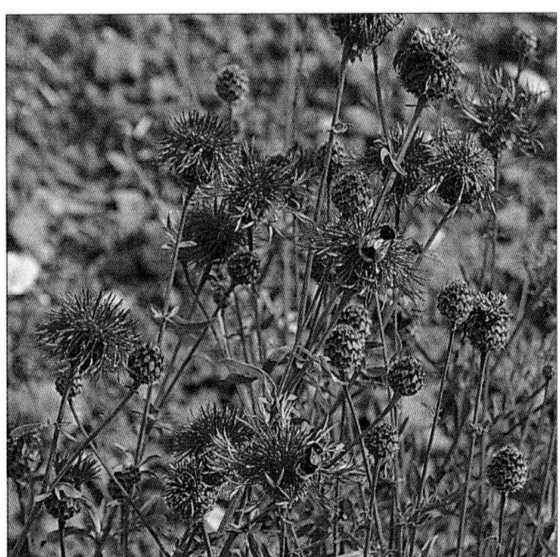

GREATER KNAPWEED, related to the cornflower, is a robust perennial plant with many stems, each topped by a single thistlelike flower head, exquisite in form with an overlapping tilelike structure. When the flower stops blooming, the seed head opens to reveal shiny black seeds whose silky hairs carry them on the wind.

In the garden, greater knapweed needs plenty of space and should not be crowded with other plants. It is best planted as a single specimen. Knapweed establishes well in grass, and is a lovely flower to grow in a wild meadow. Its flowers come later in the summer, when many others have finished blooming.

This herb has medicinal properties like many other species of knapweed. It was employed mostly as a wound herb, but was also used as a decoction to soothe sore throats and coughs. The dried heads and stems make superb winter decorations.

Perennial Zone 3
Height 1–3 ft (30–90 cm).
Spread 2 ft (60 cm).
Flowers Rich purple-crimson, with deeply cut petals.
Flowering Summer.
Foliage Dull green, deeply lobed, lower leaves stemmed and in a large rosette. Upper leaves are smaller and stalkless.
Natural habitat Grassland and scrub on chalky soil. Native of northern Europe.
Soil Fertile loam.
Site Full sun.
Propagation Sow seeds in fall or spring.
Uses Formerly medicinal; dried flowers.
Family Compositae (daisy family).
Other varieties and species
C. dealbata; *C. d.* 'Steenbergii'; *C. hypoleuca*; *C. nigra*; *C. pulcherrima.*

Centaurium erythraea

Centaury

Centaury belongs to the gentian family, and its medicinal properties are similar to those of *Gentiana lutea* (yellow gentian). This is a tiny, delicate-looking plant with bright rose-pink flowers and few leaves. The flowers are very light sensitive and open only on bright days.

Centaury is not easy to grow in the garden unless the soil is suitable; a poor, alkaline soil is ideal. Centaury grows well in fine grassland on poor soil. The seed is like dust; it is best surface sown in the fall where the plants are to grow.

Centaury is a bitter tonic herb used as a tea to stimulate digestion and reduce fevers, and as a bitter flavoring in certain liqueurs.

Annual
Height To 12in (30cm).
Spread 4in (10cm).
Flowers Rose colored, small, starlike, in dense forking cymes on top of stem.
Flowering Late summer.
Foliage Pale green, pointed, lance shaped, sparse.
Natural habitat Dry grassland, dunes, open woods. Native to most of central and northern Europe and North Africa. Naturalized in North America.
Soil Dry, rather poor, alkaline.
Site Full sun.
Propagation Sow seeds in spring or fall; self-seeds.
Uses Medicinal; liqueurs.
Family Gentianaceae (gentian family).
Other varieties and species *Sabatia angularis*; *S. campestris*; *S. elliottii*.

Centranthus ruber

Red Valerian

Red valerian, which is often called Kentranthus in the horticultural world, is a plant that flourishes on the poorest and driest soils, though it prefers alkaline conditions. It is often seen growing against, or even in, old walls and this is a habitat in which it thrives. Its extensive roots find moisture and nourishment in the stoniest, most barren situation.

Red valerian is a colorful plant. A mixture of deep red and pink shades looks spectacular with the occasional white bloom. Always plant where it can freely self-seed (which it does with a vengeance). It is far too invasive for the rock garden, yet ideal for growing in gravel or stones. Once the main flowering has finished, cut the flower stems down and a second flowering will occur later in the year. Plants will last longer if not allowed to set too much seed.

Red valerian leaves are very succulent in salads and can also be cooked. The roots are used for soup in France.

Perennial Zone 4
Height 3ft (90cm).
Spread 18in (45cm).
Flowers Pink, crimson, sometimes white, in dense clusters at top of stem.
Flowering Summer to fall.
Foliage Long, pointed, fleshy.
Natural habitat Cliffs, old walls, waste ground. Native of the Mediterranean and southwestern Asia.
Soil Dry loam and stony, alkaline soil.
Site Full sun.
Propagation Sow seeds or divide in fall or spring; self-seeds.
Uses Culinary.
Family Valerianaceae (valerian family).
Other varieties and species Shades of pink, red, and white forms.

Cheiranthus cheiri

Wild Wallflower

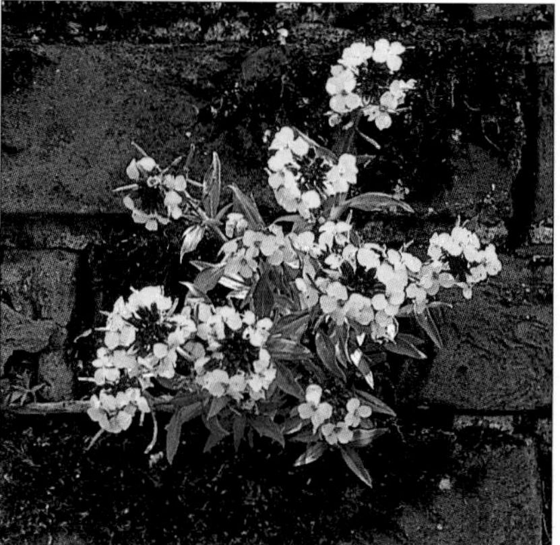

The rich golden blooms of the wild wallflower, or gillyflower, can often be seen adorning old walls. It is a wild plant that has spread far and wide from its original home in southern Europe.

The small, delicately scented flowers bloom from early through to late summer. They are followed by large quantities of small red-brown, elongated seeds that will germinate readily. The wild wallflower naturalizes well in gravel, its long taproot enabling it to survive in very inhospitable situations.

The diluted oil of the plant has a delightful perfume.

Perennial Zone 6
Height 8–24in (20–60cm).
Spread 6in (15cm).
Flowers Orange-yellow, single, borne in clusters at top of stem, fragrant.
Flowering Early to late summer.
Foliage Medium green, narrow, tapering, untoothed.
Natural habitat Rocks, walls, and sea cliffs. Native of the Aegean region and widely naturalized.
Soil Well drained.
Site Full sun.
Propagation Sow seeds in spring or late summer; self-seeds.
Uses Aromatic oil.
Family Cruciferae (cabbage family).
Other varieties and species *C. cheiri* Fair Lady Series; *C.* x *allionii*; *C.* 'Bowles Mauve'; *C.* 'Harpur Crewe'; *C.* 'Moonlight'; *Erysimum* subsp.

Chelidonium major

Greater Celandine

THE GREATER CELANDINE belongs to the poppy family and is not related to the lesser celandine. Its stem contains a latex that is bright orange and strongly irritant. Take care not to allow this juice onto the skin.

The numerous small bright yellow flowers and soft green, divided leaves create an attractive effect and texture. The distinctive long seed pods contain small, shiny black seeds.

The greater celandine is accommodating as to soil and will thrive in poor, dry conditions. Partial shade is the best habitat. Plant in the dappled shade of trees, a hedge, or a fence.

Medicinally celandine has been used for centuries to treat a variety of conditions. The yellow juice is an ancient wart remedy.

Perennial Zone 4
Height 18–36 in (45–90 cm).
Spread 18 in (45 cm).
Flowers Bright yellow, with four petals in cross form.
Flowering Spring to summer.
Foliage Pale green, slightly hairy, grayish underneath. Deeply divided, forming three leaflets with rounded teeth.
Natural habitat Woodland borders, hedges, waste ground, by walls. Native of Europe; naturalized in the eastern U.S.
Soil Most well-drained soils.
Site Full sun to partial shade.
Propagation Sow seeds in spring or fall.
Uses Medicinal.
Family Papaveraceae (poppy family).
Other varieties and species *C. majus* 'Flore Pleno.'

Warning

The whole plant is poisonous and should not be taken internally or externally without medical supervision.

Chelone glabra

Balmony

BALMONY IS ALSO known as turtlehead, as the flowers resemble the head of a turtle or tortoise. It is a native of North America, where it grows wild in low-lying wet situations from Florida to Newfoundland.

This beautiful flowering herb establishes well in any wet soil that does not dry out over the summer. Cultivated forms bear cerise blooms. For the best effect grow balmony in small groups on the margins of a pond or stream, or in a specially constructed boggy area. It is an unusual plant and not commonly cultivated, so it is sure to fascinate visitors.

Medicinally, balmony is used as a bitter tonic and appetite stimulant. It also acts as a laxative and purgative.

Perennial Zone 3
Height 2–3 ft (60–90 cm).
Spread 18 in (45 cm).
Flowers White to pink, two lipped, swollen, in tight clusters in axils of leaves, like a turtle head.
Flowering Summer to fall.
Foliage Dark green, shiny, lance shaped to oval, toothed.
Natural habitat Wet ground, edges of streams, damp forests. Native of North America.
Soil Moist loam.
Site Partial shade.
Propagation Sow seeds or divide in spring or fall; take soft tip cuttings in summer.
Uses Medicinal.
Family Scrophulariaceae (figwort family).
Other varieties and species *C. barbata* syn. *C. obliqua*.

Chrysanthemum cinerariifolium

Pyrethrum

THE PYRETHRUM flower produces an important natural insecticide that is nonpersistent in the soil and harmless to mammals. For this reason the plant is widely cultivated across the world. Pyrethrum has recently been reclassified into another genus, *Tanacetum*, by botanists.

Pyrethrum is a decorative garden plant. The white daisy flowers are produced in great profusion, and the attractive leaves give the whole plant a silvery gray appearance.

Use pyrethrum in a general planting scheme where gray foliage is required. This plant likes dry well-drained conditions; it is short lived in rich soil, especially in a humid climate, and it will not tolerate shade.

The insecticidal properties of pyrethrum were discovered in the 1920s, and it was largely cultivated in California. Another commonly grown garden flower is *T. coccineum* (Persian pyrethrum) which has similar properties but is not as potent.

Perennial Zone 4
Height 12–20 in (30–50 cm).
Spread 18 in (45 cm).
Flowers White, medium, daisylike, solitary on long stems.
Flowering Summer to fall.
Foliage Gray-green, long, oval, deeply subdivided.
Natural habitat Dry areas with poor limestone or sandy soil. Native of former Yugoslavia.
Soil Well drained and fairly poor.
Site Full sun.
Propagation Sow seeds in spring or fall.
Uses Insecticide.
Family Compositae (daisy family).
Other varieties and species *C. balsamita*; *C. parthenium*.

Chrysanthemum parthenium

Feverfew

ONCE KNOWN as flirtwort, this native of southeastern Europe has now spread far afield in gardens and naturalized in the wild over most of Europe and North America. Feverfew is a multibranched plant; the masses of white daisylike flowers have yellow centers. The whole plant is strongly aromatic, and the leaves are bitter to taste. The variety 'Aureum,' golden feverfew (illustrated opposite), is very decorative and has more compact growth than wild feverfew.

In the garden feverfew looks its best in a large group and thrives in well-drained or even dry locations. It spreads extensively from seed if not cut down after flowering.

Feverfew has a long tradition as a medicinal herb to treat fevers, indigestion, and is also a sedative. In recent years this herb, taken in tablet form or as fresh leaf, has assumed new importance in the treatment of migraine and arthritis and is now a registered medicine in Britain where it has been extensively researched. The dried leaves are also useful in the home as a moth repellent.

Feverfew has recently been reclassified into another genus and is called *Tanacetum parthenium.*

Perennial Zone 5
Height 2 ft (60 cm).
Spread 18 in (45 cm).
Flowers White, small, daisylike with a yellow center.
Flowering Early to late summer.
Foliage Yellow-green, oblong, toothed, aromatic.
Natural habitat Waste ground and rocky places. Native of southeastern Europe and naturalized over most of Europe and North America.
Soil Well drained, any type.
Site Full sun or partial shade.
Propagation Sow seeds in spring or late summer; self-seeds.
Uses Medicinal; moth repellent; dye plant.
Family Compositae (daisy family).
Other varieties and species
C. parthenium 'Aureum';
C. p. 'Flore Pleno.'

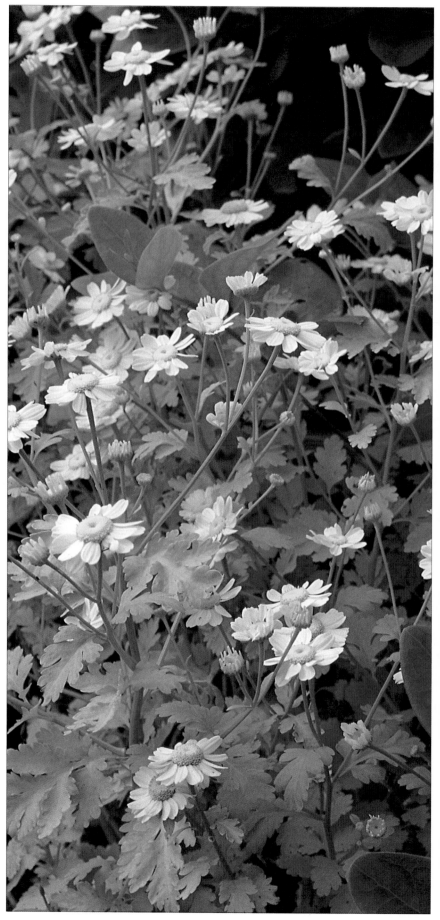

Lilium

Lily

Lilium candidum
Madonna lily

Lilium martagon
Martagon lily

The lily family includes aloe, asparagus, beetroot and garlic chives. True lilies belong to the genus *Lilium*; they include many popular species and varieties available for the garden.

Most lilies, with the exception of the madonna lily, enjoy deep planting. Bury the bulb up to 8 in (20 cm) deep. For best results the soil must be well drained so that there is no risk of waterlogging in winter. They respond to humus-rich soil and potash feed (wood ash is a good source). When planting, surround the bulbs with ½ in (1 cm) of sand to protect them from excess moisture and attack by slugs.

The madonna lily, which has been grown in gardens for centuries, is one of the most beautiful. The highly scented flowers should be positioned near the house, in a good clump, where they can be fully appreciated. The simple white blooms look their best against the dark background of a hedge. Plant them among lower-growing shrubby herbs that shade the soil and keep it cool.

L. martagon (martagon lily or purple turk's cap) has purple flowers that give off their scent at night. They have a distinctive shape, resembling a traditional Turkish turban. This is a hardy lily that enjoys a free-draining soil with lime in full sun or partial shade. The martagon lily looks especially good growing among shrubby plants or in the shade of trees. It seeds itself freely; the bulbs should be planted deep, as this lily produces roots on its lower stem.

Many species of lily bulbs are edible and are grown as vegetables in China and Japan. A soothing mucilage extracted from the bulb of *L. candidum* was used externally to treat ulcers, burns, and bruises.

Perennial bulb Zone 6
Height 3–6 ft (90–1.8 m).
Spread 12 in (30 cm).
Flowers White, fragrant, funnel shaped with recurved tips, outward facing, in groups of five to ten on a single stem.
Flowering Midsummer.
Foliage Lance shaped, scattered up stem.
Natural habitat Rocky slopes and among scrub. Native of southern and western Greece and former Yugoslavia.
Soil Humus-rich, very well-drained sandy loam. Enjoys lime.
Site Full sun, with shaded roots.
Propagation Plant small bulbs in fall; sow seeds in spring or fall.
Uses Formerly medicinal; cut flowers.
Family Liliaceae (lily family).
Other varieties and species
L. canadense; *L. chalcedonicum*; *L. martagon*; *L. philadelphicum*; *L. superbum*.

Linaria vulgaris

Toadflax

Toadflax was aptly named eggs-and-bacon on account of its many bright yellow-and-orange flowers. The charming, vivid, snapdragonlike blooms are designed for pollination by large bees, such as honeybees.

Toadflax continues flowering over many weeks and often months; it is low growing and spreads readily in a suitable light, sandy soil. However, in parts of North America the plant can be invasive, and is considered a weed.

Plant toadflax in a dry area where a colorful ground cover is required, along with taller-growing herbs. A dry bank or patch of uncultivated ground is ideal.

Toadflax is rarely used in herbal medicine today, but was once valued for diseases of the liver. The flowers make an effective fly poison and deterrent, and also yield a yellow dye.

Perennial Zone 5
Height To 2 ft (60 cm). Creeping rootstock.
Flowers Bright yellow, small, resemble a snapdragon but with a long spur and orange lower lip, in dense terminal spikes.
Flowering Summer.
Foliage Bluish green, small, long, narrow, numerous.
Natural habitat Banks, roadsides, and field margins. Native of Europe and naturalized in North America.
Soil Most soils, but must be well drained, including sandy and gravelly.
Site Full sun.
Propagation Divide in spring; sow seeds in spring or fall.
Uses Insecticidal; dye plant; formerly medicinal.
Family Scrophulariaceae (figwort family).
Other varieties and species
L. alpina; *L. dalmatica*; *L. purpurea*.

Linum perenne

Perennial Flax

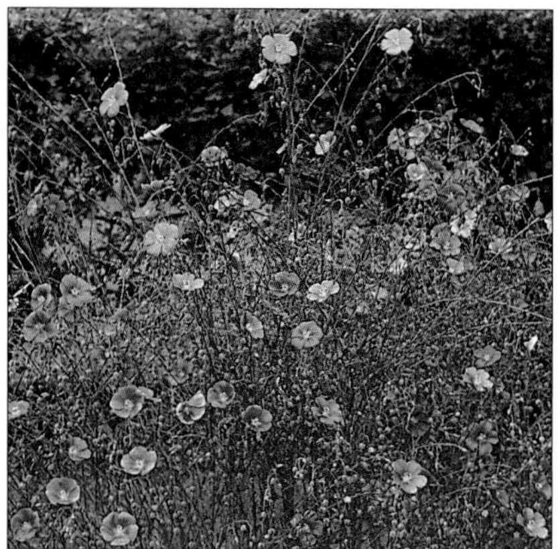

The perennial flax is a delightful, delicate-looking flower. When planted in a group with other species of various shades of blue and white and different flower sizes, it creates a beautiful, visual effect.

A lovely plant for the rock garden, perennial flax combines well with other herbs which grow in similar dry, calcareous soils. Placed near the front of the border, flax makes a graceful addition to any planting.

L. usitatissimum (the annual flax), derived from the perennial species and sharing the same properties, has been widely cultivated for thousands of years. Varieties were developed for linen cloth production and others for the valuable linseed oil, used in paints and in animal feed. Also a medicinal plant, it is used for poultices and to treat coughs and urinary infections.

Perennial Zone 3
Height 2ft (60cm).
Spread 12in (30cm).
Flowers Clear, pale blue, delicate, open funnel shape, in terminal clusters.
Flowering Early summer.
Foliage Grasslike, on slender stems.
Natural habitat Dry pastures and stony south-facing slopes. Native of Europe and western Asia. Naturalized in North America.
Soil Humus-rich, well-drained, alkaline, dryish loam.
Site Full sun.
Propagation Sow seeds in fall or spring.
Uses Medicinal; fodder; industrial; linen manufacture.
Family Linaceae (flax family).
Other varieties and species *L. perenne* 'Album'; *L. austriacum*; *L. grandiflorum* 'Rubrum'; *L. narbonense* 'Six Hills'; *L. usitatissimum*.

Lobelia cardinalis

Cardinal Flower

Cardinal flower, also known as red lobelia, is a spectacular plant with brilliant scarlet blooms. It requires rich, moist soil during the summer months, and any soil that dries out is unsuitable. In its native habitat in the eastern U.S., this plant is hardy and will withstand extremely low winter temperatures; but for full hardiness it should be grown in water. Its scarlet flowers look stunning on the margin of a pond and it is also particularly striking combined with other waterside plants.

Medicinally cardinal flower was well utilized by the Cherokee Indians to treat cramps, nosebleeds, syphilis, and rheumatism, as a nerve tonic, to expel worms, and as a love potion. The plant was considered a substitute for *L. inflata* (Indian tobacco), but the latter was the more effective medicinal.

Perennial Zone 5
Height 2–3ft (60–90cm).
Spread 12in (30cm).
Flowers Vibrant scarlet, two lipped, in one-sided racemes.
Flowering Mid- to late summer.
Foliage Fresh green or bronze-red, lance shaped, toothed.
Natural habitat Marshy riverbanks, shallow water, wet meadows. Native of North America.
Soil Deep, moist, fertile.
Site Full sun or partial shade.
Propagation Sow seeds or divide crowns in spring.
Uses Medicinal.
Family Lobeliaceae (lobelia family).
Other varieties and species *L. fulgens*; *L. inflata*; *L. siphilitica*.

Lobelia syphilitica

Great Lobelia

Great lobelia is often used as a medicinal substitute for *L. inflata* (Indian tobacco), an annual of no great decorative value. Great lobelia, on the other hand, is a handsome and colorful plant and is useful in the garden because it flowers so late – at the summer's end, when flowering plants are becoming scarce. It can be grown in any good soil that retains moisture, but in its natural habitat it is associated with water. Grow it in the bog garden or near the edge of a pond, where its roots will search out moisture throughout the summer. In a large clump it will give welcome color when other waterside flowers have stopped blooming.

As its Latin name indicates, this was a herb that the Iroquois Indians employed to treat venereal disease: they made the root into a tea. Leaf tea was also employed for colds, fevers, and stomach trouble.

Perennial Zone 3
Height 1–3ft (30–90cm).
Spread 18in (45cm).
Flowers Blue-lavender, tubular, with white-striped throat, on narrow spires.
Flowering Late summer.
Foliage Light green, crinkled, in whorls on lower half of stem.
Natural habitat Wet meadows and stream banks. Native of the northeastern U.S.
Soil Rich, moist or moisture retaining.
Site Full sun.
Propagation Sow seeds in spring, surface sow.
Uses Formerly medicinal.
Family Lobeliaceae (lobelia family).
Other varieties and species *L. siphilitica* 'Alba'; *L. cardinalis*; *L. inflata*.

Lonicera periclymenum

Wild Honeysuckle

THERE ARE MORE than 100 species and varieties of the honeysuckle, including climbers and bush types, although not all are hardy. The wild honeysuckle, or woodbine, grows in woods and hedgerows, filling the summer air with its seductive eastern perfume. In the evening and at night, the fragrance is particularly intense, so plant woodbine near the house or climbing up a wall to release its scent into open-windowed bedrooms. Many poets, from Shakespeare to Tennyson, have immortalized this sweet-scented herb. It has always been associated with love and affection.

Honeysuckle also looks attractive if it is planted in hedgerows or twining around old trees. In the more formal herb garden or vegetable garden, it may be grown on a surrounding fence or to make a fragrant arbor, often a feature of old gardens. With renewed interest in the potager, or decorative vegetable garden, traditional arbors may be due for a welcome revival. However, honeysuckle can be invasive and must be kept within bounds.

Honeysuckle grows best in a soil enriched with compost or leaf mold. The ground should be well prepared before planting. Old wood can be thinned out to maintain a good-looking plant. There are many varieties of honeysuckle suitable for the garden. *L.caprifolium* (perforate honeysuckle) flowers in the spring and early summer, before the other varieties.

Over time perhaps a dozen of the many species of honeysuckle have been used in medicine. A decoction or ointment from the flowering herb is now used mainly externally, to treat skin infections.

Perennial climber Zone 3
Height To 30ft (9.1m). Climbing.
Flowers Creamy white to yellow, tinged with red, trumpet shaped, very fragrant, in terminal whorls. Followed by bright red, poisonous fruit.
Flowering Mid- to late summer.
Foliage Gray-green, oval, untoothed, pointed, in pairs.
Natural habitat Mixed woodlands and hedgerows. Native of Europe, western Asia, and North Africa.
Soil Fertile loam to sandy soils.
Site Full sun to partial shade.
Propagation Take woody cuttings in early fall; layer in late summer; sow seeds in fall (stratify).
Uses Medicinal; bee plant; cut flowers.
Family Caprifoliaceae (honeysuckle family).
Other varieties and species
L.periclymenum 'Graham Thomas'; *L.p.*'Serotina'; *L.*x *americana*; *L.caprifolium*; *L.etrusca*; *L.fragrantissima*; *L.japonica*.

Warning

The berries are very poisonous.

Lysimachia nummularia

Creeping Jenny

CREEPING JENNY has many other old country names, the most common of which is moneywort, referring to the round, pennylike leaves, and possibly to the golden flowers that resemble cascading coins.

This is a decorative ground-cover plant for moist or wet ground that gets some shade. It thrives if grown in a woodland-edge or pond-edge site, and provides early green ground cover followed by profuse, brilliant gold flowers. A cover of leaf mold mulch, about 6in (15cm) deep, every fall will do it good. Allow this plant space to spread. In warmer climates creeping Jenny can become too rampant for the small garden.

An old medicinal herb, it was supposed to have many virtues and was used as a compress for wounds.

Perennial Zone 5
Height Very low growing (trailing).
Spread 2ft (60cm) or more.
Flowers Bright golden yellow, cuplike, growing in the leaf axils.
Flowering Summer.
Foliage Light green, smooth, rounded, set in pairs along stem.
Natural habitat Meadows, streamsides, moist hedgebanks and woods. Native of Europe and the Caucasus. Naturalized in North America.
Soil Moist, humus-rich loam.
Site Shade or partial shade.
Propagation Divide in spring.
Uses Formerly medicinal.
Family Primulaceae (primrose family).
Other varieties and species *L. nummularia* 'Aurea'; *L. ciliata*; *L. clethroïdes*; *L. punctata*; *L. quadrifolia*.

Lysimachia vulgaris

Yellow Loosestrife

YELLOW LOOSESTRIFE is a colorful and picturesque waterside plant found in wetlands. It is not related to purple loosestrife, being a member of the primrose family.

A tall, upright-growing plant, over the years yellow loosestrife will spread into a sizable clump in damp ground. Grow it with other wetland plants (see page 61). *L. vulgaris* looks its best if planted in light shade, as its golden flowers are more intense out of the strong sun.

Yellow loosestrife is no longer used in medicine. The plant was believed to possess insect-repellent qualities, especially as regards flies and gnats, and was, in folklore, supposed to hold a special attraction for horses.

Perennial Zone 5
Height To 4ft (1.2m).
Spread 2ft (60cm).
Flowers Golden yellow, five petaled, starlike, forming a mass of blossoms at the end of each main stem.
Flowering Mid- to late summer.
Foliage Marked with black dots (glands) on the upper surface, downy underneath, lance shaped, rather large, broad, sharply tapering, untoothed.
Natural habitat Roadsides, riverbanks, and marshes. Native of Europe; naturalized in North America.
Soil Fertile, moisture-retaining loam.
Site Full sun or partial shade.
Propagation Sow seeds in spring.
Uses Formerly medicinal; insect repellent.
Family Primulaceae (primrose family).
Other varieties and species *L. brachystachys*; *L. clethroïdes*; *L. nummularia*; *L. punctata*; *L. quadrifolia*.

Lythrum salicaria

Purple Loosestrife

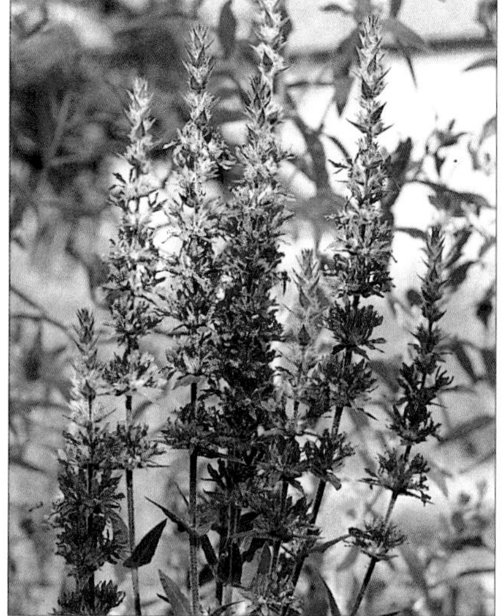

PURPLE, OR SPIKED, loosestrife is a handsome waterside plant for the pond, though in warm climates it can be invasive. In parts of North America it has taken over, and should always be introduced with caution.

The long purple flower stems look stunning beside water and produce thousands of tiny red-brown dustlike seeds. This plant should always be encouraged to form a good stand.

Purple loosestrife is still valued in herbal medicine; it has tonic, antibacterial, and hemostatic properties. The plant rapidly stops bleeding, is a good wound cleanser, and makes an effective gargle.

Perennial Zone 3
Height 2–4ft (60cm–1.2m). Spreading.
Flowers Reddish purple to pink, in whorls, forming long terminal spikes.
Flowering Mid- to late summer.
Foliage Dark green, long, slender, pointed, untoothed, willowlike.
Natural habitat Marshes, banks of rivers and streams, ditches, and wet meadows. Native of Europe, western Asia, and Russia. Naturalized in North America and Australia.
Soil Fertile, moist or wet.
Site Full sun or partial shade.
Propagation Sow seeds or divide in spring.
Uses Medicinal.
Family Lythraceae (loosestrife family).
Other varieties and species *L. salicaria* 'Firecandle'; *L. s.* 'Mordens Pink'; *L. s.* 'Robert'; *L. s.* 'Zigeunerblut'; *L. virgatum* 'Rose Queen.'

Malva moschata

Muskmallow

THE MUSKMALLOW is a little-known, exceptionally beautiful plant. In the summer its attractive, dense, bright green foliage is followed by a display of brilliant pink flowers in great profusion. The seed heads are distinctive and decorative enough for use in winter arrangements.

It looks its best in bright shade and stunning against a backdrop of trees and shrubs. The white form, 'Alba,' is particularly recommended: its flowers are delicately flushed with pink, and the plant bears even more blooms than the wild pink species.

Muskmallow enjoys most of the medicinal properties of *M.sylvestris* (common mallow), though its action is weaker. The leaves and flowers are used in fomentations and poultices.

Perennial Zones 4–5
Height To 2ft (60cm).
Spread 18in (45cm).
Flowers Bright rose-pink, one to two in leaf axils and in dense terminal clusters. Followed by distinctive seed heads.
Flowering Early to midsummer.
Foliage Basal leaves kidney shaped, upper leaves deeply cut into narrow segments, musk scented.
Natural habitat Grassy and rocky places, dry meadows, and hedgebanks. Native of Europe.
Soil Fertile or sandy loam, well drained.
Site Full sun or light shade.
Propagation Sow seeds in late summer or spring; take cuttings of basal shoots in spring or summer.
Uses Medicinal; dried seed heads.
Family Malvaceae (mallow family).
Other varieties and species
M.moschata 'Alba'; *M.cretica*; *M.mauritiana*; *M.neglecta*; *M.sylvestris*; *M.verticillata* var. *crispa*.

Marrubium vulgare

Horehound

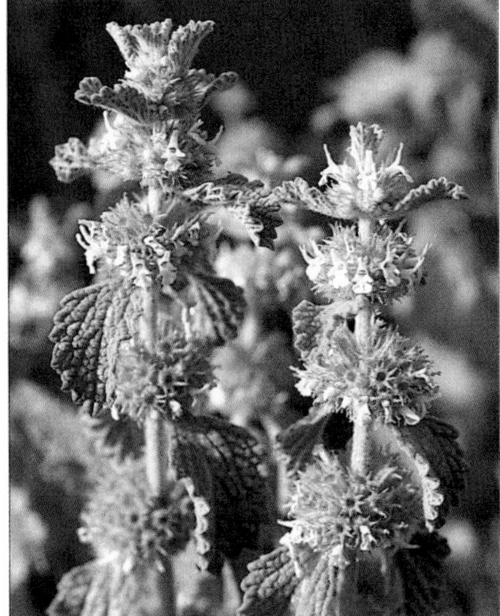

USEFUL IN THE herb garden for its distinctive texture and color, horehound's soft silvery-green foliage and "frosted" appearance have a subtle charm. It is an undemanding plant to grow and prefers the poorest conditions. Take advantage of its drought-resistant qualities.

Horehound is a useful foliage plant that blends well with a wide range of herbs and makes an attractive foil for brighter-colored flowers.

In England horehound beer was formerly very popular and candy was made from the juice of the plant. Medicinally the herb's greatest value is in the treatment of bronchitis, coughs, and sore throats and as a bitter digestive tonic.

Perennial Zone 3
Height 2–3ft (60–90cm).
Spread 18in (45cm).
Flowers White, two lipped, dense whorls.
Flowering Summer.
Foliage Greenish gray, oval, opposite, deeply veined on the upper surface, woolly underneath, aromatic.
Natural habitat Dry pastures, sandy and waste ground. Native of southern and central Europe, North Africa, and Asia. Naturalized in the U.S.
Soil Well drained, sandy, dry and poor.
Site Full sun.
Propagation Take cuttings in summer; divide roots in spring; sow seed in spring or fall (erratic), stratify.
Uses Medicinal; confectionery; beer.
Family Labiatae (mint family).
Other varieties and species
M.cylleneum; *M.supinum*.

Melissa officinalis

Lemon Balm

AN EASY AND undemanding herb to grow, lemon balm will withstand considerable heat and drought, and will even flourish at the base of a sunny wall. It is not a particularly decorative plant, but if cut down after flowering it will remain neat and green, and will also produce more leaf for cutting. However, *M.officinalis* 'Aurea' (golden lemon balm) is worth growing for its pretty gold-and-green, variegated leaves, and the variety *M.officinalis* 'All Gold' is also highly recommended. These golden balms look and do best in a little shade; otherwise the leaves tend to brown.

The Arabs regard lemon balm as a valuable medicinal plant, with particular benefit for treating anxiety and depression and as a sedative and tonic tea. The ancient Greeks grew it as an important bee plant and for its scented foliage.

Perennial Zones 4–5
Height 2ft (60cm).
Spread 18in (45cm).
Flowers White tinged yellow, tiny, two lipped, in axillary clusters.
Flowering Mid- to late summer.
Foliage Light green, heart shaped, toothed, opposite, on a slightly hairy, square stem; strongly lemon scented.
Natural habitat Dry soils, especially in mountainous regions in scrub. Native of southern Europe; naturalized in the U.S.
Soil Fairly fertile, well-drained loam.
Site Full sun or partial shade.
Propagation Divide roots or sow seeds in spring (erratic); take cuttings in spring and early summer.
Uses Medicinal; bee plant.
Family Labiatae (mint family).
Other varieties and species
M.officinalis 'All Gold'; *M.o.*'Aurea.'

Mentha

Mint

Mentha spicata 'Moroccan'
Moroccan spearmint

Mentha pulegium
Pennyroyal

Mentha suaveolens
Apple mint

M. x *piperita* var. *crispa*
Crisp black peppermint

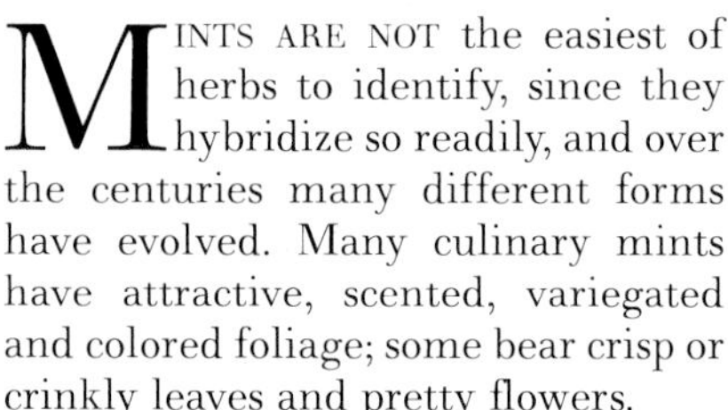

MINTS ARE NOT the easiest of herbs to identify, since they hybridize so readily, and over the centuries many different forms have evolved. Many culinary mints have attractive, scented, variegated and colored foliage; some bear crisp or crinkly leaves and pretty flowers.

Mints worth growing are: *M. spicata* 'Moroccan,' the best for mint sauce and mint drinks; *M.* x *piperita piperita* (peppermint), is also available with decorative crisped leaves; *M.* x *piperita* var. *citrata* (bergamot or eau de Cologne mint), with red-tinged, scented foliage; *M. suaveolens* (apple mint), and also its white-variegated form, *M. suaveolens* 'Variegata,' often known as pineapple mint; and the vigorous, woolly leaved *M.* x *villosa alopecuroides* 'Bowles' (Bowles mint), which gives a superb flavor to mint sauce and new potatoes.

Mints require a rich, well-drained loam that will retain moisture in summer. If they are put under stress with too few nutrients or, more important, too little moisture, they become unhealthy and susceptible to rust and – in the case of woolly leaved mints – to mildew (see page 41). To stop mints from spreading beyond their patch, either grow them in a bottomless old can or pail sunk into the ground, or use some other physical barrier sunk about 12 in (30 cm) into the soil around the plant.

Two superb ground-cover plants are *M. requienii* (Corsican mint) with minute bright green leaves and tiny mauve flowers; and *M. pulegium* (pennyroyal), which is much more vigorous (the prostrate form gives the best ground cover). Both plants do best in a moisture-retentive sandy soil. Do not try to grow mint from seed since, except for *M. aquatica*, all culinary mints are hybrids and do not come true from seed.

Mints, especially peppermint and spearmint, are valuable medicinals and make a delightful and soothing tea. Eau de Cologne or bergamot mint is used in perfumes and soaps. In the home, mints have many applications: for instance, both peppermint and spearmint make refreshing additives to the bath.

Perennial Zone 5
Height To 2 ft (60 cm). Spreading.
Flowers Pale lilac to white, dense, in close whorls on narrow, cylindrical, terminal spikes.
Flowering Late summer.
Foliage Strong green, spear shaped, smooth to crinkled with serrated margin, very aromatic, growing opposite, on square branched stems.
Natural habitat Damp, shady sites near habitations. Native of southern Europe and naturalized in North America.
Soil Fertile, well-drained, moist or moisture-retaining loam.
Site Full sun or partial shade.
Propagation Divide runners in fall; root cuttings in water or compost in spring and early summer.
Uses Culinary; medicinal; cosmetic.
Family Labiatae (mint family).
Other varieties and species
M. aquatica; *M.* x *gentilis* 'Variegata'; *M.* x *piperita*; *M.* x *p.* var. *citrata*; *M.* x *p.* var. *officinalis*; *M.* x *p.* var. *piperita*; *M. pulegium*; *M. requienii*; *M.* x *smithiana* 'Rubra'; *M. spicata* 'Moroccan'; *M. suaveolens*; *M. s.* 'Variegata'; *M.* x *villosa* var. *alopecuroides* 'Bowles.'

Menyanthes trifoliata

Bogbean

BOGBEAN, also known as buckbean, marsh trefoil, or water shamrock, is an attractive plant that will grace any medium-size to large pond. It grows in shallow water and spreads by means of its thick, black, horizontal roots. In spring the delicate fringed, white flowers and large trefoil leaves are a splendid sight. This is primarily a transitional plant from land to water, particularly useful for hiding or just covering the pond edge with its scrambling habit. Plant it at a depth of 2–4 in (5–10 cm).

In ancient Greece it was the flower of the month, used to treat menstrual pain. It was also considered something of a panacea for all ills, but is now employed as a tonic to relieve indigestion. It is mildly sedative and helps to ease rheumatic pain.

Perennial water plant Zone 3
Height To 9 in (23 cm). Spreading.
Flowers White and pink in bud, with distinctive, shaggy petals.
Flowering Late spring.
Foliage Medium green, large, cloverlike with pale prominent midribs forming a sheath at the base.
Natural habitat Freshwater marshes, bogs, and ponds. Native of northern temperate regions from North America to Siberia.
Soil Pond soil, preferably peaty and slightly acid.
Site Full sun.
Propagation Divide rhizomes in fall or spring.
Uses Medicinal; tobacco substitute.
Family Menyanthaceae (bogbean family).
Other varieties and species None.

Meum athamanticum

Spignel

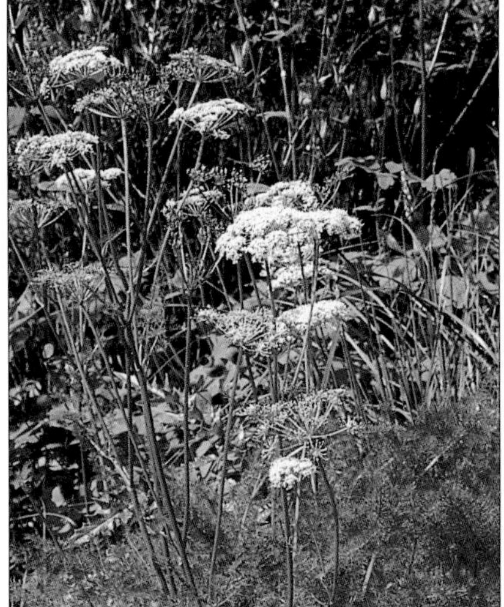

SPIGNEL WAS sometimes known by country folk as bald or baldmonay. It is rare in the wild, where it is confined to mountainous areas of northern Europe. It is a pretty plant, which in leaf resembles a small fennel; indeed, it belongs to the same family. The flowers are attractive and dainty. Grow it with other herbs that prefer lime-free soil and some shade.

Spignel is a popular culinary herb in Scandinavian countries. In Norway, where the plant is known as bjørnerot or bear root, it is dedicated to the Norse god Balder. Add the leaves and seeds to egg dishes, salads, cheese, soups, and stews. The herb's flavor is difficult to describe, but has a hint of curry. The thick white roots were once eaten as a vegetable in Scotland.

Perennial Zone 3
Height 12–18 in (30–45 cm).
Spread 9 in (23 cm).
Flowers Pinkish white, tiny, in compound umbels. Followed by aromatic fruits.
Flowering Early summer.
Foliage Strong green, fennellike, with needlelike leaflets, strongly scented.
Natural habitat Mountainous pastures. Native of northern Europe.
Soil Sandy to sandy loam, lime-free.
Site Full sun or light shade.
Propagation Sow seeds in late summer or spring.
Uses Culinary.
Family Umbelliferae (carrot family).
Other varieties and species None.

Monarda didyma

Bee Balm

BEE BALM, also known as Oswego tea or red bergamot, is a colorful North American herb whose deep scarlet, ragged flowers bloom over a long period in late summer.

Grow bee balm in a fertile, moist soil, preferably out of the hottest sun, with a backdrop of trees or shrubs. None of the numerous, colorful garden varieties has the strong scent of the wild species. In hard winters without snow cover, give bee balm a thick mulch, about 6 in (15 cm) deep, to protect it from severe frosts.

A tea made from bee balm was drunk by the Oswego Indians, as well as the colonists. The plant is invaluable in potpourri, both for its strong citrus scent and the deep red flower color, and the dried blooms are attractive in arrangements. Bee balm flowers are loved by bees, humming birds, and butterflies.

Perennial Zones 4–9
Height 18 in–3 ft (45–90 cm).
Spread 18 in–3 ft (45–90 cm).
Flowers Scarlet red, ragged, tubular, in solitary, terminal whorls.
Flowering Late summer.
Foliage Dark green tinged red, ovate, with toothed margins, opposite, very aromatic.
Natural habitat Moist open woodlands, thickets, and stream banks. Native of North America.
Soil Fertile, moist to moisture retaining.
Site Partial shade or full sun.
Propagation Divide in fall or spring.
Uses Tea; potpourri; dried flowers; bee and butterfly plant.
Family Labiatae (mint family).
Other varieties and species *M. didyma* 'Alba'; *M.* 'Blue Stocking'; *M.* 'Cambridge Scarlet'; *M.* 'Croftway Pink.'

Monarda

Bergamot

Monarda fistulosa
Wild bergamot

Monarda citriodora
Lemon bergamot

Monarda citriodora
Lemon bergamot

WILD BERGAMOT, also known as purple bee balm, is in some respects similar to bee balm but has mauve flowers and thrives in quite different conditions. It enjoys dryish soils but is a woodland-edge plant, so give it some shade from the hottest midday sun and grow it in a situation where trees, shrubs, or a hedge form a background feature. For a striking effect plant wild bergamot in a good size clump. Grow it with other drought-tolerant herbs that enjoy light shade like *Galium verum* (lady's bedstraw), *Origanum vulgare* (wild marjoram), and the popular *Digitalis grandiflora* (yellow foxglove).

Monardas can easily be propagated by 3–4 in (6–10 cm) tip cuttings taken from late spring to late summer. The roots of mature plants can also be divided into smaller sections to make new plants. Monardas benefit from division every 2 or 3 years.

The wild bergamot crossed with red bergamot has produced many different colored garden hybrids. It is not surprising, therefore, that these hybrid plants often prefer growing in conditions that are different from those required by either of their parents. A compromise is usually the best answer. Provide them with good drainage but a moisture-retaining loam and, ideally, some shade.

Medicinally, wild bergamot has similar properties to bee balm. A refreshing tea can be made from the leaves and this was also once used by North American Indians and colonial settlers to treat colds and sore throats.

M. citriodora (lemon bergamot) is a beautiful annual plant that bears stunning pink-purple flowers in tiers up the stems, ending in a pin-cushion crown. The bracts are mauve and green, and the leaves are scented with a spicy lemon fragrance. This is well worth growing in the herb garden. The leaves provide a delicious lemon-flavored tea.

Perennial Zones 4–9
Height 2–3 ft (60–90 cm).
Spread 18 in (45 cm).
Flowers Lavender, narrow-lipped tubes in crowded terminal heads.
Flowering Late summer.
Foliage Triangular to oval, toothed, in pairs on stalks, aromatic.
Natural habitat Dry thickets, woodland edges, and roadsides. Native of North America.
Soil Well-drained, dryish loam or sandy soil.
Site Partial shade or full sun.
Propagation Sow seeds in spring; take cuttings from late spring to late summer; divide in fall or spring.
Uses Formerly medicinal; tea.
Family Labiatae (mint family).
Other varieties and species
M. didyma; *M. bradburyana*; *M. citriodora*; *M. menthifolia*; *M. punctata*; *M. stipitatoglandulosa*.

Myrrhis odorata

Sweet Cicely

SWEET CICELY, with its soft green, fernlike leaves and white flower heads, is a lovely herb for the wild or woodland-edge garden. It has an aniseed scent. The masses of large shiny seeds become a rich brown color as they ripen. After seeding it can be cut down and within a few weeks will grow fresh foliage.

All parts of the plant are edible. The leaves can be added to salads and take the tartness from cooked fruit. The white, fibrous roots may be eaten raw or boiled. The ripe seeds were also traditionally ground to give a perfume to furniture polish.

Sweet cicely was once valued for medicinal purposes, the leaves as a sugar substitute for diabetics, for the treatment of coughs and flatulence, and as a gentle stimulant. The roots are antiseptic.

Perennial Zone 3
Height 2–3 ft (60–90 cm).
Spread 2 ft (60 cm).
Flowers White, in flat compound umbels, each composed of up to 10 smaller umbels.
Flowering Late spring to early summer.
Foliage Soft green, fernlike, downy, aromatic, leaf stalks wrapped around stem.
Natural habitat Roadsides and mountain pastures. Native of Europe and northern Britain.
Soil Rich, moist to moisture-retaining loam.
Site Full sun or partial shade.
Propagation Sow seeds in fall (stratify); divide in spring.
Uses Culinary; medicinal; bee and dye plant.
Family Umbelliferae (carrot family).
Other varieties and species None.

Nepeta mussinii

Catmint

THERE ARE MANY catmints suitable for the herb garden. They make lovely soft edging plants, with masses of summer blooms. Catmint will flower again in the fall if cut back after the first long flowering.

This plant looks best when it is tumbling over the edge of a path or low wall, and is suitable for planting in an open border or a rock garden. The soft gray-green foliage is a wonderful foil for brighter flowers.

N. cataria (catnip) is the traditional herbal catmint. It grows tall and bears white flowers dotted with purple and strongly scented, nettlelike leaves. Cats love this herb.

Catmint was traditionally a medicinal plant and is also used for tea.

Perennial Zones 3–4
Height 1–2 ft (30–60 cm).
Spread 18 in (45 cm).
Flowers Lavender-blue, in spikes.
Flowering Midsummer to early fall.
Foliage Gray-green, small, oval, wrinkled, toothed, downy underneath, aromatic.
Natural habitat Rocky or disturbed dry ground. Native of the Caucasus and Caspian Sea area of Europe. Naturalized in the U.S.
Soil Sandy or well-drained loam, moist to dry.
Site Full sun or light shade.
Propagation Sow seeds or divide in spring; take cuttings in early summer.
Uses Bee plant; formerly medicinal.
Family Labiatae (mint family).
Other varieties and species *N.* x *faasenii* 'Six Hills Giant'; *N. grandiflora* 'Blue Beauty'; *N. nervosa*.

Nigella sativa

Fennel Flower

FENNEL FLOWER, or nutmeg flower, is a decorative annual herb closely related to *N. damascena* (love-in-a-mist), but bears paler blue to nearly white flowers. The blooms have a fascinating construction: the globular, horned seed pods are carried above the flowers. The herb is in no way related to fennel.

Fennel flower looks best when grown in a patch or drift, possibly in a rock garden or in an open border. In early spring the seedlings make a brilliant, light green carpet. It self-seeds profusely.

The Romans used the black seeds in cooking. The aromatic nutmeg-scented seeds are valued today as a seasoning in curries and many other dishes, for spreading on bread or cakes, and as a substitute for pepper. The seeds also have some medicinal properties and were employed to treat indigestion. The dried seed heads are highly decorative.

Hardy annual Zone 3
Height 18 in (45 cm).
Spread 6 in (15 cm).
Flowers Pale blue, five petaled, followed by decorative, globular seed vessels, aromatic seeds.
Flowering Midsummer.
Foliage Gray-green, long, threadlike.
Natural habitat Stony areas. Native of Syria.
Soil Medium to light, well drained.
Site Full sun.
Propagation Sow seeds in fall or spring.
Uses Culinary; medicinal; dried seed heads.
Family Ranunculaceae (buttercup family).
Other varieties and species *N. damascena*.

Nymphaea alba

White Water Lily

THE WHITE water lily is a truly magnificent plant. Its handsome flowers emit a sweet fruity perfume. The plant is beneficial to wildlife, affording shade and sanctuary for fish, and other water creatures.

Many cultivars and hybrids in a diverse range of colors and shades are readily obtainable from water-plant specialists and some are ideal for growing in small ponds or tubs. The vigorous white water lily is suitable only for large ponds and lakes. It needs a depth of 15–36 in (38–90 cm).

Water lily leaves were once used as a vegetable. The leaves and rhizomes yield a brown dye, and the rhizomes also produce a soap substitute and are valued for treating sore throats and ulcers. The leaves and flowers are said to be an anaphrodisiac.

Perennial water plant Zone 3
Height 6 in (15 cm). Spreading.
Flowers White, cup shaped, open wide in sunlight, 20 or more petals and numerous golden stamens, fragrant.
Flowering Summer.
Foliage Reddish when young and then dark green, shiny, heart shaped, very large, floating.
Natural habitat Ponds, lakes, and rivers. Native of Europe and North America.
Soil Humus rich, silty.
Site Full sun.
Propagation Separate plantlets or divide rhizomes in spring or early summer; sow seeds in fall or spring.
Uses Medicinal; culinary; dye plant.
Family Nymphaceaceae (water lily family).
Other varieties and species *N. alba* var. *rubra*; *N. odorata*; *N. o.* var. *minor*; *N. o.* var. *rosea*; *N. pygmaea* 'Alba'; *N. p.* 'Rubra.'

Ocimum

Basil

Ocimum basilicum 'Genovese'

Ocimum basilicum 'Bush'

Ocimum basilicum 'Rubin'

Ocimum basilicum 'Cinnamon'

THE SWEET BASIL was brought to Europe from India in the 16th century and has become one of the most popular culinary herbs. The best basil for cooking is the sweet *O. basilicum* 'Genovese'; other popular varieties are Greek or miniature bush, 'Dark Opal,' 'Purple Ruffles,' and 'Green Ruffles.' More exotic types include those with lemon, cinnamon, and anise scents, and holy basil.

Many other species, some of which are medicinal only, originate from across the world. There is much confusion in catalogs with botanical and common names, and until this is resolved, common names have mostly been used here.

All varieties and species of basil are decorative, particularly those with purple or ruffled foliage, and they provide an attractive range of leaf and flower. Their distinctive scents are an added bonus. Many can be used as decorative edgings, especially the miniature Greek bush basil.

Grow basil in small troughs or pots indoors, on the windowsill, or outside during the summer either in the soil or in containers. It is happiest in clay pots (rather than plastic) and should be watered around midday, to enable it to dry out before the cool of the evening. Containers look especially ornamental if planted with a variety of basil plants.

Keep the larger sweet basil bushy by frequent cutting. Allow some types to flower, especially the colored-leaf basils, as they look pretty in bloom.

Sweet basil has a strongly aromatic, clovelike scent and is used extensively in the kitchen to season tomatoes, salads, vegetables, poultry, and fish, and to make Italian pesto sauce. The leaves are best fresh, but may be dried or, better still, preserved in olive oil or as a frozen paste. They have medicinal properties, especially with regard to digestion. Basil is valuable as an insect repellent, and as a companion plant with tomatoes.

Tender annual
Height 18–24in (45–60cm).
Spread 12in (30cm).
Flowers White, pink, or lavender, in whorls in the leaf axils.
Flowering Mid- to late summer.
Foliage Leaves of various colors, textures, and scent.
Natural habitat Native of southern Asia, Iran, and the Middle East.
Soil Rich, well drained, moisture retaining.
Site Hot, sunny, sheltered from wind.
Propagation Sow seeds in late spring.
Uses Culinary; medicinal; insect repellent.
Family Labiatae (mint family).
Other varieties and species
O. basilicum 'Anise'; *O. b. citriodorum*; *O. b.* 'Dark Opal'; *O. b.* 'Genovese'; *O. b.* 'Green Ruffles'; *O. b.* 'Mammoth'; *O. b.* 'Napoletano'; *O. b.* 'Purple Ruffles'; *O. b.* 'Rubin'; *O. b. minimum* 'Finissimo verde a palla'; *O. b. m.* 'Greek'; *O. b.* var. *m.* 'Green Bouquet'; *O. b. m.* 'Spicy Globe'; *O. sanctum*.

Oenothera biennis

Evening Primrose

EVENING PRIMROSE is something of a misnomer as, although many species open their flowers at dusk, they are often open for much of the day, especially in cloudy weather. Their wonderful, intense fragrance is most noticeable at night. The tall *O. biennis* is most suited to any dry situation or stony ground, where a selection of evening primroses can be grown.

Evening primrose has recently become an important medicinal herb used in capsules to treat premenstrual syndrome, multiple sclerosis, and other conditions. The thick root of the plant has been used as a vegetable.

Biennial Zone 3
Height To 4 ft (1.2 m).
Spread 18 in (45 cm).
Flowers Yellow, four petaled, fragrant, on spikes, long, distinctive seed capsules.
Flowering Midsummer to fall.
Foliage Flat rosette in first year, then alternate, lance shaped to oval, up tall, rough, reddish stems.
Natural habitat Dry, stony or sandy soil on roadsides and waste ground. Native of North America.
Soil Well drained.
Site Full sun.
Propagation Sow seeds in late summer; self-seeds.
Uses Medicinal; culinary.
Family Onagraceae (evening primrose family).
Other varieties and species
O. fruticosa 'Yellow River'; *O. missouriensis*; *O. speciosa*; *O. stricta* syn. *O. odorata*.

Ononis spinosa

Spiny Restharrow

RESTHARROW WAS so called because the roots are so thick and well anchored that even the harrow struggled with it. Spiny restharrow is the only variety with thorns, and a hedge of this herb could keep out rabbits. It might be worth a try, since this is an attractive plant that bears rich pink, pealike flowers.

Spiny restharrow is a meadow plant and will readily naturalize with other wild flowers and grasses in a flowering meadow area, preferably with a heavy, moisture-retaining soil. Without the competition of grasses, it will grow larger and lusher. However, in a warm climate it could become invasive if introduced into certain wild situations.

Medicinally an infusion of spiny restharrow was used as a diuretic to treat kidney and bladder disorders, gout, and rheumatism. At one time the young shoots were eaten cooked or raw as a green vegetable. Use the flowers to decorate salads.

Perennial Zone 3
Height 18 in (45 cm).
Spread 12 in (30 cm).
Flowers Pink, pealike, in loose leafy inflorescences.
Flowering Summer.
Foliage Dark green, narrow, pointed, trifoliate, on hairy stems with long spines.
Natural habitat Grassland, often heavy and calcareous. Native of Europe.
Soil Heavy, moisture retaining.
Site Full sun.
Propagation Sow seeds in spring (scarify).
Uses Medicinal; culinary.
Family Leguminosae (pea family).
Other varieties and species
O. fruticosa; *O. natrix*; *O. repens*.

Onopordum acanthium

Cotton Thistle

THIS MAGNIFICENT plant has been the national emblem of Scotland since the early 16th century – hence its alternative name, Scotch thistle.

The plant is biennial. In the first year it produces a large, impressive rosette of leaves a few inches above the ground. In the second year it reaches its stately proportions.

This herb requires plenty of space in the garden to self-seed freely, and one specimen alone will provide an architectural and focal point in an area of waste ground or gravel.

The seeds contain an oil that was used in lamps and for cooking. The heads and young stalks, stripped of their rind, can be eaten. A decoction of the flower heads was used to treat baldness and ulcers.

Biennial Zone 7
Height To 8 ft (2.4 m).
Spread 4 ft (1.2 m).
Flowers Light purple, solitary, surrounded by a flattened globe with narrow, green bracts tipped with yellowish spines.
Flowering Late summer.
Foliage Large, waved, with sharp spines on edge; stout, much-branched stems with spiny, winglike appendages, whole covered with thick, white down.
Natural habitat Waste ground, dry banks, and roadsides. Native of Europe and Asia.
Soil Most soils, prefers poor, sandy loam.
Site Full sun.
Propagation Sow seeds in spring and early summer.
Uses Formerly medicinal; culinary; household.
Family Compositae (daisy family).
Other varieties and species
O. arabicum; *O. argolicum*; *O. bracteatum*; *O. nervosum*; *O. salteri*; *O. tauricum*.

Origanum

Oregano

BOTH OREGANO AND MARJORAM are among the most popular of seasoning herbs, but in spite of this there is much confusion over their correct naming. They are botanically the same, but oregano is the name (with variations) usually used to describe the herb employed for cooking. *O. majorana* (sweet marjoram) is a half-hardy perennial and is quite distinct in appearance and flavor from the hardy marjoram/oregano.

Origanum growing on the chalk downs of England tastes different from the botanically similar herb growing in the hot Mediterranean climate. *O. vulgare* (wild marjoram or oregano), it should be emphasized, has many variations in habit, leaf and flower colors, and flavor. These variations might be described as subspecies of oregano.

The flowers of oregano are colorful and abundant. They are a magnet for many bees and butterflies and also of decorative value in the garden. The plant enjoys the hottest situation in a calcareous, well-drained but nutrient-rich soil, although it will grow well in semishade. The pretty variegated and golden varieties, however, look and grow best out of the hottest sun, which browns the leaves. They also benefit from more moisture in the soil. Cut back the stems of oregano after flowering to leave an attractive leafy mound until the herb grows up again in the following spring.

The herbs mainly used for culinary purposes are: *O. onites* (often called pot marjoram), although it is not easy to obtain; *O. hirtum* (Greek marjoram or oregano), which has a fiery hot taste; *O. majorana* (sweet marjoram); and *O. vulgare* (wild marjoram or oregano).

Sweet marjoram, is referred to as marjoram (not oregano) in cooking. Its scent is sweet and floral rather than spicy and sharp like that of oregano. This is not a native of the Mediterranean, although often found there, but comes from North Africa and southwestern Asia and is not hardy. Sweet marjoram grows well outside during the summer months but will not survive the frost. It is an ideal herb to grow in a container, where it can be stood outside near the kitchen in warm weather and brought inside for protection during winter and spring.

Origanum vulgare
Oregano or wild marjoram

O. hirtum
Greek marjoram

O. vulgare 'Aureum Crispum'

O. vulgare 'Gold Variegated'

O. majorana
Sweet marjoram

Perennial Zone 5
Height To 2 ft (60 cm).
Spread 12 in (30 cm).
Flowers Rose-purple or pink to white, with purple bracts, two lipped, forming dense, terminal clusters, aromatic.
Flowering Summer.
Foliage Dark green, sometimes reddish, broadly ovate, normally untoothed and opposite, aromatic.
Natural habitat Dry hills, hedgebanks, and bushy places. Native of Europe and the Middle East.
Soil Nutrient rich, well drained to dry, calcareous.
Site Full sun or light shade.
Propagation Sow seeds in spring; take cuttings in early summer; self-seeds.
Uses Culinary; medicinal; cosmetic; bee plant.
Family Labiatae (mint family).
Other varieties and species *O. vulgare* 'Aureum'; *O. v.* 'Gold Tip'; *O. amanum*; *O. calcaratum*; *O. compactum*; *O. dictamnus* (Dittany of Crete); *O. hirtum* syn. *O. heracleoticum*; *O. x hybridinum* 'Kent Beauty'; *O. laevigatum* 'Hopleys'; *O. majorana*; *O. microphyllum*; *O. onites*; *O. pulchellum*; *O. rotundifolium*; *O. scabrum*.

Paeonia officinalis

Peony

THE PEONY is a robust shrub that was developed for its beautiful blooms. Most of the forms of peony now available bear spectacular double flowers in many colorful shades.

Essentially a plant of the woodland edge, the peony looks its best associated with trees and shrubs. Grow it as a specimen plant and give it space and a rich, woodland soil, with plenty of leaf mold. The peony will withstand periods of drought in summer, drawing on reserves in its thick rootstock.

P. officinalis, sometimes called the apothecaries' peony, is an early cultivated plant, named by the ancient Greeks after Paen, the physician to the gods. The herb is still valued medicinally by the Chinese.

Perennial shrub Zone 5
Height 2–3 ft (60–90 cm).
Spread 2 ft (60 cm).
Flowers Crimson, pink, or white, single, large, with eight petals, five sepals.
Flowering Summer.
Foliage Dark green, large, with several unequal lobes cut into segments.
Natural habitat Among trees and shrubs in woodland conditions. Native of southern and western Europe.
Soil Humus rich, moisture retaining but well drained.
Site Partial shade or full sun (avoid early-morning sun).
Propagation Sow seeds in fall; divide roots with a bud in early fall.
Uses Medicinal.
Family Paeoniaceae (peony family).
Other varieties and species
P. officinalis 'Alba Plena'; *P. o.* 'China Rose'; *P. lactiflora*; *P. mollis*.

Warning

The flowers are poisonous.

Papaver

Poppy

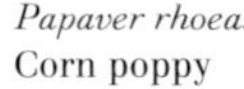

Papaver rhoeas
Corn poppy

P. somniferum
Opium poppy

P. orientale
'Cedric Morris'

OF ALL THE many members of the poppy family, the genus *Papaver* is the largest. The red corn poppy, or Flanders poppy (*Papaver rhoeas*) is immortalized as the Poppy of Remembrance, and is the most common and best loved.

The seeds of the corn poppy can remain viable in the soil for many decades, but the earth must be disturbed or cultivated for the plant to appear. It will not grow well among established thick vegetation. Seed a patch of waste ground for a quick and colorful display, perhaps with other bright cornfield flowers like *Anthemis arvensis* (chamomile) and *Centaurea cyanus* (cornflower).

The seeds of the corn poppy may be sprinkled on breads and cakes, and their oil can be used in cooking. The petals yield a red dye which is used in medicine, and they have been used to color wine. Medicinally the flowers are beneficial for treating irritable coughs, colic, and bronchitis.

P. somniferum (opium poppy) is a larger plant. The flowers are big and handsome, in a range of colors with a large dark blotch at the base. Many varieties have been developed with double, peonylike or fringed carnationlike flowers in various shades. The decorative opium poppy self-seeds readily. In some areas it is illegal to grow this plant.

This is an invaluable medicinal plant, once used by the ancient Egyptians and Greeks, and today utilized in the manufacture of pain-killers such as codeine and morphine. The dried seed capsules can be used to make stunning winter decorations.

Annual
Height 10–36 in (25–90 cm).
Spread 9 in (23 cm).
Flowers Scarlet, bowl shaped, with four large, overlapping petals, each usually with a black blotch at the base, and bearing stamens with purple filaments, growing on thin, wiry, hairy stems. Followed by ovoid seed capsules.
Flowering Summer.
Foliage Mainly at base of stem, deeply divided into segments and toothed; basal leaves are stalked.
Natural habitat Cultivated, disturbed, and bare soil. Native of Europe, North Africa, and western and central Asia.
Soil Most soils, including chalk.
Site Full sun.
Propagation Sow seeds in late summer, fall or early spring; self-seeds.
Uses Medicinal; culinary; dye plant; dried seed heads.
Family Papaveraceae (poppy family).
Other varieties and species *P. rhoeas* 'Mother of Pearl'; *P.* Shirley Series; *P. orientale* 'Beauty of Livermere'; *P. o.* 'Cedric Morris'; *P. o.* 'Perry's White'; *P. somniferum*: *P. s.* 'Giganteum'; *P. s.* 'Hen and Chickens'; *P. s.* 'White Cloud.'

Passiflora incarnata

Passionflower

PASSIONFLOWER, or maypop, must be among the most exotic of flowers. It makes a superb dense cover for sheds or fences, and can also be trained through a large tree. When mature the plant produces many flowers, followed by edible fruits.

In a small garden or patio, growth will be restricted. The plant can be grown successfully in a container. *P. incarnata* will not stand temperatures below freezing; the species *P. caerulea* is a hardier plant and more suitable for northern climates.

Far from arousing "passion," as its name suggests, *P. incarnata* is in fact a sedative and tranquilizer with a mild narcotic effect. It is still much used in European herbal medicine.

Perennial vine Zone 7
Height 25–30 ft (7.6–9.1 m). Climbing.
Flowers White with a pink or purple calyx and a very distinctive, brilliant pink-purple corona, with threadlike filaments radiating from the center, scented; followed by yellow-orange, egg-shaped fruit called granadilles.
Flowering Summer to late summer.
Foliage Three to five lobed, finely toothed, alternate, stalked with tendrils from the leaf axils.
Natural habitat Thickets, hedgerows, and woodland edges on dry, sandy soils. Native of the southern U.S.
Soil Fertile and well drained.
Site Partial shade.
Propagation Sow seeds in spring, presoak; keep moist (erratic).
Uses Medicinal; culinary.
Family Passifloraceae (passionflower family).
Other varieties and species *P. caerulea*; *P. lutea*; *P. quadrangularis*.

Pelargonium

Scented Pelargonium

THERE ARE MANY varied species of pelargonium with foliage scented of rose, lemon, nutmeg, apple, peppermint, and coconut, to name a few, all with attractive, sometimes variegated, leaves and delicate flowers.

In frost-free climates, pelargoniums can be grown outside in the garden in well-drained, sandy loam. They also make beautiful container plants, and grow well in the house.

The scented leaves can be used to flavor sweets, cakes, and other dishes. The flowers are decorative in salads, and both flowers and leaves make an important addition to potpourri.

Half-hardy perennial evergreen
Zones 8–10
Height To 4 ft (1.2 m).
Spread To 3 ft (90 cm).
Flowers Cyclamen-purple (sometimes lighter pink or darker) with purple stripes on the two upper petals, 8 to 20 small flowers in dense, terminal heads.
Flowering Summer.
Foliage Three to six lobed, with toothed margin, crinkled, covered with soft hairs, fragrant.
Natural habitat Sand dunes and low, stony hillsides near the sea, disturbed areas. Native of coastal South Africa and widely naturalized.
Soil Light, well-drained to sandy loam.
Site Full sun.
Propagation Take cuttings of non-flowering shoots in summer; sow seeds in spring.
Uses Culinary; perfume; potpourri.
Family Geraniaceae (geranium family).
Other varieties and species *P.* 'Attar of Roses'; *P. citrosum* 'Prince of Orange'; *P. clorinda*; *P. crispum* var. *minor*; *P.* x *fragrans*; *P. graveolens*; *P. grossularioïdes*; *P. quercifolium*; *P. tomentosum*.

Perilla frutescens

Perilla

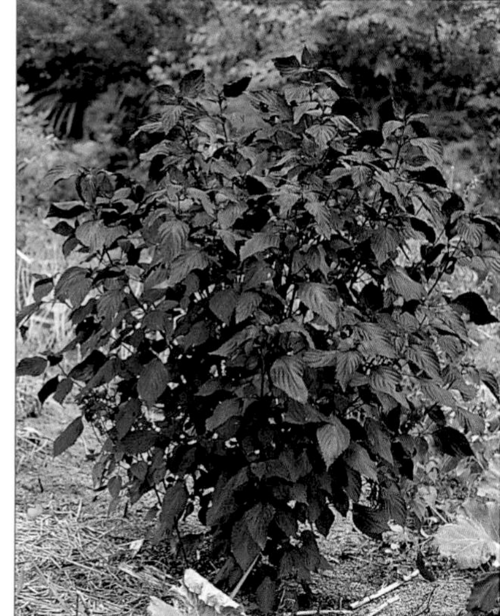

THIS COLORFUL annual is valued in bedding schemes for its beautiful purple-bronze foliage. Perilla adds a splash of rich color to any planting and is beautifully set off by some of the soft green and silver herbs. It can be used as a colorful edging in the formal garden and is invaluable in the potager. Plant it in bold groups to give dramatic color and accent.

Used extensively in Japan, where it is known as shiso: the cinnamon-scented leaves provide a flavoring; the green variety is popular for sushi and tempura; the purple form is favored for pickling, as it imparts its color to the liquid. Use also in salads, soups, and with vegetables. The leaves have an added hint of curry.

Annual
Height 1–2 ft (30–60 cm).
Spread 9 in (23 cm).
Flowers White to lavender, small, tubular, in terminal spikes.
Flowering Late summer to fall.
Foliage Green or reddish purple, oval, long toothed, nettlelike, aromatic.
Natural habitat Moist, open woods. Native of China and Japan.
Soil Rich, moisture-retaining loam.
Site Partial shade.
Propagation Sow seeds in spring at 70°–80°F (21°–27°C), leave seed uncovered; (prechill seed in moist sand at 40°F (5°C) for three days).
Uses Culinary.
Family Labiatae (mint family).
Other varieties and species *P. frutescens* 'Crispa'; *P. f.* var. *nankinensis*; *P. f.* 'Shiso green'; *P. f.* 'Shiso red.'

Petroselinum

Parsley

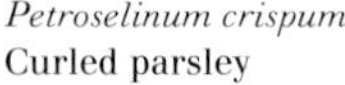

Petroselinum crispum
Curled parsley

Petroselinum crispum
Plain-leaved parsley

Petroselinum crispum
Plain-leaved parsley

PARSLEY IS OUR best-known and most used seasoning herb. The flavor is reminiscent of its close relative, celery, as is the foliage of plain-leaved varieties.

Plain-leaved, or French, parsley is strongly aromatic and hardier than the curled types. *P.c.* var. *tuberosum* (turnip-rooted or Hamburg parsley), the same in leaf as the plain-leaved types, is a good substitute but with the added advantage of a thick root that can be eaten raw or cooked. The root has a sweet parsley-celery flavor; this is the hardiest parsley.

The most popular parsleys are the curled or moss curled varieties. In the last century many were available, including a fern-leaved variety. Today there are fewer from which to choose. They should be protected from snow and hard frost.

As well as being an indispensable garnishing and flavoring herb, parsley is also highly decorative in its curled form. Traditionally, it has been used as an attractive edging to the herb garden or small bed, and planted in a thick clump is eye-catching along a border. It makes a decorative container plant, suitable for growing on the patio or windowsill.

Parsley is notoriously difficult to germinate. It does best if sown direct in the soil or in plugs, as it dislikes root disturbance. Because it requires a high temperature (60°F/15°C or higher) to germinate, sowing is not recommended before early summer for late-summer, fall, and winter harvesting, or late summer for early-spring harvesting.

Medicinally parsley is valuable in the treatment of urinary disorders, as a diuretic. It is a rich source of iron and vitamin C, and makes an effective breath freshener.

Biennial Zone 6
Height 1–2 ft (30–60 cm).
Spread 12 in (30 cm).
Flowers Greenish yellow, very small, in compound umbels. Followed by long, ribbed, ovoid seeds.
Flowering Summer to fall.
Foliage Rich green, aromatic, much divided into featherlike leaflets, crisp and curled or flat and celerylike.
Natural habitat Native of Sardinia and the eastern Mediterranean; widely naturalized.
Soil Fertile, moisture-retaining loam.
Site Full sun or partial shade.
Propagation Sow seeds in early and late summer; self-seeds.
Uses Culinary; medicinal; breath freshener.
Family Umbelliferae (carrot family).
Other varieties and species *P. crispum* 'Champion Moss Curled'; *P.c.* 'Bravour'; *P.c.* 'Darki'; *P.c.* var. *neopolitanum* 'French'; *P.c.* var. *neopolitanum* 'Italian Giant'; *P.c.* var. *tuberosum*.

Phacelia tanacetifolia

Phacelia

PHACELIA HAS RECENTLY come to the notice of gardeners as a good green manure crop. It is also a superb beekeeper's plant, being especially attractive to the honeybee.

This herb has the advantage of rapid growth, providing quick ground cover and a shallow, extensive root system that produces a fine soil. Dig in, or prolong its life span by cutting before flowering. Beekeepers should leave the plant to flower over a long period, and it will then self-seed. In mild areas phacelia will overwinter as young self-sown seedlings; in colder areas, however, it should be sown anew each year by broadcasting the seeds and raking in. The more thickly it is sown, the lower it will grow.

Phacelia is extremely decorative. Sow a good-size patch in any area of the garden that you do not intend to use for a few months and wait for a wonderful display of color.

Annual
Height To 3 ft (90 cm).
Spread 12 in (30 cm).
Flowers Lavender-blue spikes, followed by curled, scorpionlike seed heads.
Flowering Summer.
Foliage Deep green, finely divided, feathery, alternate.
Natural habitat Brush and grassy areas. Native of North America.
Soil Most soils, prefers some moisture.
Site Full sun or partial shade.
Propagation Sow seeds in spring after frost; self-seeds.
Uses Green manure crop; bee plant.
Family Hydrophyllaceae (waterleaf family).
Other varieties and species
P. bipinnatifida; *P. campanularia*; *P. fimbriata*; *P. linearis*; *P. purshii*.

Phytolacca americana

Pokeweed

POKEWEED HAS OVER 30 common names, including inkweed, and is a dramatic-looking specimen. The whole plant has a purplish hue, and when the small flowers are over the thick spikes of pink and then purple-black berries are spectacular. In a good soil it can grow to massive proportions.

Pokeweed is poisonous, especially the juicy-looking berries. Keep it out of any garden where children play.

Medicinally pokeweed is a valuable herb, but it should not be used in any way for home treatment. Juice from the berries has been employed as ink, to dye fabric, and as a food coloring.

Perennial Zone 3
Height 4–8 ft (1.2–2.4 m).
Spread 4 ft (1.2 m).
Flowers White and green, sometimes pink flushed, small, shallow, cup shaped, borne in terminal racemes. Followed by large head of purplish-black berries.
Flowering Summer to late summer.
Foliage Medium-green tinged purple, on pinkish-red stems, ovate or lanceolate, toothless, alternate, unpleasant scent.
Natural habitat Waste ground, fields, and roadsides. Native of eastern and southern U.S.
Soil Humus rich and light to moisture retaining, well drained.
Site Full sun or partial shade.
Propagation Sow seeds or divide in spring or fall.
Uses Medicinal; dye plant.
Family Phytolaccaceae (phytolacca family).
Other varieties and species
P. polyandra syn. *P. clavigera*.

Warning

All parts of this plant are poisonous. Wear gloves when handling.

Platycodon grandiflorus

Balloon Flower

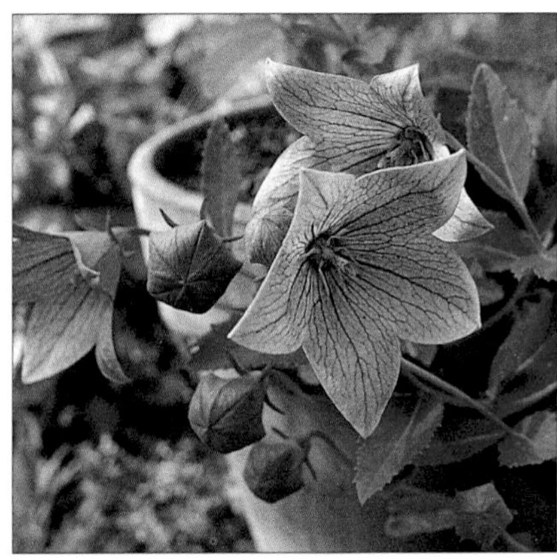

BALLOON FLOWER, a native of China and Japan, is an impressive herb when in flower. The conspicuous, 10-faceted "balloons" slowly open into large, stunning, pure blue flowers.

This herb makes a lovely border plant and looks superb blooming among gray- and silver-leaved herbs where its tall flower stems ensure that its flowers are well displayed. When the blooms are over, the stems can be cut down. It also makes a beautiful container plant, its slender stems trailing over the edge.

Balloon flower enjoys moisture in early summer. It does best in a fertile loam but requires good drainage over the winter months.

In China and Japan the root of the plant is used to prepare a remedy for coughs. The young leaves are eaten in Chinese salads.

Perennial Zone 3
Height 18–24 in (45–60 cm).
Spread 12–18 in (30–45 cm).
Flowers Clear blue, pointed, five petaled, open bell shaped, opening from balloonlike buds in terminal clusters.
Flowering Summer.
Foliage Green with lighter blue-green underside, ovate, toothed.
Natural habitat Mountainous areas. Native of China and Japan.
Soil Deep, fertile, moist, well drained.
Site Full sun or light shade.
Propagation Sow seeds in spring.
Uses Medicinal; culinary.
Family Campanulaceae (bellflower family).
Other varieties and species
P. grandiflorus var. *albus*; *P. g.* 'Florist Blue'; *P. g.* 'Florist Mixed'; *P. g.* 'Florist Rose'; *P. g.* 'Florist Snow'; *P. g.* 'Park's Double Blue'; *P. apoyana*; *P. mariesii*.

Polemonium caeruleum

Jacob's Ladder

JACOB'S LADDER is so called because of the ladderlike formation of its bright green leaves. This is a cottage flower that has been grown for many centuries in country gardens.

Jacob's ladder requires moisture in the soil to flourish and grows well in partially shaded areas. It associates well with water, and with trees and shrubs. For a long flowering, cut down the stems before they go to seed. One stem will be more than adequate for self-seeding, since seeds are produced in abundance.

In times past the herb was used to treat fevers, headaches, epilepsy, and nervous complaints.

Perennial Zone 3
Height 2–3 ft (60–90 cm).
Spread 12 in (30 cm).
Flowers Deep blue, five petaled, with prominent, orange stamens, in drooping panicles.
Flowering Summer.
Foliage Bright green, pinnate, in a ladder formation.
Natural habitat Damp soils by streams, meadows, and open woodland. Native of northern and central Europe, central Asia, and Siberia. Naturalized in central and eastern U.S.
Soil Humus-rich, moist to moisture-retaining, calcareous loam.
Site Full sun or partial shade.
Propagation Sow seeds in spring or fall; divide roots in spring; self-seeds.
Uses Formerly medicinal.
Family Polemoniaceae (Jacob's ladder family).
Other varieties and species
P. caeruleum var. *album*; *P. c.* 'Blue Bell'; *P. c.* 'White Pearl'; *P. c.* subsp. *himalayanum*; *P. carneum*; *P. foliosissimum*; *P.* x *richardsonii*.

Polemonium reptans

Greek Valerian

GREEK VALERIAN is a native of North America, growing in damp areas from New York to Wisconsin. It has several common names, including Jacob's ladder (its leaves, in common with other members of the genus, have a ladderlike construction); false Jacob's ladder; abscess root; sweetroot; and bluebells. The North American Indians called it "smells-like-pine," which refers to the scent of its root. Why it is also known as Greek valerian is a mystery, because it is no relation to valerian and does not grow in Greece. The logic of common plant names is sometimes obscure.

Greek valerian is a sprawling, low-growing plant that makes a good ground cover and bears its bluebell-like flowers in profusion. In the moist conditions that it enjoys, the creeping roots spread quickly and a few plants will soon create a full clump. Grow this herb in the damper areas of the garden, by the edge of a pond or stream. On moisture-retaining soils it grows well in a border or the edge of a woodland and is successful in semishade in association with trees and shrubs. If it is cut down after blooming, another flush of flowers is likely to appear later in the season. It produces little seed.

Greek valerian was valued medicinally by North American Indians for the root tea and root extract, which they used to treat a number of ailments, including pleurisy, bronchitis, fevers, and snakebites.

Perennial Zone 3
Height 8–18 in (20–45 cm).
Spread 18 in (45 cm).
Flowers Violet-blue, bell-like, in loose clusters on wiry stems.
Flowering Spring to early summer.
Foliage Bright green, pinnate, in ladder formation like *P. caeruleum* (Jacob's ladder).
Natural habitat Moist valleys, damp woods, and shady riverbanks. Native of North America.
Soil Humus-rich, moist to moisture-retaining loam.
Site Full sun and partial shade.
Propagation Sow seeds in spring or fall; divide in spring.
Uses Formerly medicinal.
Family Polemoniaceae (Jacob's ladder family).
Other varieties and species
P. reptans 'Blue Pearl'; *P. r.* 'Lambrook Manor'; *P. r.* 'Pink Beauty'; *P. caeruleum*; *P. carneum*; *P. cashmerianum*; *P. foliosissimum*; *P.* x *richardsonii*; *P. vanbruntia*.

Primula veris

Cowslip

THE NODDING FLOWERS of the cowslip were once seen in their thousands in wild meadows. Today this lovely spring flower is more often found on roadsides, on chalky soil.

Seed or plant in drifts, in a weed-free area of soil mixed with other suitable meadow grasses and flowers. On the right soil cowslips establish easily, but to wait two or three seasons for flowers is not unusual. The plants seed profusely and spread vigorously.

Cowslip leaves were once eaten in salads, the roots and flowers were used medicinally, and the flowers to make an excellent wine.

Perennial Zone 3
Height 4–12 in (10–30 cm).
Spread 8 in (20 cm).
Flowers Deep yellow, with an orange marking and inflated green calyx, drooping, sweetly scented, in nodding umbels on a stalk.
Flowering Late spring to early summer.
Foliage Medium green, similar to that of the primrose but not as spoon shaped or as wrinkled, downy on both sides.
Natural habitat Meadows, grassy banks, and open woods. Native of northern and central Europe; naturalized in North America.
Soil Fertile, calcareous loam to clay soil.
Site Full sun or partial shade.
Propagation Sow seeds as soon as ripe or stratify; divide in fall; self-seeds.
Uses Formerly medicinal; culinary.
Family Primulaceae (primrose family).
Other varieties and species *P. veris* Mixed Hybrids; *P. auricula*; *P. elatior*; *P. veris* 'Red.'

Primula vulgaris

Primrose

THE PRIMROSE is one of the earliest spring flowers. It once grew in great profusion in the wild, but many of its natural habitats have now been destroyed. Primroses enjoy a rich soil with moisture and a thick mulch of leaf mold. They always look their best associated with woodland and can be successfully naturalized in woodland and partial shade or in grass which should be left uncut until after seeding in midsummer. Primrose stems curve over to the ground when the seeds are ready. If seed is sown when fresh, germination will occur during the fall; otherwise, it needs the winter cold to stimulate germination.

The plant has medicinal properties similar to those of the cowslip, and the leaves are likewise edible in fresh salads. The flowers can be candied.

Perennial Zone 3
Height To 8 in (20 cm).
Spread 8 in (20 cm).
Flowers Pale yellow with a deep yellow center, sweetly scented, growing on fine, pink, curved stems.
Flowering Winter to late spring.
Foliage Medium green, very crinkly, spoon shaped, prominent veins, form a basal rosette.
Natural habitat Damp, woodland soils; hedges and ditches. Native of Europe.
Soil Humus-rich, moisture-retaining loam.
Site Shade to partial shade.
Propagation Sow seeds as soon as ripe or stratify; divide in fall.
Uses Medicinal; culinary.
Family Primulaceae (primrose family).
Other varieties and species *P. vulgaris* 'Alba Plena'; *P. v.* 'Cornish Pink'; *P. v.* 'Double Sulphur'; *P. v.* 'Gold-Laced Hose'; *P. v.* 'Hose-in-Hose'; *P. v.* 'Wanda'; *P. farinosa*; *P.* Gold Lace Group.

Pulmonaria officinalis

Lungwort

LUNGWORT IS A useful ground-cover plant with decorative foliage. Bright pink buds open in early spring to produce tubular flowers in changing colors of blue through red, which is why the plant has also been called soldiers-and-sailors.

Lungwort thrives in the shade of trees and shrubs. Plant over an extensive area to achieve the best effect in a soil that retains some moisture, along with leaf mold.

Lungwort was once thought to be effective for treating lung complaints because of the lunglike markings on the leaves, according to the principle of the Doctrine of Signatures (see page 180). Surprisingly, the leaves are of some benefit in the treatment of bronchial catarrh, but their use has now been superseded by more effective remedies.

Perennial Zone 5
Height To 12 in (30 cm). Spreading.
Flowers Pink, red, violet, to blue; cowsliplike; in terminal cymes.
Flowering Spring.
Foliage Dark green with white spots, rough, hairy, oval, slightly pointed.
Natural habitat Woodlands and thickets. Native of Europe and widely naturalized.
Soil Most well-drained, calcareous soils with humus.
Site Shade or partial shade.
Propagation Divide after flowering or in fall.
Uses Medicinal.
Family Boraginaceae (borage family).
Other varieties and species *P. officinalis* 'Alba'; *P. o.* 'Bowles' Blue'; *P. o.* 'Sissinghurst White'; *P. angustifolia* 'Azurea'; *P. a.* 'Munstead Blue'; *P. longifolia*; *P. rubra*; *P. saccharata*; *P. vallarsae* 'Margery Fish.'

Pulsatilla vulgaris

Pasqueflower

PASQUEFLOWER is so named as it flowers around Easter; the ancient Greeks knew it as windflower. It has rich purple-violet flowers, though there are varieties with white, red, or mahogany blooms. The silky seed heads, with their own "feather" to carry them on the wind, make eye-catching dried arrangements.

This is a perfect rock-garden plant, and it can be naturalized in dry grassland where competition is not too vigorous. Allow it to self-seed and do not crowd it with other plants.

Pasqueflower is of great value in homeopathic and herbal medicine.

Perennial Zone 5
Height To 12in (30cm).
Spread 9in (23cm).
Flowers Purple-violet with yellow anthers, very silky underneath, borne singly on stalks, distinctive ruff below flowers. Copper feathery seed heads.
Flowering Spring.
Foliage Silky (especially when young), deeply divided into long linear segments.
Natural habitat Dry meadows on chalk and sand. Native of northern and central Europe.
Soil Well-drained calcareous loam or sandy loam.
Site Sun.
Propagation Sow seeds in spring or fall (erratic). May require stratification. Best sown with "feather" attached to seed; divide after flowering.
Uses Medicinal; dried seed heads.
Family Ranunculaceae (buttercup family).
Other varieties and species *P.vulgaris* var. *alba*; *P.v.*'Flore Pleno'; *P.v.* var. *rubra*; *P.alpina*; *P.grandis*; *P.halleri*.

Warning
The fresh plant is poisonous.

Pycnanthemum pilosum

Mountain Mint

A NORTH AMERICAN herb, mountain mint grows mostly on dry soils, often in shady situations. It will withstand considerable drought, but in a fertile, moist soil it grows lusher and spreads more rapidly, making an imposing garden plant.

Mountain mint is an attractive fall-flowering plant, which looks natural at the edge of a woodland with other North American native herbs, such as *Echinacea angustifolia* (purple coneflower) or *Asclepias tuberosa* (pleurisy root). All these flowers will attract fall butterflies. Mountain mint is also loved by honeybees.

Botanically this herb is not a true mint, though it is a member of the mint family. The strongly peppermint-scented leaves can be used to impart a delicious flavor to tea.

Perennial Zone 4
Height 2–4ft (60–120cm). Spreading.
Flowers Lilac-white, spotted purple, in dense, terminal clusters.
Flowering Late summer to fall.
Foliage Light green, lance shaped, opposite, strongly aromatic.
Natural habitat Dry thickets. Native of North America.
Soil Fertile, sandy loam.
Site Full sun or partial shade.
Propagation Sow seeds in early spring; divide in spring or fall; take tip cuttings in early summer.
Uses Culinary; bee and butterfly plant.
Family Labiatae (mint family).
Other varieties and species *P.incanum*; *P.tenuifolium* syn. *P.flexuosum*; *P.muticum*; *P.virginianum*.

Ranunculus ficaria

Lesser Celandine

LESSER CELANDINE is a beautiful wild member of the buttercup family. It is not related to greater celandine (*Chelidonium majus*).

This early spring plant forms dense mats of attractive foliage in shades of green, bronze, and purple, and the shiny flowers come in shades of yellow and white, and in double forms.

These accommodating plants enjoy shady conditions under trees and shrubs, with a humus-rich soil and a plentiful supply of moisture in spring. Reproduction is by the tiny bulbils produced on the stem, which detach themselves as the plant dies.

Another name for this herb is pilewort, indicating one of its former medicinal uses. The plant should, however, never be taken internally.

Perennial Zone 3
Height 2–9in (5–23cm). Spreading.
Flowers Bright yellow, glossy, with 8 to 12 petals, solitary, on long stalks.
Flowering Early spring.
Foliage Glossy, with dark markings, some heart shaped on long stalks, some serrated and ivylike.
Natural habitat Moist soils in woodlands, meadows, and ditches. Native of Europe, North Africa, and western Asia.
Soil Moist to wet soils rich in nitrogen.
Site Shade and partial shade.
Propagation Sow seeds (erratic) or divide tubers in fall; bulbils in early summer.
Uses Formerly medicinal.
Family Ranunculaceae (buttercup family).
Other varieties and species *R.ficaria* var. *albus*; *R.f.* 'Brazen Hussey'; *R.f.* 'Flore pleno'; *R.f.* 'Foliis Purpureis.'

Warning
This plant is poisonous, and the juice can cause skin irritation.

Rosa

Rose

Rosa gallica var. *officinalis*
Apothecary's rose

Rosa gallica 'Versicolor'
syn. 'Rosa Mundi'

Rosa rugosa
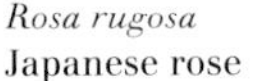
Japanese rose

Rosa eglanteria
Sweetbrier rose

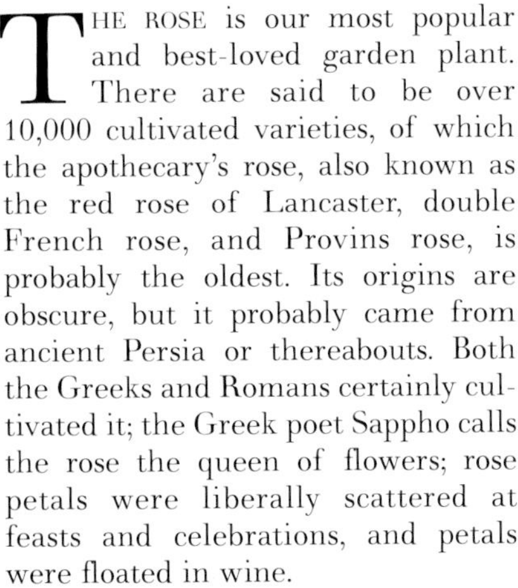

THE ROSE is our most popular and best-loved garden plant. There are said to be over 10,000 cultivated varieties, of which the apothecary's rose, also known as the red rose of Lancaster, double French rose, and Provins rose, is probably the oldest. Its origins are obscure, but it probably came from ancient Persia or thereabouts. Both the Greeks and Romans certainly cultivated it; the Greek poet Sappho calls the rose the queen of flowers; rose petals were liberally scattered at feasts and celebrations, and petals were floated in wine.

The rose is an extremely versatile plant: there is one for every garden. Most prefer a rich, fertile loam soil which is clay based and retains moisture. However, there are varieties that will grow in sandy or poor conditions, and many that will tolerate some shade. Many roses make excellent decorative hedges, but most are used in the garden as specimen shrubs, climbers, or ramblers. A mixed selection can also be planted into a specially prepared bed. The old-fashioned and specie roses normally have only one flowering season, but often produce hips in the fall. The foliage alone is decorative in either color or texture. More modern roses are repeat flowering, and many retain the beautiful form and scent of the older types.

Today attar of rose is the most popular ingredient of perfume, soaps, and cosmetics. Although the rose is now little used medicinally, the essential oil is valued in aromatherapy to treat many conditions. Rose hips are extensively used as a rich source of vitamin C. Rose petals are indispensable in potpourri; they retain their fragrance for a long period and also keep their color well when dried. *R.* x *centifolia* and *R.* x *damascena* are used for the production of essential oil. The musk-scented rose, *R. moschata*, is said in India to be an aphrodisiac.

Perennial shrub Zone 6
Height 3–4 ft (90 cm–1.2 m).
Spread 3 ft (90 cm).
Flowers Light crimson, semidouble, strongly perfumed.
Flowering Summer.
Foliage Dark gray-green, dense.
Natural habitat Sunny hills and bushy places. Probably a native of ancient Persia. Widely grown in North America.
Soil Tolerant of soil type but does best in clay-based loam.
Site Sun or partial shade.
Propagation Sow seeds of species in fall (stratify); budding onto wild rootstock or layering in midsummer; take cuttings of current year's growth in early fall.
Uses Medicinal; culinary; cosmetic; perfume; essential oil.
Family Rosaceae (rose family).
Other varieties and species
R. gallica 'Belle de Crécy'; *R. g.* 'Complicata'; *R. g.* 'Juno'; *R. g.* 'Versicolor' syn. 'Rosa Mundi'; *R. canina*; *R.* x *centifolia*; *R.* x *damascena* 'Kazanlik'; *R. eglanteria*; *R.* 'Eugène Furst'; *R. indica*; *R. laevigata*; *R. moschata*; *R.* 'à Parfum de l'Hay'; *R. rugosa*; *R. r.* 'Alba.'

Rosmarinus

Rosemary

Rosmarinus officinalis
Rosemary

R. officinalis
'Sawyers'

R. officinalis
'Prostratus'

R. officinalis
'Severn Sea'

WHERE ROSEMARY flourishes, the woman rules: so goes an old saying. Traditionally a symbol of love and loyalty, rosemary is for remembrance and to strengthen the mind and memory. The name *Rosmarinus* translates as "dew of the sea," and this is a plant that grows naturally by the seaside.

The flowers attract bees, but the herb often comes into flower in winter, when no bees are around. Flower color varies from the palest blue to a rich, deep blue according to variety. There are also white and pink forms, and one with gold-marked foliage.

Although most rosemaries will tolerate cold conditions, they are not particularly hardy and should be planted in the optimum position, with shelter from cold winds and a hot sunny site. They also require sharp drainage and some lime in the soil. The base of a wall is ideal; in areas of heavy, wet soil and cold winters, this is the place to grow rosemary.

In suitable soil evergreen rosemary looks superb all year round in a bed or border. Give it plenty of space to grow to its full size unhampered. There are many varieties from which to choose. Some have a neat compact habit, others are sprawling, prostrate, or miniature, and some grow upright. The 'Majorca Pink,' prostrate, and some of the true dwarf kinds are much less hardy and in cold climates must be grown in containers. In fact, rosemary makes a decorative container plant; it is best grown in a clay pot, in a gritty compost with added lime.

Rosemary does not reshoot from the old wood like other shrubby herbs, such as lavender and santolina, so prune or cut back only lightly into the current season's growth. If a whole branch dies, as sometimes happens, cut it out to the base or joint.

Rosemary is a flavorful, aromatic herb to use in cooking, especially with meat dishes, and can be picked fresh all year. It is also extensively used in the cosmetics industry. Fresh or dried rosemary has some insect-repellent properties and is a natural antioxidant. Medicinally rosemary has tonic, antiseptic, nervine, antispasmodic, fungicide, and paraciticide properties. It is valued especially for the treatment of headaches, poor circulation, digestion, and as a hair tonic.

Perennial evergreen shrub Zones 6–10
Height 3–6 ft (90 cm–1.8 m).
Spread To 4 ft (1.2 m).

Flowers Pale to dark blue, sometimes white or pink, small, two lipped in small clusters along a branch.
Flowering Winter through spring and often again.
Foliage Dark green, white felted underneath, inrolled, needlelike, leathery, very aromatic.
Natural habitat Among rocks and on stony ground. Native of the Mediterranean coastal region.
Soil Sharply drained, sandy to loamy, calcareous with low fertility.
Site Full sun.
Propagation Sow fresh seeds in summer, best at a high temperature, 70°–80°F (21°–27°C); take semiripe cuttings or layer in summer.
Uses Culinary; medicinal; cosmetic; insect repellent; essential oil.
Family Labiatae (mint family).
Other varieties and species
R. officinalis var. *albiflorus*; *R.o.* var. *angustissimus* 'Corsican Blue'; *R.o.* 'Arp'; *R.o.* 'Aureus'; *R.o.* 'Benenden Blue'; *R.o.* 'Blue Boy'; *R.o.* 'Corsicus'; *R.o.* 'Lockwood Variety'; *R.o.* 'Majorca Pink'; *R.o.* 'Miss Jessopp's Upright'; *R.o.* 'Primley Blue'; *R.o.* Prostratus Group; *R.o.* 'Rex'; *R.o.* 'Sawyers'; *R.o.* 'Severn Sea'; *R.o.* 'Sissinghurst Blue'; *R.o.* 'Sudbury Blue'; *R.o.* 'Tuscan Blue.'

Ruta graveolens

Rue

RUE, ONCE CALLED the herb of grace, has long been used medicinally. It is a decorative garden plant, particularly the variety 'Jackman's Blue,' which has more ample, blue-green foliage and blends particularly well with silver and gray herbs.

It will grow on the poorest, driest of soils, and although it will do well in rich, fertile soil it will be less hardy. It enjoys a hot sunny site in the bed, or border and also thrives in gravel.

Rue has long been regarded as an excellent antiflea herb. In homeopathic medicine it is used as an ointment for sprains and strains. It is too powerful to use as a home remedy.

Perennial semievergreen subshrub
Zones 4–9
Height To 3 ft (90 cm).
Spread 18 in (45 cm).
Flowers Yellow-green, small, in loose terminal clusters.
Flowering Summer.
Foliage Blue-green, waxy, deeply subdivided, with spatulate segments, alternate, very strongly aromatic.
Natural habitat Poor, rocky, and limestone soils. Native of southern Europe.
Soil Well drained, calcareous, and not too fertile.
Site Full sun.
Propagation Sow seeds in spring; take cuttings in early summer.
Uses Medicinal; insecticide.
Family Rutaceae (rue family).
Other varieties and species
R. graveolens 'Harlequin'; *R. g.* 'Jackman's Blue'; *R. g.* 'Variegata'; *R. chalepensis.*

Warning

Rue can cause a phototoxic rash. Wear gloves when handling, especially in sunlight.

Salvia

Sage

Salvia officinalis
Common sage

Salvia officinalis 'Icterina'
Gold variegated sage

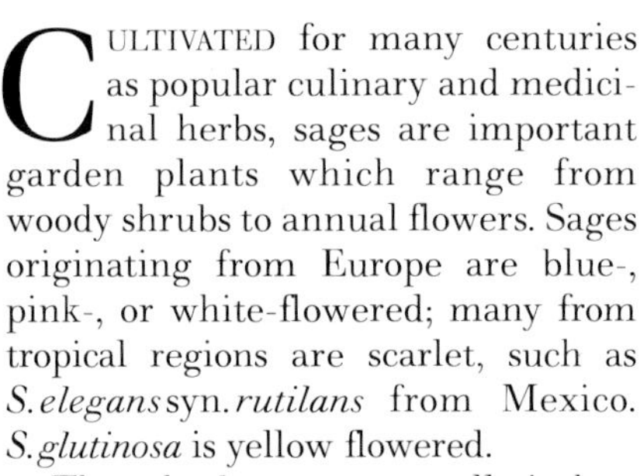

CULTIVATED for many centuries as popular culinary and medicinal herbs, sages are important garden plants which range from woody shrubs to annual flowers. Sages originating from Europe are blue-, pink-, or white-flowered; many from tropical regions are scarlet, such as *S. elegans* syn. *rutilans* from Mexico. *S. glutinosa* is yellow flowered.

These herbs grow naturally in hot, dry, harsh conditions and must have good drainage if they are to survive hard, wet winters. They also require plenty of space and good air circulation to keep them dry at the base. The soil is best prepared with a proportion of coarse sand and stones, or gravel. Cut the plants back lightly after flowering and, if more drastic action is needed, cut harder back in spring.

For use in the garden *S. officinalis* 'Purpurascens' (red or purple sage) is very decorative, as is *S. o.* 'Icterina' (gold variegated sage). Both keep their foliage through the winter. *S. candelabrum*, with its large gray leaves, tall flower stems, and violet-blue flowers is a dramatic plant but it needs space. *S. sclarea* (clary sage) is also known as muscatel sage, as it provides muscatel oil used in the perfume industry.

S. officinalis and its broad-leaved form are indispensable in the kitchen. Medicinally common sage is valuable for treating colds, sore throats, mouth ulcers, and hot flushes and strengthens the nervous system. Common sage and red or purple varieties make a good infusion that relieves indigestion.

Perennial evergreen subshrub
Zones 4–8
Height 12–30 in (30–75 cm).
Spread 2 ft (60 cm).
Flowers Violet-blue, two lipped, in terminal spikes.
Flowering Summer.
Foliage Gray-green, oblong, rounded at the ends, finely wrinkled, with a prominent venue on both sides, softly hairy, stalked, strongly aromatic.
Natural habitat Limestone soils, usually on hillsides. Native of the Mediterranean region.
Soil Well-drained calcareous or sandy loam.
Site Full sun.
Propagation Sow seeds in spring; take semiripe tip cuttings in early summer or fall; layer in spring.
Uses Culinary; medicinal; bee plant.
Family Labiatae (mint family).
Other varieties and species
S. officinalis 'Albiflora'; *S. o.* 'Aurea'; *S. o.* 'Broad leaved'; *S. o.* 'Icterina'; *S. o.* 'Purpurascens'; *S. o.* 'Rosea'; *S. o.* 'Tricolor'; *S. candelabrum*; *S. fruticosa*; *S. glutinosa*; *S. horminum*; *S. lavandulifolia*; *S. pratensis*; *S. prostratus*; *S. reptans*; *S. sclarea*; *S. viridis.*

Salvia elegans syn. *rutilans*

Pineapple Sage

Pineapple sage is an unexciting-looking herb for much of the year, but it is always a surprise to crush a leaf and smell the unmistakable scent of pineapple. Then, in late fall, the plant bursts into flower with spectacular, scarlet blooms, and these often continue right into spring.

Grow pineapple sage in a container in all areas subject to frost, place outside over the summer months and bring into the house when the nights start to turn cold. The plant is easily kept in bounds by cutting back after flowering. In frost-free areas, *S.elegans* can take its place with other tender herbs in the garden. Semiripe shoots root easily in a sandy mixture and often root well in water, too.

The leaves give a subtle tang of pineapple to fruit salads, cakes, and other sweet dishes.

Half-hardy perennial Zones 7–10
Height 2–3 ft (60–90 cm).
Spread To 2 ft (60 cm).
Flowers Scarlet, long, sagelike.
Flowering Fall.
Foliage Soft green, lance shaped, pineapple scented.
Natural habitat Native of Mexico.
Soil Fertile, well-drained loam or sandy loam.
Site Full sun.
Propagation Take tip cuttings in summer, root in sandy compost or water.
Uses Culinary.
Family Labiatae (mint family).
Other varieties and species *S.elegans* 'Scarlet Pineapple'; *S.coccinea*; *S.dorisiana*; *S.fulgens*; *S.guaranitica*.

Sambucus nigra

Elder

When the musk-scented flowers of the elder bloom, summer has arrived. Elder is a most useful shrub, and almost every part is of value.

In the garden, coppice elder every two or three years to keep it bushy and attractive, it will produce a mass of fragrant flowers every year.

The flowers make a light wine, or even "champagne." They are used in summer drinks, to make fritters and for a delicate tea. The shiny berries form the basis of a superb red wine, are excellent in fruit pies, and for making jam. The close-grained, hard wood has many uses.

Perennial tree or shrub Zone 4
Height To 15 ft (4.5 m).
Spread To 8 ft (2.4 m).
Flowers Creamy white, tiny, in a much-branched, flat-topped cyme, very fragrant. Followed by many small, purple-black, edible fruits.
Flowering Early summer.
Foliage Dull green, subdivided into five elliptical, toothed leaflets, with an unpleasant odor.
Natural habitat Hedgerows, edges of woodlands, and near human habitation. Native of Europe, North Africa, and western Asia.
Soil Nitrogen-rich, moisture-retaining loam or clay loam.
Site Full sun or partial shade.
Propagation Sow cleaned seeds in spring; take hardwood cuttings and insert into sandy soil over winter.
Uses Culinary; wine; medicinal; dye plant.
Family Caprifoliaceae (honeysuckle family).
Other varieties and species *S.nigra* 'Aurea'; *S.n.laciniata*; *S.n.*'Marginata'; *S.canadensis*.

Sanguinaria canadensis

Bloodroot

Bloodroot, a beautiful flower of North American woods, blooms early in spring soon after the snow has melted. It requires woodland conditions where the soil is rich in leaf mold or humus and does not bake dry in summer. Shade shows off the pale flowers to full advantage.

The plant spreads slowly and in time forms a thick clump. The leaves unfurl after the flowers are finished, creating attractive ground cover. The rhizomes grow near the surface: when dividing them cut off sections without disturbing the whole plant, and make sure that each one has a bud.

The rhizome of this old medicinal herb was used by American Indians, and is valued mainly for the treatment of chronic bronchitis. When cut it yields a red juice.

Perennial Zone 3
Height 6–12 in (15–30 cm).
Spread 9 in (23 cm).
Flowers White or pinkish, with pale yellow stamens, usually eight petaled, solitary, star shaped.
Flowering Spring.
Foliage Bluish green above, paler beneath, heart shaped, with shallowly lobed and scalloped margin, stalked.
Natural habitat Rich woodland and rocky slopes. Native of eastern North America.
Soil Humus-rich, moist to moisture-retaining loam.
Site Shade, partial shade, or sun.
Propagation Divide in fall.
Uses Medicinal; dye plant.
Family Papaveraceae (poppy family).
Other varieties and species *S.canadensis* 'Plena.'

Warning

All parts of this plant are poisonous.

Sanguisorba minor

Salad Burnet

SALAD BURNET has been used and planted for many centuries in herb gardens. It is also a foliage plant, as the flowers are modest. The attractive leaves stay green for most of the year, especially if the plant is cut down after flowering. Burnet makes decorative ground cover for dry areas and can be used in herb beds as an edging. The foliage also provides an effective contrast in color and texture to the gray-leaved herbal shrubs like santolina and curry plant.

Burnet has a delicate cucumber flavor. The young leaves make a tasty addition to salads and soups, and can be used as a good substitute for borage in fruit cups. The herb was employed as a medicine by the ancient Greeks. Burnet is recommended in Gerard's famous herbal for steeping in drinks as a guard against infection and as a wound herb.

Perennial Zone 3
Height To 18 in (45 cm).
Spread 12 in (30 cm).
Flowers Green, tiny, with crimson-tufted stigmas, in compact globular heads.
Flowering Summer.
Foliage Divided into 4 to 12 pairs of oval, deeply toothed leaflets, cucumber scented, on red stems; basal leaves form a rosette.
Natural habitat Chalky grassland and roadsides. Native of Europe and parts of Asia. Naturalized in North America.
Soil Well-drained, alkaline loam.
Site Full sun or partial shade.
Propagation Sow seeds in spring or fall; self-seeds.
Uses Culinary; medicinal.
Family Rosaceae (rose family).
Other varieties and species
S. canadensis; *S. officinalis*.

Santolina

Santolina

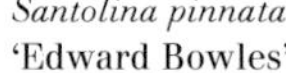

Santolina pinnata
'Edward Bowles'

S. chamaecyparissus
Cotton lavender

S. chamaecyparissus
'Lemon Queen'

SANTOLINA, OR cotton lavender, looks nothing like *Lavandula* (lavender) and is in no way related to it. But its finely cut foliage is just as decorative and as useful in the herb garden.

Santolina grows naturally on dry, stony soils which are baked by the hot Mediterranean sun, so this is a plant that will survive heat and dry soil conditions. Although it is basically gray leaved, new growth is much greener, giving the growing plant a softer appearance, and there is also a bright green form (*S. virens*) that provides an interesting contrast.

There is a good variety of santolinas available for the garden, each with its own distinctive texture, such as *S. chamaecyparissus* 'Lemon Queen.' This has lovely, soft lemon-colored flowers and a low spreading habit, which provides excellent ground cover in dry stony areas; it is a decorative rock garden plant. Santolina makes a superb hedge, especially the compact form: it can be kept tightly clipped and shaped and looks good all year round. The best time of year to do the main clipping is early spring. Santolina hedges are especially favored for outlining a formal knot garden or herb garden. The foliage is also delightfully fragrant.

The shrub was used medicinally but nowadays is more valued for decorative use, in both fresh and dried forms, and as an insect repellent; the dried stems kept among clothes will keep moths away. It is also a dye plant, yielding golds and yellows.

Perennial evergreen shrub Zones 6–8
Height To 2 ft (60 cm).
Spread 18 in (45 cm).
Flowers Yellow, small, buttonlike, on slender, gray stems.
Flowering Summer.
Foliage Silver-gray, very finely cut, linear, forming long spikes, very aromatic.
Natural habitat Stony slopes on chalk, often by the sea. Native of the western and central Mediterranean region.
Soil Well drained, alkaline, dry in summer.
Site Full sun.
Propagation Take tip cuttings in spring or summer.
Uses Formerly medicinal; household; insect repellent; dye plant; cut and dried flowers.
Family Compositae (daisy family).
Other varieties and species
S. chamaecyparissus 'Lambrook Silver'; *S. c.* 'Lemon Queen'; *S. c.* var. *nana*; *S. pinnata* subsp. *neapolitana*; *S. p.* subsp. *n.* 'Edward Bowles'; *S. p.* subsp. *n.* 'Sulphurea'; *S. rosmarinifolia*; *S. virens* syn. *S. viridis*.

Saponaria officinalis

Soapwort

Soapwort is a very pretty tumbling plant that in rich, moist soil can spread vigorously. If planted on the edge of a border, it will spread into the grass and is unaffected by mowing. Soapwort's lovely pinkish-white flowers bloom at the end of summer and well into the fall.

An old medicinal plant, it was introduced to American Indians by European settlers. It is no longer used in medicine, but is well known as a gentle soap substitute. It is used to clean old fabrics and tapestries, and is an ingredient of herbal shampoos.

Perennial Zones 3–8
Height To 2 ft (60 cm). Spreading.
Flowers Pale pink to white, carnation-like, with a distinctive green calyx, in dense, terminal clusters.
Flowering Late summer.
Foliage Oval to lance shaped, smooth, with three linear veins, opposite.
Natural habitat Waste ground, roadsides, hedgebanks, and grassland. Native of Europe and western Asia; naturalized in North America and elsewhere.
Soil Moisture-retaining loam.
Site Full sun or partial shade.
Propagation Sow seeds or divide in spring or fall.
Uses Formerly medicinal; household.
Family Caryophyllaceae (pink family).
Other varieties and species
S. officinalis 'Alba Plena'; *S. o.* 'Dazzler'; *S. o.* 'Variegata'; *S. ocymoïdes*.

Warning

This plant is poisonous, especially to grazing animals and to fish.

Satureja montana

Winter Savory

Winter savory has been used as a culinary herb since the 9th century. This is a decorative foliage plant, ideal for growing in the rock garden or gravel. The more delicate, creeping variety will tumble over rocks and spread over gravel. As a native of mountain regions, it will survive cold winters only if it is given sharp drainage and rather poor soil.

Winter savory is the perfect flavoring for beans. The annual *S. hortensis*, summer savory, with its thymelike flavor, is used in many dishes and is easily grown from seed sown in situ in late spring. Make use of gaps between the shrubby herbs.

Perennial evergreen shrublet Zone 6
Height 6–12 in (15–30 cm).
Spread 15 in (38 cm).
Flowers White or pale lilac, with lower lip spotted purple, in terminal spikes.
Flowering Summer.
Foliage Dark green, glossy, small, lance shaped, highly aromatic.
Natural habitat Dry, rocky hillsides, cliffs, and mountains, usually on chalk. Native of southeastern Europe and North Africa.
Soil Well-drained to dry, alkaline or sandy loam.
Site Full sun.
Propagation Surface sow seeds in fall (erratic); take semiripe cuttings in early summer.
Uses Culinary; bee plant.
Family Labiatae (mint family).
Other varieties and species
S. montana 'Prostrate White'; *S. m.* 'Purple Mountain'; *S. coerulea*; *S. hortensis*; *S. spicigera* syn. *S. repandra*; *S. thymbra*.

Scutellaria lateriflora

Skullcap

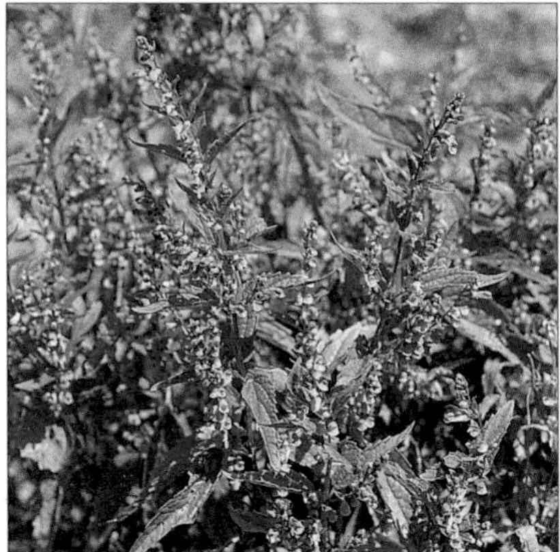

Skullcaps grow all over the world although the majority are native to North America. The plant is known as mad-dog skullcap in the U.S., where it was considered a treatment for rabies. The name skullcap comes from the miniature seed capsule, which opens like a helmet when the seed is ripe and ready for dispersal.

The mad-dog skullcap is a modest plant whose main use in the garden is as ground cover in moist, shady areas among trees and shrubs. It spreads rapidly in damp soils by pale yellow underground runners. There are many other species, some of which are well worth growing in the garden.

The plant is now considered an effective medicinal for the treatment of the nervous system, on which it acts as a tonic.

Perennial Zone 5
Height 1–3 ft (30–90 cm). Spreading.
Flowers Violet-blue, small, hooded, lipped, in one-sided racemes from the leaf axils.
Flowering Summer.
Foliage Oval to lance shaped, toothed, opposite.
Natural habitat Damp woods and moist thickets, wet meadows, and streamsides. Native of North America from Connecticut to Florida.
Soil Moist to moisture-retaining, fertile loam.
Site Shade or partial shade.
Propagation Sow seeds or divide in spring.
Uses Medicinal.
Family Labiatae (mint family).
Other varieties and species
S. altissima; *S. amanus*; *S. baicalensis*; *S. galericulata*; *S. hastifolia*; *S. scordiifolia*.

Sedum reflexum

Reflexed Stonecrop

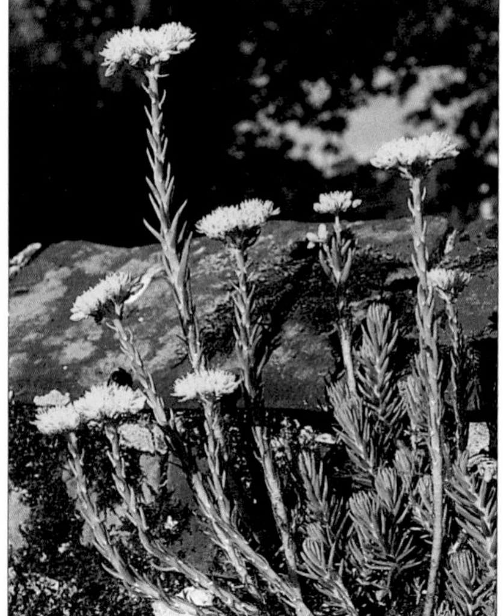

THERE ARE MANY garden varieties of sedums, some have pink, red, or purple flowers. *S. reflexum* is an excellent ground-cover plant and, like other small species, should be grown in a gravel or rock garden. Larger-flowered plants, like *S. spectabile* (ice plant), are magnets for butterflies in late summer. All look their best in stony soil, and some will grow on tiled or flat roofs, and walls.

The succulent leaves and shoots of reflexed stonecrop can be used in fresh salads. *S. acre* (biting stonecrop), so named because of its acrid juice, is used to treat warts and remove corns but should not to be taken internally. Rosewater was once produced from the scented roots of *S. rosea* (roseroot).

Perennial Zone 5
Height 9–12 in (23–30 cm). Spreading.
Flowers Bright yellow, tiny, in flat, terminal, nodding heads on leafy stems.
Flowering Summer.
Foliage Green-gray, fleshy, narrow, reflexed up flowering stem.
Natural habitat Rocks, old walls, and rooftops. Native of central and southern Europe, the Ukraine, and North America.
Soil Rocky or sandy soil, well drained.
Site Full sun.
Propagation Divide rooting stems in spring or fall; sow seeds in fall (stratify); self-seeds.
Uses Culinary; medicinal; butterfly plant.
Family Crassulaceae (stonecrop family).
Other varieties and species *S. acre*; *S. album*; *S. rosea* syn. *Rhodiola rosea*; *S. spectabile*; *S. telephium*; *S. ternatum*.

Silybum marianum

Milk Thistle

MILK THISTLE, St. Mary's thistle or holy thistle, is so called because of the ornamental white markings on its leaves, said to represent the milk of the Virgin Mary. This striking plant is grown mainly for its foliage.

In the first year it produces a huge rosette of bright green, white-veined, spiny leaves. During the second year its long stems are topped with bright purple-pink flowers, surrounded by vicious but decorative spines.

The flower heads (like artichokes), the leaves (trimmed of spines), young shoots, and peeled stems can all be cooked as a vegetable. It is also used medicinally to stimulate appetite, aid digestion, to relieve travel sickness, and for cardiovascular disorders.

Biennial Zone 5
Height To 5 ft (1.5 m).
Spread 3 ft (90 cm).
Flowers Purple-pink, thistlelike, surrounded by long, spiny bracts, sweet scented.
Flowering Summer.
Foliage Bright green, with conspicuous white veins, shiny, wavy edged and lobed, very spiny.
Natural habitat Rocky and stony soil, waste ground, and roadsides. Native of the Mediterranean, Asia Minor, and the Caucasus. Naturalized in North America.
Soil Most well-drained soils.
Site Full sun.
Propagation Sow seeds in fall or spring; self-seeds.
Uses Culinary; medicinal.
Family Compositae (daisy family).
Other varieties and species None.

Stachys officinalis

Betony

AN ANCIENT HEALING herb once held in high repute, betony, which is also known as bishopswort or wood betony, was said to be endowed with magical powers against evil spirits. It was grown in many herb gardens and churchyards in the middle ages.

A good-size clump in grassland, or in association with trees and shrubs, looks superb in full bloom. It enjoys the partial shade of the woodland edge. However, betony will also grow successfully in open borders, and the varieties *S. officinalis* 'Rosea Superba' and *S. o.* 'Alba' are well worth planting in this garden site for a brilliant summer display. Although betony is found mainly on light sandy soils of an acid or alkaline nature, it also thrives on heavier soils.

Today the herb is little used in medicine, but it has a mildly sedative action and is used as a tea and in herbal smoking mixtures.

Perennial Zone 4
Height 1–2 ft (30–60 cm).
Spread 12 in (30 cm).
Flowers Pink-purple, two lipped, growing in dense, interrupted terminal spikes.
Flowering Summer.
Foliage Dark green, rough, ovate, round toothed, opposite.
Natural habitat Wood clearings, hedgebanks, and meadowland. Native of Europe and the Caucasus.
Soil Moist to fairly dry or sandy loam.
Site Partial shade or full sun.
Propagation Sow seeds in spring or fall.
Uses Medicinal; tea; dye plant.
Family Labiatae (mint family).
Other varieties and species *S. officinalis* 'Alba'; *S. o.* 'Rosea Superba'; *S. macrantha*.

Succisa pratensis

Devil's-bit Scabious

DEVIL'S-BIT SCABIOUS is so named because the root was supposed to have been bitten by the devil. The root does looks as if it has been eaten away. Its violet-blue globular blooms hover above other plants, long after their flowers have faded. No other plant attracts late-summer butterflies in such profusion.

Plant devil's-bit scabious in the border or with other moisture-loving flowers and some meadow grasses to create a patch of flowering meadow. In areas of high summer rainfall, it will grow well in much lighter soil.

In Culpeper's day this herb was recommended for treating scabies, for the removal of pimples and freckles, for protection against plague and venomous bites, as a gargle for sore throats, and as a bruise herb. It is now rarely used in herbal medicine.

Perennial Zone 4
Height To 3 ft (90 cm).
Spread 12 in (30 cm).
Flowers Mauve to violet-blue, hemispherical, with conspicuous stamens, on long thin stalks.
Flowering Late summer.
Foliage Gray-green, oblong, in a basal rosette, sparse on the stem.
Natural habitat Moist ground in woods, pastures, marshes, and lowland. Native of Europe, North Africa, and western Siberia. Naturalized in North America.
Soil Moist to moisture-retaining loam.
Site Full sun or partial shade.
Propagation Sow seeds in spring; self-seeds.
Uses Butterfly plant; formerly medicinal.
Family Dipsacaceae (teasel family).
Other varieties and species
S. pratensis (dwarf form).

Symphytum x *uplandicum*

Russian Comfrey

GROW RUSSIAN comfrey in a plot of its own for use in composting. Well manured, it can be cut down up to six times a season. Other species also make attractive garden plants: *S. grandiflorum*, with creamy-pink flowers, produces excellent ground cover; *S. peregrinum* has intense blue flowers; and *S. orientale* bears cream-colored blooms.

Comfrey, also known as knitbone, boneset, and bruisewort, is an old and valuable medicinal plant. A leaf poultice is used externally for bruises, burns, wounds, and ulcers, and a leaf tea given for gastric ulcers, pleurisy, and bronchitis.

Perennial Zone 3
Height To 4 ft (1.2 m).
Spread 3 ft (90 cm).
Flowers Blue, purplish pink, bell shaped, in one-sided, drooping clusters.
Flowering Summer.
Foliage Rough, bristly, hairy, ovate, and very large at base, upper leaves smaller.
Natural habitat Damp, shady places by streamsides and rivers. Native of Europe and temperate Asia; widely naturalized.
Soil Rich, moisture-retaining loam.
Site Sun or partial shade.
Propagation Sow seeds in summer or fall; divide roots in spring.
Uses Compost; medicinal; dye plant.
Family Boraginaceae (borage family).
Other varieties and species
S. x *uplandicum* 'Variegatum'; *S. asperum*; *S. grandiflorum*; *S. officinale*.

Warning
This plant is phototoxic.

Tagetes patula

French Marigold

BOTH FRENCH and African species of marigold are valued by organic gardeners for their insecticidal and companion properties (see page 40). *T. patula* is an excellent decorative companion plant for tomatoes to deter whiteflies. *T. erecta* (African marigold) is an attractive and pleasantly scented flower with similar properties, ideal for the vegetable garden. All French marigolds enjoy well-drained, fertile loam and tolerate dry conditions.

T. lucida (mint marigold) is well worth growing for decoration, but especially for its tarragon-tasting leaves, which make a stimulating tea. *T. tenuifolia* is a lacy-leaved annual with a citrus scent, which bears small orange or lemon flowers.

Tender annual
Height To 12 in (30 cm).
Spread To 12 in (30 cm).
Flowers Yellow, orange, or bronze, often bicolor, with five square-ended petals, terminal.
Flowering Summer.
Foliage Dark green, deeply divided, aromatic.
Natural habitat Cultivated ground and wasteland. Native of Mexico.
Soil Well-drained loam.
Site Full sun.
Propagation Sow seeds in spring.
Uses Companion plant; potpourri.
Family Compositae (daisy family).
Other varieties and species *T. patula* 'Cinnabar'; *T. erecta*; *T. lucida*; *T. minuta*; *T. tenuifolia* 'Lemon Gem'; *T. t.* 'Tangerine Gem.'

Tanacetum coccineum

Persian Pyrethrum

THIS PICTURESQUE garden flower was, until the introduction of *C. cinerariifolium*, an important crop plant grown for the production of pyrethrum insecticide.

Also called painted daisy, Persian pyrethrum comes in a range of pinks and reds that are colorful to grow in a border among gray-leaved herbs like artemisias and lavender.

Persian pyrethrum is an effective, safe insecticide. Collect the fully developed flower buds when dry, dry them out of the sun until crisp, then powder them and store in sealed containers. This insecticide is not toxic to animals and humans, but is lethal to insects. Another advantage is that its toxic power breaks down rapidly in the sun. Use after sundown when beneficial insects, such as bees and hover flies, have stopped flying.

Perennial Zone 5
Height 24 in (60 cm).
Spread 18 in (45 cm).
Flowers Magenta-pink, daisylike, with a yellow center, solitary on a fine stem, aromatic.
Flowering Early to late summer.
Foliage Dark green, finely divided, feathery.
Natural habitat Mountain slopes. Native of Iran and the Caucasus.
Soil Well-drained or sandy loam.
Site Full sun.
Propagation Sow seeds in spring or fall.
Uses Insecticide.
Family Compositae (daisy family).
Other varieties and species
Chrysanthemum balsamita; *C. cinerariifolium*; *C. parthenium*; *Tanacetum coccineum* 'Brenda'; *T. c.* 'Eileen May Robinson'; *T. c.* 'James Kelway'; *T. vulgare*.

Tanacetum vulgare var. *crispum*

Crisp Tansy

CRISP OR FERN-LEAVED tansy, an old cottage-garden herb, is one of the best herbaceous foliage plants. Allow tansy to form clumps in the border or woodland edge. It withstands periods of drought, and dislikes wet soils. Cut the plant down to the base when the leaves lose their freshness.

Tansy has long been valued as an insecticide; it was used as a strewing herb. It is valued medicinally for expelling intestinal worms and to treat scabies. In Britain, tansy cakes and pudding were traditional at Easter. The flowers and leaves yield yellow and green dyes for wool.

Perennial Zone 4
Height To 4 ft (1.2 m).
Spread 3 ft (90 cm).
Flowers Yellow, buttonlike, in a flat-topped, terminal corymb.
Flowering Late summer.
Foliage Dark green, fernlike, with crisped edges, much divided into many pairs of deeply pinnatified leaflets with serrated edges, very aromatic.
Natural habitat Wasteland, wood clearings, and roadsides. Native of Europe and Asia. Naturalized in North America.
Soil Most soils, but rich loam preferred.
Site Full sun or partial shade.
Propagation Divide in spring or fall; sow wild tansy seed in spring or fall.
Uses Culinary; medicinal; insecticide; dye plant.
Family Compositae (daisy family).
Other varieties and species
T. vulgare; *T. v.* var. *crispum* 'Isla Gold'; *T. v.* var. *c.* 'Silver Lace'; *T. coccineum*.

Warning
This plant is potentially toxic.

Teucrium chamaedrys

Wall Germander

WALL GERMANDER is a sprawling plant that produces a delightful mat of bright green, glossy foliage. In summer it is covered with purple-pink flowers much visited by bees. An herb from dry, hot situations, it is ideal in a rock garden, gravel bed, or on walls. It has a spreading rootstock.

Traditionally germander was used as an evergreen edging plant for formal herb and knot gardens, since its growth is dense and it can be closely clipped. It is said that George Washington loved the plant and introduced it to Mount Vernon.

Germander is an ingredient of various liqueurs and tonic wines. Medicinally it has been valued for treating indigestion and gallbladder disorders but is little used today.

Perennial evergreen Zones 5–9
Height To 12 in (30 cm).
Spread 2 ft (60 cm).
Flowers Rose to purple, dotted red, two lipped, in whorls in the leaf axils.
Flowering Summer.
Foliage Bright green, shiny, paler underneath, opposite, stalked, oval, with serrated edges like a very small oak leaf.
Natural habitat Dry thickets, rocky terrain, old walls on chalk. Native of Europe and southwest Asia. Naturalized in North America; widely introduced.
Soil Sharply drained, alkaline.
Site Full sun.
Propagation Divide in fall; take cuttings in spring and summer; sow seeds in spring.
Uses Liqueurs; bee plant; medicinal.
Family Labiatae (mint family).
Other varieties and species
T. chamaedrys 'Nanum'; *T. c.* 'Rose Carpet'; *T. c.* 'Variegatum'; *T. canadense*; *T. fruticans*.

Thymus
Thyme

Thymus vulgaris
Common thyme

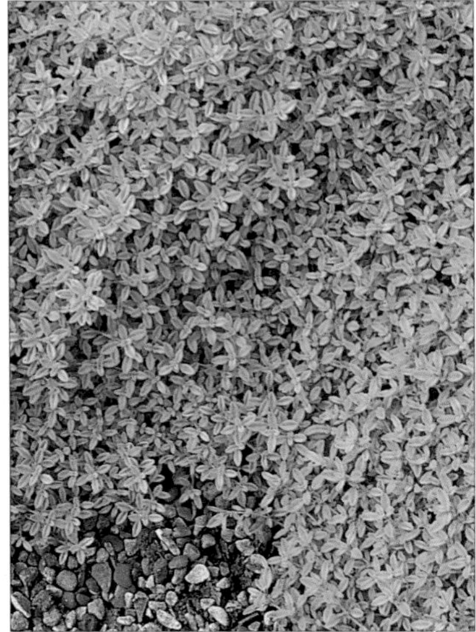

Thymus x *citriodorus aureas*
Golden thyme

Thymus serpyllum var. *coccineus*

Thymus serpyllum
'Pink Chintz'

There are innumerable species and varieties of this popular and useful herb. There are the thymes scented of lemon, caraway, pine, orange, and other fragrances; bushy and creeping thymes, and those that form a decorative mound. Flower colors vary from white to pale and rich pink, purple, and deep red-purple. The small foliage is always attractive and comes in a variety of colors, scents, and textures: gray- and woolly-leaved, gold, and all shades of green with gold or silver variegations.

A "lawn" composed of carpeting thymes of mixed colors and textures looks spectacular in bloom. Thymes will cascade over a low wall and if planted between paving slabs, they will spread and soften the edges.

Thymes thrive in extremely dry conditions, most preferring a gritty or gravelly soil. Surround creeping thymes with a layer of sand, gravel, or small stones placed on the soil's surface so that the mat of leaves is kept dry and clean.

The many creeping thyme varieties can be easily propagated by division. Most of the "decorative" thymes do not produce seed or do not come true from seed. Lightly trim back bushy thymes after they have flowered.

T. vulgaris is the main culinary thyme, but *T. pulegioïdes* is a good substitute. It is a popular seasoning for meat, fish, and vegetable dishes; an ingredient of *bouquet garni* and is used in Creole and Cajun cooking. *T. herba-barona* (caraway thyme) is a traditional flavoring for beef. Thyme honey is very popular. The herb is also used to flavor Benedictine liqueur.

Medicinally thyme is valuable as a strong antiseptic. Kept among linens, the herb is an insect repellent and is also widely used as an aromatic for colognes, aftershaves, and soaps.

Perennial subshrub Zones 5–9
Height To 12 in (30 cm).
Spread 12 in (30 cm).
Flowers Lilac to white, tiny, two lipped, in dense or loose terminal inflorescences.
Flowering Early summer.
Foliage Gray-green, with pale underside, small, linear, opposite, highly aromatic.
Natural habitat Rocky hillsides and dry, chalky slopes. Native of the western Mediterranean and southern Italy.
Soil Well-drained, alkaline, sandy or gritty loam.
Site Full sun.
Propagation Sow seeds in spring; take greenwood cuttings in spring or summer.
Uses Culinary; liqueur; medicinal; household; cosmetic; bee plant.
Family Labiatae (mint family).
Other varieties and species Upright, bushy: *T. vulgaris albus*; *T. v. aureus*; *T.* x *citriodorus*; *T.* x *c.* 'Silver Posie'; *T.* x *c.* 'Archer's Gold'; *T. erectus*; *T. fragrantissimus*; *T. odoratissimus*. Spreading, creeping: *T. azoricus*; *T. caespititius*; *T. doerfleri* 'Bressingham Pink'; *T.* 'Doone Valley'; *T. herba-barona*; *T. praecox* subsp. *arcticus*; *T. p.* 'Porlock'; *T. pseudolanuginosus*; *T. pulegioïdes*; *T. serpyllum*; *T. s. albus*; *T. s.* 'Annie Hall'; *T. s.* var. *coccineus* 'Major' and 'Minor'; *T. s.* 'Elfin'; *T. s.* 'Lemon Curd'; *T. s.* 'Pink Chintz'; *T. s.* 'Russetings'; *T. s.* 'Snowdrift.'

Trillium erectum

Birthroot

BIRTHROOT IS ALSO known as purple trillium, bethroot, and Indian balm. All the trilliums are native to North American woodlands. This beautiful, graceful plant is slow to establish and requires the appropriate conditions of shade, moisture, and rich woodland-type soil to thrive.

A shady area covered in a variety of trilliums mixed with other woodland plants is a lovely sight. Birthroot is also suitable for a shady rock garden in areas that have summer rainfall.

An old medicinal herb, birthroot was used by the Indians as well as by the settlers. It was considered an aphrodisiac and is an antispasmodic, tonic, and expectorant made from a decoction of dried rhizome.

Perennial Zone 4
Height To 18 in (45 cm).
Spread 18 in (45 cm).
Flowers Red-brown, triangular, three petaled and three sepaled, solitary, followed by pink or red berries.
Flowering Late spring to early summer.
Foliage Large, triangular, pointed, prominently veined, three in a single whorl just beneath the flower.
Natural habitat Moist, rich woods. Native of North America.
Soil Humus-rich, moist to moisture-retentive loam, neutral to acid.
Site Shade or partial shade.
Propagation Sow fresh seeds in summer in moist shade; divide roots in late summer to fall.
Uses Medicinal.
Family Liliaceae (lily family).
Other varieties and species
T. erectum albiflorum; *T. e. luteum*; *T. chloropetalum*; *T. grandiflorum*; *T. g.* 'Flore Pleno'; *T. nivale*; *T. sessile*.

Tropaeolum majus

Nasturtium

THE NASTURTIUM, or Indian cress, is among the brightest and most colorful of garden flowers. This decorative herb makes an excellent companion plant for the vegetable garden (see page 40). The dwarf form looks attractive around shrubs, in the border, or in a container.

The vivid flowers make a colorful decoration for green salads, and the leaves add a peppery flavor. The seeds can be pickled when still green. The nasturtium also has some medicinal properties. The seeds are antibacterial and an infusion of the leaves is used to treat infections of the genito-urinary tract and bronchitis.

Tender annual/perennial Zones 8–10
Height To 12 in (30 cm).
Spread To 18 in (45 cm).
Flowers Red, orange, yellow, and cream, funnel shaped, spurred, followed by fat seeds in threes.
Flowering Summer.
Foliage Medium to dark green, succulent, glossy above, pale beneath, unevenly circular, with radiating veins, borne on slender stems.
Natural habitat Scrub, wasteland, and wood margins. Native of South America.
Soil Dry to moisture-retaining loam.
Site Full sun and partial shade.
Propagation Sow seeds in spring.
Uses Culinary; medicinal.
Family Tropaeolaceae (nasturtium family).
Other varieties and species *T. majus* 'Alaska'; *T. m.* 'Empress of India'; *T. m* 'Jewel'; *T. m.* 'Tom Thumb.' Climbing, trailing: *T. m.* 'Gleam'; *T. tuberosum*.

Valeriana officinalis

Valerian

VALERIAN, ALSO known as all-heal, is an old medicinal plant whose use dates back to the 10th century.

It is very ornamental, with masses of frothy pink flowers and attractive foliage, and looks its best planted near water, alongside other herbs from a similar habitat (see page 61). Valerian will spread and form a large clump in time. It self-seeds to a limited extent.

Medicinally valerian is used as a herbal tranquilizer to treat insomnia, hypertension, nervous exhaustion, and anxiety. Herbal preparations that contain valerian are widely favored in Europe. In the U.S., however, this natural medicine is prohibited.

The native American valerian (*Cypripedium calceolus*), a species of orchid, has medicinal properties that are similar to those of *V. officinalis*.

Perennial Zone 4
Height To 5 ft (1.5 m).
Spread 3 ft (90 cm).
Flowers Pink to white, small, tubular, in large, terminal inflorescences, frothy looking when fully open, scented.
Flowering Summer to fall.
Foliage Dark green, opposite, pinnate, with leaflets, narrow, lanceolate, toothed.
Natural habitat Riversides, wet meadows, and moist woodland. Native of Europe and western Asia. Naturalized in North America.
Soil Fertile, moist to moisture-retaining loam.
Site Sun or partial shade.
Propagation Sow seeds in spring; divide roots in spring or fall.
Uses Medicinal.
Family Valerianaceae (valerian family).
Other varieties and species
V. officinalis subsp. *sambucifolia*; *V. dioica*; *V. edulis*; *V. montana*; *V. phu*; *V. sitchensis*.

Verbascum thapsus

Great Mullein

THE GREAT MULLEIN has many local names, including flannel plant, Aaron's rod, and donkey's ears. The long dried flower stems were once dipped in tallow and lit as torches. Poor country children placed the felted leaves in their shoes to keep their feet warm.

Grow this striking plant alone, or give it space and allow it to self-seed. Many mulleins that grow wild in Europe have great ornamental value for the gardener, and are easy to raise from seed. The leaves are frequently eaten by the mullein moth caterpillar; pick these off by hand.

Medicinally great mullein is used mainly to treat respiratory disorders and is also analgesic and antiseptic. The flowers yield a yellow dye.

Biennial Zone 5
Height To 6 ft (1.8 m).
Spread To 30 in (75 cm).
Flowers Bright yellow, with five rounded petals, borne in clusters on dense erect spikes.
Flowering Summer.
Foliage Gray-green, woolly, soft to touch, ovate to spoon shaped, faintly scented, basal leaves very large, stemmed and in rosettes, upper leaves stalkless; smaller.
Natural habitat Wasteland, wood clearings, and stony or chalky well-drained ground. Native of Eurasia, but widely naturalized in North America.
Soil Most well-drained or sandy soils.
Site Full sun.
Propagation Sow seeds when ripe or in spring.
Uses Dye plant; medicinal.
Family Scrophulariaceae (figwort family).
Other varieties and species *V. bombyciferum*; *V. chaixii*; *V. nigrum*; *V. olympicum*; *V. phlomoïdes*; *V. phoeniceum*.

Verbena hastata

Blue Vervain

BLUE VERVAIN, also known as wild hyssop, and simpler's joy, is much showier than *V. officinalis*. The charm of verbenas is their very thin, spiky flower stems, which in the case of some species, such as *V. hastata*, form a candelabralike head. The flowers open on a small length of the stems at a time and, although brightly colored, they are never overpowering.

Blue vervain thrives in a variety of soils and withstands intermittent dryness in summer. Plant in a good-size clump to obtain the best and longest effect of flowering.

It was a medicinal plant of North America, employed by the Indians to treat colds, coughs, and fevers – the root being most valuable. The leaves provided a tonic tea for women.

Perennial Zone 5
Height 2–4 ft (60 cm–1.2 m).
Spread 18 in (45 cm).
Flowers Blue-violet, in whorls on candelabralike spikes.
Flowering Summer.
Foliage Narrow, lance shaped, and sharp toothed.
Natural habitat Fields and thickets. Native of North America.
Soil Well drained, rich, moisture retaining to dry.
Site Sun.
Propagation Sow seeds in spring; self-seeds.
Uses Formerly medicinal.
Family Verbenaceae (verbena family).
Other varieties and species *V. hastata* 'Alba'; *V. h.* 'Rosea'; *V. canadensis*; *V. officinalis*; *V. peruviana*.

Vinca major

Greater Periwinkle

GREATER PERIWINKLE is a vigorous plant with many long arching stems growing from the root. The clear blue flowers are sparse, but against the dark backdrop of foliage appear jewellike. There are numerous beautiful varieties with different-colored, even double, flowers and variegated or gold foliage.

This is a plant for dense ground cover in a woodland site, under a thick natural hedgerow, among shrubs, or on a shady bank. Periwinkle thrives in dry conditions.

Periwinkle has many medicinal uses, including as a styptic, to reduce blood pressure, as a tonic, and to treat catarrh. Greater periwinkle was once considered a magic plant and was used for making love potions.

Perennial evergreen Zone 5
Height 1–3 ft (30–90 cm).
Spread Trailing to 5 ft (1.5 m).
Flowers Purple-blue to pale blue, five-petaled, solitary, growing on a stalk from leaf axils.
Flowering Late spring to early summer.
Foliage Dark green, shiny, ovate, short stemmed, opposite, widely spaced.
Natural habitat Mixed woodland. Native of Europe.
Soil Well-drained calcareous loam.
Site Shade or partial shade.
Propagation Divide in early spring; take greenwood cuttings in fall (stems root at the tip).
Uses Medicinal.
Family Apocynaceae (periwinkle family).
Other varieties and species *V. major* var. *alba* 'Variegata'; *V. minor*; *V. m.* 'Atropurpurea'; *V. m.* 'Pleno'; *V. rosea*.

Viola odorata

Sweet Violet

THIS LOVELY HERB has always been the harbinger of spring. The scented sweet violet was cultivated commercially in ancient times; the Greeks used the flower as the symbol of Athens. William Shakespeare loved the violet and referred to it on many occasions in his plays and sonnets; it is immortalized in the lines from *A Midsummer Night's Dream*: "I know a bank whereon the wild thyme blows, where oxlips and the nodding violet grows." For centuries bunches of violets were sold on the streets of London, and violet scent was long the most popular perfume.

Every garden, however small it is, should have sweet violets growing in some shady corner, perhaps around a tree, among shrubs, or at the edge of woodland where there is shade during the hottest part of the day. Violets will also establish themselves in short grass. They need some moisture and enjoy a woodland-type soil with plenty of leaf mold. A few plants will soon spread in suitable conditions. Sweet violets look best growing with other wild woodland herbs, such as primroses, oxlips, hellebores, wild strawberries, and lungwort. Grow violets in earthenware containers, which can be brought into the house in winter and placed on a windowsill.

Medicinally sweet violet is valued for its soothing expectorant properties in the treatment of respiratory disorders, including bronchitis. It alleviates and cools hot swellings, and is also mildly sedative. The flowers are extensively used in perfumery. In Britain the flowers were cooked with meat and game and can be candied.

Perennial Zones 5–8.
Height To 6 in (15 cm). Spreading.
Flowers Violet, white, or pink, distinctive, five petaled, spurred, sweetly scented.
Flowering Spring.
Foliage Dark green, glossy, downy, oval to kidney shaped, bluntly toothed, on short stalks.
Natural habitat Shady woodland, wood clearings, hedgerows. Native of Europe, North Africa, and Asia.
Soil Moisture retaining to moist, humus rich, alkaline.
Site Shade or partial shade.
Propagation Sow seeds in fall (stratify); divide in late winter or early spring.
Uses Perfume; medicinal; culinary.
Family Violaceae (violet family).
Other varieties and species
V. odorata 'Alba'; *V. o.* 'Alba Plena'; *V.* 'Admiral Avallon'; *V. canadensis*; *V.* 'Coeur d'Alsace'; *V. cornuta*; *V. cucullata*; *V.* 'Czar'; *V. elatior*; *V.* 'Freckles'; *V. gracilis*; *V. labradorica*; *V.* 'Opera'; *V. palmata*; *V.* 'Princess of Wales'; *V.* 'Queen Charlotte'; *V. rupestris*; *V. septentrionalis*; *V. sororia*; *V. tricolor*.

Viola tricolor

Heartsease

HEARTSEASE, or Johnny-jump-up, is a delightful wildflower that blooms continuously all summer and well into the fall. It readily cross-pollinates with other violas to produce a wide range of color combinations. Hundreds of varieties of violas and violettas are available from specialized growers and suppliers.

Heartsease self-seeds everywhere. It will thrive in the rock garden, in gravelly or sandy areas, and in a border or even a formal herb garden. It enjoys hot sun.

Medicinally it was used as a blood purifier, for fevers, as a gargle, and to treat ulcers and sores. It is fed to racing pigeons as a tonic and blood purifier. The dainty little blooms can be sprinkled on green salads.

Annual
Height 4–12 in (10–30 cm).
Spread To 8 in (20 cm).
Flowers Yellow, blue-violet, and white, small, flat faced, pansylike, scented, on straight stems from the leaf axils.
Flowering Spring, summer, and fall.
Foliage Dark green, toothed, elongated, lance shaped, comprised of three leaflets.
Natural habitat Waste ground and cultivated fields. Native of Europe, naturalized in North America and elsewhere.
Soil Fertile to sandy loam.
Site Full sun.
Propagation Sow seeds in spring or late summer; take cuttings in summer; self-seeds.
Uses Formerly medicinal; culinary.
Family Violaceae (violet family).
Other varieties and species *V. tricolor* subsp. *curtisii*; *V. t.* subsp. *macedonica*; *V. t.* 'Bowles' Black'; and many other named varieties: *V. cornuta*; *V. lutea*.

Yucca filamentosa

Yucca

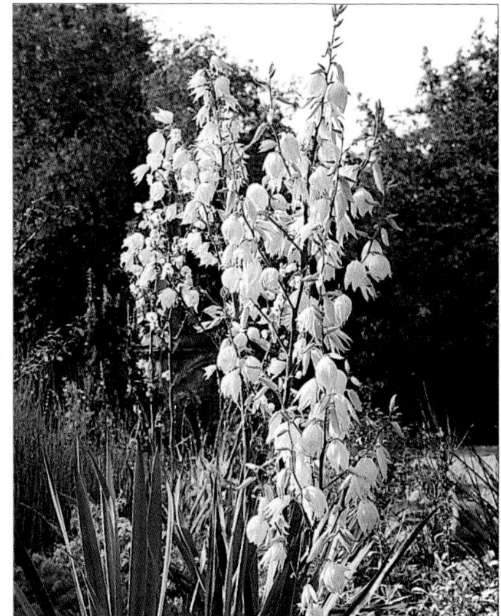

YUCCA, OR ADAM'S needle, an exotic-looking desert plant, enjoys heat and dry stony soil but will not survive persistent damp in winter. Given its preferred conditions, the plant will live to a great age. The tall flower spikes look spectacular; grow them as architectural features. Cut back flower spikes hard when the flowers are over to encourage new leaves.

Yucca has many uses. The leaves make a strong fiber, and the roots contain saponin used in shampoos and natural soaps. The fruits provided food for North American Indians, who also used the roots in poultices for skin diseases, sprains, and sores.

Perennial Zone 5
Height To 9 ft (2.7 m).
Spread 5 ft (1.5 m).
Flowers White, waxen, large, bell shaped, pendulous, on tall panicles.
Flowering Summer.
Foliage Dark green, glaucous, long, pointed, swordlike; forming a large basal rosette with fraying twisted threads on the leaf margins.
Natural habitat Dry, rocky, or sandy ground. Native of the southeastern U.S.
Soil Well drained, alkaline, stony or sandy.
Site Full sun.
Propagation Take root cuttings, divide roots, or sow seeds in spring.
Uses Medicinal, culinary, household.
Family Liliaceae (lily family).
Other varieties and species *Y. filamentosa* 'Bright Edge'; *Y. f.* 'Elegantissima'; *Y. f.* 'Variegata'; and other selections: *Y. glauca*.

Zanthoxylum piperitum

Japan Pepper

JAPAN PEPPER, also known as sansho, is a graceful, spiny shrub or small tree. It thrives in full sun or partial shade, although in hot climates it does best in shade. Both male and female forms are needed to produce the edible fruits. To keep the tree compact, prune it lightly in the first year in fall and regularly thereafter.

In Japan the berries, flowers, and leaves of the pepper are valued as a flavoring ingredient for spices. Young fruits and spring leaves are used with vinegar, tofu, and miso (soya bean paste), and in soup. In China the dried seedless berries with a wood spicy flavor, called Fagara or Sichuan pepper, are used as a condiment. Medicinally the plant is valuable for treating digestive disorders.

Perennial shrub or tree Zone 5
Height To 10 ft (3 m).
Spread To 8 ft (2.4 m).
Flowers Greenish-yellow, tiny, in axillary clusters followed by red fruits.
Flowering Spring.
Foliage Medium glossy, composed of many leaflets with spine at the base of leafstalk; faintly aromatic.
Natural habitat Woodlands and mountains. Native of the Far East.
Soil Humus-rich, moisture-retaining loam to well-drained sandy loam.
Site Full sun or partial shade.
Propagation Sow fresh seeds in fall (stratify); take root cuttings in late winter; greenwood cuttings in early summer.
Uses Culinary; medicinal.
Family Rutaceae (rue family).
Other varieties and species *Z. piperitum* var. *brevispinosume*; *Z. p.* var. *inerme*; *Z. americanum*; *Z. clava-herculis*; *Z. simulans*.

Plant Hardiness Zones

PLANT HARDINESS ZONES are determined by the average number of annual frost free days and the minimum winter temperatures. They indicate the lowest winter temperature that a plant is likely to survive. Most herbs will tolerate a maximum temperature of about 96°F (35°C).

The zone for each perennial or biennial plant is given in the "Herb Directory" (pages 100-77). Annual plants are not given a zone reference as they complete their growing cycle within one season. The zone gives an indication of the plant's tolerance but it is important to bear in mind other influential factors such as rainfall, wind, and altitude. There may be many variations within the zone created by local conditions. These microclimates can also be created in the garden where there is shelter from icy winds, or shade from intense sun, for example.

Most European herbs grow in zones 6, 7, and 8 but there are many that will survive colder zones with special care. In the North American prairies covered by zones 2 and 3, conditions are often very harsh and many perennial herbs from the Mediterranean region will have to be treated as annuals, or brought inside over the hard winter.

Herbs are surprisingly adaptable. It is worth experimenting using the zones as a rough guide.

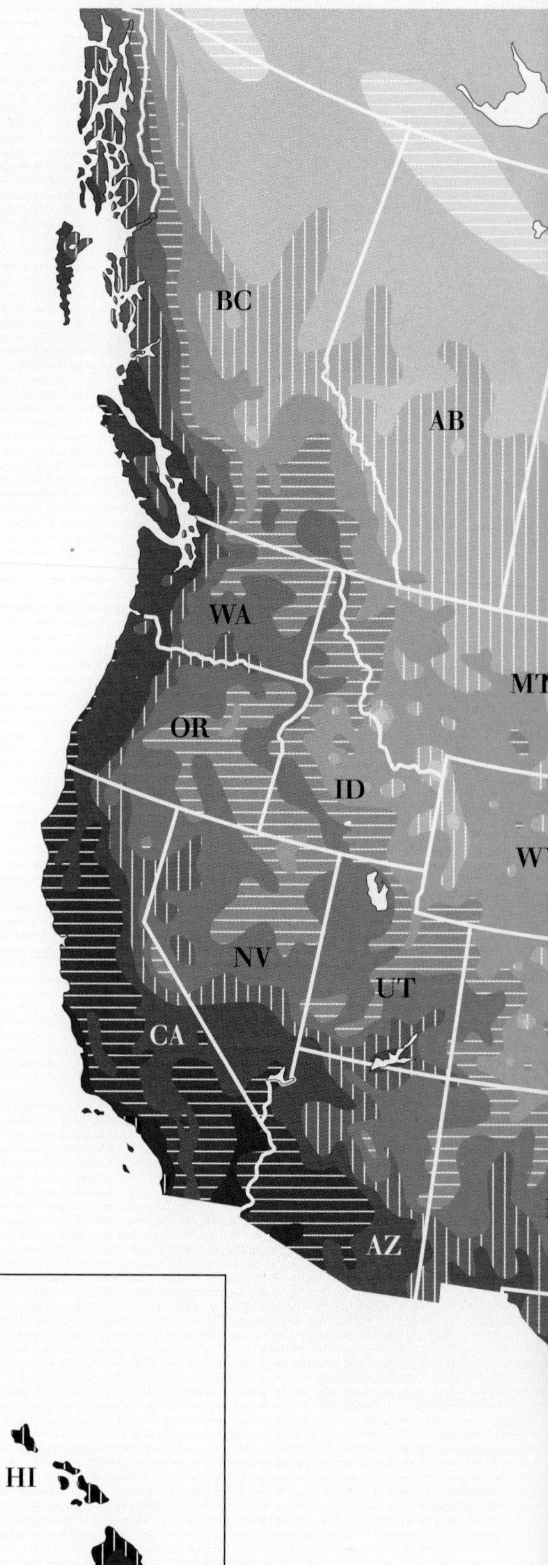

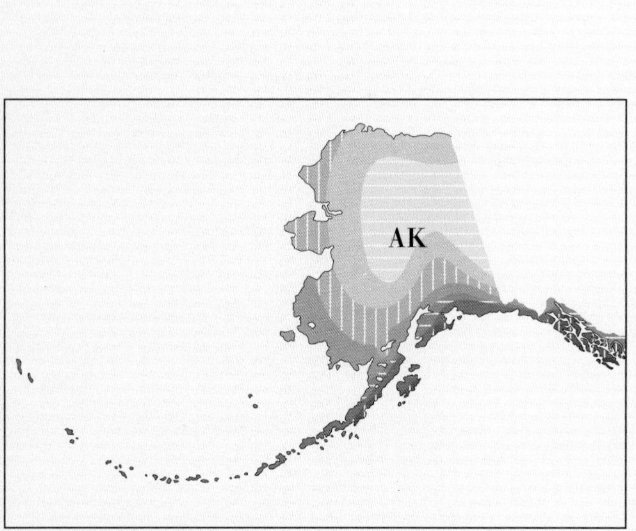

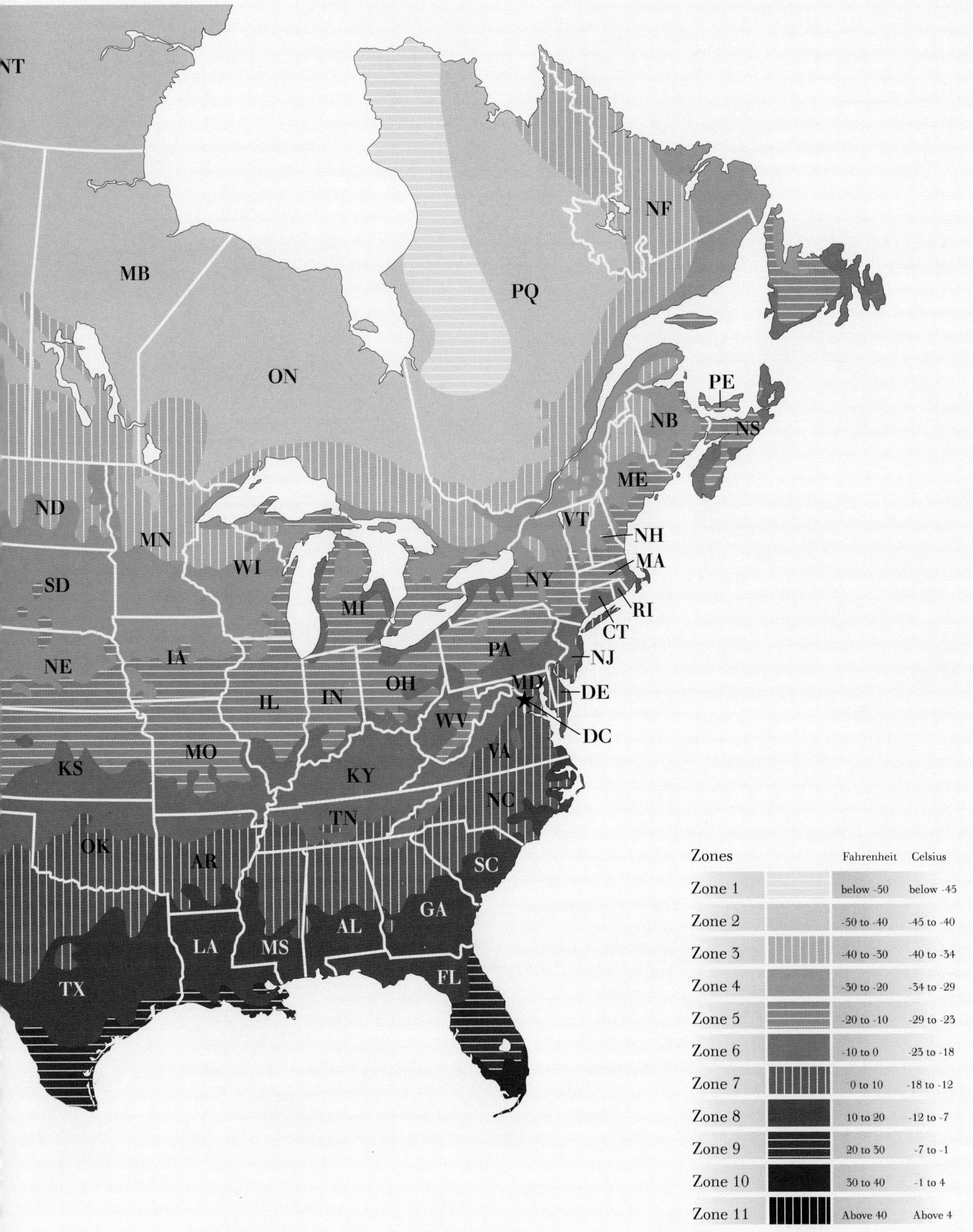
NT
MB
ON
PQ
NF
PE
NB
NS
ME
VT
NH
MA
NY
RI
CT
NJ
PA
DE
MD
DC
ND
MN
SD
WI
MI
NE
IA
IL
IN
OH
WV
VA
KS
MO
KY
NC
TN
OK
AR
SC
GA
AL
MS
LA
TX
FL
Zones Fahrenheit Celsius
Zone 1 below -50 below -45
Zone 2 -50 to -40 -45 to -40
Zone 3 -40 to -30 -40 to -34
Zone 4 -30 to -20 -34 to -29
Zone 5 -20 to -10 -29 to -23
Zone 6 -10 to 0 -23 to -18
Zone 7 0 to 10 -18 to -12
Zone 8 10 to 20 -12 to -7
Zone 9 20 to 30 -7 to -1
Zone 10 30 to 40 -1 to 4
Zone 11 Above 40 Above 4

Glossary

acid soil Soil with a **pH** below 7.

alkaline soil Soil with a **pH** above 7.

alternate leaves Borne singly at each node alternating up the stem

annual A plant that completes its growing cycle – from **germination** to flowering, setting seed, and dying – in one growing season, usually between early spring and late summer. (See also **biennial** and **perennial**.)

aromatherapy The use of plants' **essential oils** for healing and the maintenance of vitality.

axil The upper angle formed between the leaf or flower stalk and the stem.

Bach's remedies A system of natural healing developed by Dr. Edward Bach, a homeopathic doctor and Harley Street physician in the 1920s and 1930s in Britain. The remedies are prepared from wildflowers, shrubs, and trees and are used to treat the state of mind, restoring equilibrium and harmony.

biennial A plant that requires two growing seasons to flower and produce seed, after which it usually dies. (See also **annual** and **perennial**.)

broadcasting Sowing seed by scattering freely by hand over the planting area.

bud An embryonic growth on a stem or shoot that grows into a leaf or flower.

bulb A storage organ consisting mainly of fleshy scales and swollen modified leaf bases that enclose the following year's growth **buds**. Usually formed underground.

bulbil Small **bulbs** or bulblike growths found in the leaf **axils** or in place of flowers in the **inflorescence**. May be used for **propagation**.

capsule A dry fruit that splits open when ripe to release its seeds.

climber Upward- and outward-growing plants that use other plants or objects as supports. Their stems are usually lax and the plant will creep along the ground in the absence of something to grow up.

compost A crumbly soillike substance produced by the breaking down of a variety of organic wastes by bacterial action. Used as a natural fertilizer and soil improver.

compound leaves Two or more leaflets arranged on a thin leaf stalk.

coppice To cut back shrubs or small trees to ground or near ground level, either annually or at regular intervals, to encourage new, straight growth.

corm Underground storage organ consisting mainly of a swollen stem base. It is similar to a **bulb** but is in one piece, without scales or layers. It is **annual**: the next year's corm forms from a **bud** close to the original corm.

corymb An **umbel**-like **inflorescence**, with a flat-topped flower cluster, and flower stalks coming from different points up the stem.

crown Found at the base of a **herbaceous** plant, where the roots and stem join. Herbaceous plants die down to the crown in winter to re-emerge in spring.

Culpeper Nicholas Culpeper was a late 17th-century popular herbalist and astrologer who published his best-selling herbal, *The English Physician*, in 1652.

cutting A length of stem taken from the parent plant in order to **propagate** a new plant.

cyme A flower cluster in which the terminal flower is the first to open followed in succession by lateral flowers that grow from **axils** lower down the flowering stalk.

division A method of **propagation** that involves splitting up a plant clump while **dormant** into smaller pieces, each with a portion of roots and shoots, or dormant **buds**, attached.

Doctrine of Signatures A theory developed by the Swiss physician Paracelsus in the 15th century and promoted by **Culpeper**, which suggested that God had created plants with markings to indicate their medicinal use.

dormancy A short or extended period when a seed is alive but unable to germinate. Dormancy can last for many years.

essential oils Highly concentrated, volatile and aromatic liquids extracted from a single species or botanical form that are used in cosmetics and perfumes, as flavoring agents, in pharmaceutical preparations, and extensively in **aromatherapy**.

evergreen Plant that retains its leaves at the end of the growing season but sheds older leaves through the year.

family A group of plants contained in several related genera (or occasionally a single **genus**). Classification is based on flower structure, fruits (seeds), stems, and leaf arrangements.

fibrous roots Fine, dense, and multi-branched roots, often forming a thick matted mass.

flower Contains the reproductive organs of a plant. Usually consists of petals, surrounded by sepals.

flower head A mass of small flowers that appear as one **flower**.

genus A distinct group within a **family** of plants with shared characteristics, but which are not necessarily similar in appearance, e.g. *Salvia* (sage). Each genus is subdivided into **species**.

Gerard's Herbal The *Generall Historie of Plants*, produced by the eminent Elizabethan herbalist and gardener John Gerard, in 1597.

germination The sprouting of a seed into a seedling.

greenwood The stage of soft growth on the new shoots of a woody plant between **softwood** and **semiripe shoots**. See **cutting.**

habitat The natural home of a plant with specific growing conditions.

half hardy A plant that does not tolerate persistent frost but withstands temperatures down to freezing.

hardening off Acclimatizing plants that have been raised in a greenhouse or cold frame to cooler conditions by placing them outside for increasing lengths of time over a period of a week or more before planting them out.

hardwood By the end of the growing season, **semiripe** shoots on woody plants have matured with tough, fibrous hardwood stems.

hardy A plant that is tolerant of year-round climatic conditions in temperate climates, including frost without protection.

heel cutting A cutting that leaves a small portion of old wood at the base of the stem.

herbaceous A plant with nonwoody stems that dies down to a **rootstock** at the end of the growing season.

homeopathy A system of holistic medicine developed by the German physician Samuel Hahnemann in the early 19th century.

humus Dark colored, partially decomposed organic matter in the top few inches of the soil. Improves the fertility and water-holding capacity.

hybrid The offspring of genetically different parents usually produced artificially in cultivation, but occasionally in the wild.

inflorescence The arrangement of flowers on a stem. Examples include **panicles** and **racemes**.

layering The method of **propagation** in which a stem is induced to form roots, so creating a separate plant. Woody plants can be persuaded to root by pinning their stems to the soil. Once roots have formed, the stem is severed from the parent plant.

leaf mold A **humus**-rich, fibrous, flaky material, the end product of decaying leaves. It is used as a soil improver.

lime Compounds of calcium. The lime content of soil determines its **pH**.

micro-climate A comparatively small area experiencing different climatic conditions to those locally prevalent. Usually found where there is protection from the weather. Can be created by land contours, humanmade structures, hedges, trees, and even a group of plants.

mulch A layer of material added to the surface of the soil. Mulches can be used to improve fertility, to retain moisture, and to suppress weeds.

naturalized Plants established in the wild that are of foreign origin or those that grow in a natural situation without any need for maintenance and increase of their own accord.

nematode A microscopic worm. Although some are useful in the garden in breaking down vegetable matter, others may cause damage by burrowing into and eating the roots, leaves, or flowers of plants.

node The point on a stem from which a leaf or leaves arise.

opposite leaves Leaves that are positioned at the same level on either side of the stem. (See also **alternate leaves**.)

overwinter To keep a plant in a sheltered place through winter.

pan (of soil) A layer of soil that has become tightly packed through over-cultivation or heavy rain, hampering root growth and preventing free drainage of water. They also form naturally on some clay soils.

panicle A branched **raceme**; flowers develop on stalks from the main stem.

perennial A plant that lives for more than two seasons. (See also **annual** and **biennial**.)

pH The measure of acidity or alkalinity on a scale from 1 to 14. In horticulture, lower numbers indicate **acid soil** while higher numbers indicate **alkaline soil**; pH 7 is neutral.

propagation The means by which plants are reproduced. Methods include **cuttings**, **division**, **layering**, and sowing seeds.

pruning Method of cutting back a stem, particularly a woody stem, of a shrub or tree.

puddled clay A mixture of compacted wet clay and straw that is impervious to water and is used to line and seal ponds.

raceme An unbranched, usually elongated **inflorescence**. Flowers open in sequence from the bottom upward.

repot To transfer a seedling from a seed tray or flat into an individual pot or a containerized plant into a larger pot.

rhizome An underground stem that acts as a storage organ for the plant. It may be swollen, usually grows horizontally, and is often creeping. Plant roots and stems grow from the rhizomes.

root cutting A method of **propagation** using a length of fleshy root that is planted vertically in the soil and will produce a growing shoot. Taken at the mid-point in the growing season.

rootstock The general root system of a plant.

rosette A group of leaves radiating from a single point.

runner Long, slender stem that spreads horizontally away from the parent plant. It roots at intervals and new plants arise at these **nodes**.

scarify To scratch the outer surface of a seed with a tough coat to enable water to penetrate the coat and so improve the chances of **germination**.

scree A deep layer of stone chippings and small rocks mixed with coarse sand and a small amount of loam, providing **sharp drainage**.

semiripe shoots Stems in late summer whose growth is becoming woody.

sharp drainage Good drainage required by many rock and alpine plants, especially in high rainfall areas. Provided by a special mix of soil, coarse sand, and small stones; naturally available in gravelly soil.

softwood The young immature stems produced during the first flush of spring growth.

species A group of closely related plants within a **genus** that resemble one another in important structural features and are capable of breeding with other plants of the same species.

stratify To expose moist seed to a period of cold in order to break **dormancy**.

strewing herbs Fragrant and often insect-repellent herbs that were spread over earth floors of old dwellings to mask unpleasant smells and deter insects and vermin.

subshrub A low-growing plant that is woody at the base but whose terminal shoots die back in winter.

subspecies A subdivision of a **species**.

sucker A strong shoot that arises in a mature plant at the base of the main stem, or from the root system below ground, and may appear at some distance from the parent plant.

tannin A plant substance with an astringent action. Used to cure animal skins (tanning) and fix dyes and in herbal medicine.

tender A plant that is unable to survive low temperatures and usually cultivated as an **annual** or grown in a sheltered environment such as a greenhouse or conservatory.

thin out The removal of some seedlings after **germination** to provide enough space for the others to grow.

tilth The fine crumbly surface layer of soil produced by cultivation.

transplant To move a plant from one setting to another.

umbel An **inflorescence** where the flowers are borne on stalks all arising from the same point at the top of the flowering stem. Umbels are usually flat-topped in appearance.

variegated Leaves, flowers, or bark marked with different colors.

variety (var.) A plant with a distinct and permanent variation to its type such as variation in flower color, habit of growth, or leaf.

Further Reading

GARDENING

Brickell, Christopher ed. *Royal Horticultural Society's Concise Encyclopedia of Gardening Techninques*. London: Chancellor Press, Reed Comsumer Books, 1993.

Caplan, Basil ed. *The Complete Manual of Organic Gardening*. London: Headline Book Publishing, 1990.

Chatto, Beth. *The Dry Garden*. London: J. M. Dent & Sons, 1993.

Chatto, Beth. *The Damp Garden*. London: J. M. Dent & Sons, 1990.

Hansen, Richard and Friedrich Stahl. *Perennials and their Garden Habitats*. Cambridge: Cambridge University Press, 1993. US edition: Beaventon, OR: Timber Press Inc, 1993.

Kublick, Lyn. *The Prairie Herb Garden*. Saskatchewan: Western Producer Prairie Books, 1996.

Phillips, Harry R. *Growing and Propagating Wild Flowers*. Chapel Hill, NC: The University of North Carolina Press, 1985.

Royal Horticultural Society. *The Plant Finder*. Whitbourne: Headmain, for Royal Horticultural Society, 1996, and updated annually.

Stevens, John. *The National Trust Book of Wild Flower Gardening*. London: Dorling Kindersley, 1994.

HERBS

Bremness, Lesley. *The Complete Book of Herbs*. London: Dorling Kindersley, 1988.

Kowalchick, Claire and William H. Hylton eds. *Rodale's Illustrated Encyclopedia of Herbs*. Pennsylvania: Rodale Press, 1987.

MEDICINAL

Foster, Steven and James A. Duke. *Peterson Field Guides. Medicinal Plants: Eastern and Central North America*. Boston: Houghton Mifflin Company, 1990.

Mabey, Richard ed. *The Complete New Herbal*. London: Penguin Books, 1991.

Magic and Medicine of Plants. Pleasantville, NY: Reader's Digest, 1986.

SPECIALIST

Buchanan, Rita. *A Dyer's Garden*. Loveland, CO: Interweave Press, 1995.

Casselman, Karen, L. *Craft of the Dyer*. New York: Dover Publications, 1993.

Goodwin, Jill. *A Dyer's Manual*. London: Pelham Books, 1982.

Williams, Betsy. *Potpourri and Fragrant Crafts*. Pleasantville, NY: Reader's Digest, 1996.

Uses for Herbs

The following lists suggest the most suitable herbs for a range of uses in both the garden and the home. You can incorporate them into an existing garden or plant an area specifically with herbs that have a similar use. See the "Herb Directory" (pages 100–77) for cultivation information.

ARCHITECTURAL HERBS

Add height and emphasis to planting designs; often visually stunning.

Acanthus mollis
Acanthus

Althaea rosea
Hollyhock

Angelica archangelica
Angelica

Atriplex hortensis var. *rubra*
Red orache

Cynara scolymus
Globe artichoke

Digitalis purpurea
Purple foxglove

Dipsacus fullonum
Teasel

Eupatorium purpureum
Joe-pye weed

Foeniculum vulgare
Fennel

Gentiana lutea
Yellow gentian

Helianthus annuus
Sunflower

Inula helenium
Elecampane

Lythrum salicaria
Purple loosestrife

Onopordum acanthium
Cotton thistle

Phytolacca americana
Pokeweed

Silybum marianum
Milk thistle

Verbascum thapsus
Great mullein

Yucca filamentosa
Yucca

AROMATIC CULINARY HERBS

Use either fresh or dried to flavor and garnish many culinary dishes.

Allium schoenoprasum
Chives

Allium tuberosum
Garlic chives

Anethum graveolens
Dill

Anthriscus cerefolium
Chervil

Artemisia dracunculus
French tarragon

Carum carvi
Caraway

Coriandrum sativum
Coriander (cilantro)

Laurus nobilis
Sweet bay

Levisticum officinale
Lovage

Mentha spicata
Spearmint

Meum athamanticum
Spignel

Nigella sativa
Fennel flower

Ocimum
Basil

Origanum
Oregano

Perilla frutescens
Perilla

Petroselinum
Parsley

Rosmarinus
Rosemary

Salvia officinalis
Common sage

Sanguisorba minor
Salad burnet

Satureja hortensis
Summer savory

Satureja montana
Winter savory

Thymus
Thyme

Zanthoxylum piperitum
Japan pepper

BEE AND BUTTERFLY HERBS

Attract bees for pollination and honey production, and also colorful butterflies in search of nectar.

Agastache foeniculum
Anise hyssop

Borago officinalis
Borage

Calendula officinalis
Pot marigold

Calluna vulgaris
Heather

Centaurea scabiosa
Greater knapweed

Cynara scolymus
Globe artichoke

Echinacea purpurea
Purple coneflower

Eupatorium cannabinum
Hemp agrimony

Eupatorium purpureum
Joe-pye weed

Hesperis matronalis
Sweet rocket

Hyssopus officinalis
Hyssop

Knautia arvensis
Field scabious

Lavandula
Lavender

Lythrum salicaria
Purple loosestrife

Nepeta mussinii
Catmint

Origanum
Oregano

Phacelia tanacetifolia
Phacelia

Pycnanthemum pilosum
Mountain mint

Rosmarinus
Rosemary

Salvia
Sage

Succisa pratensis
Devil's-bit scabious

Teucrium chamaedrys
Wall germander

Thymus
Thyme

Valeriana officinalis
Valerian

DRIED FLOWERS

Retain their varied colors and textures; make attractive flower arrangements.

Achillea millefolium
Yarrow

Allium tuberosum
Garlic chives

Amaranthus cruentus
Amaranth

Anthemis
Chamomile

Armeria maritima
Thrift

Artemisia
Artemisia

Calluna vulgaris
Heather

Centaurea cyanus
Cornflower

Chrysanthemum parthenium
Feverfew

Consolida ambigua
Larkspur

Dianthus
Pink

Lavandula
Lavender

Liatris spicata
Blazing star

Mentha
Mint

Monarda
Bergamot

Origanum
Oregano

Salvia sclarea
Clary sage

Santolina
Santolina

Verbena hastata
Blue vervain

DRIED SEED HEADS

Useful in fall and winter flower arrangements; also add interest to the garden over the winter.

Achillea millefolium
Yarrow

Allium schoenoprasum
Chives

Anethum graveolens
Dill

Angelica archangelica
Angelica

Atriplex hortensis var. *rubra*
Red orache

Carthamus tinctoria
Safflower

Centaurea scabiosa
Greater knapweed

Clematis vitalba
Travelers' joy

Cnicus benedictus
Blessed thistle

Cynara scolymus
Globe artichoke

Daucus carota
Wild carrot

Dipsacus fullonum
Teasel

Echinacea purpurea
Purple coneflower

Helianthus annuus
Sunflower

Humulus lupulus
Hop

Isatis tinctoria
Woad

Linum perenne
Perennial flax

Nigella sativa
Fennel flower

Oenothera biennis
Evening primrose

Papaver somniferum
Opium poppy

DYE HERBS

Produce a range of subtle, beautiful colors that can be used to dye natural fabrics, especially wool.

Angelica archangelica
Angelica

Anthemis tinctoria
Dyer's chamomile

Berberis vulgaris
Barberry

Calluna vulgaris
Heather

Carthamus tinctoria
Safflower

Convallaria majalis
Lily of the valley

Coreopsis tinctoria
Coreopsis

Cytisus scoparius
Broom

Daucus carota
Wild carrot

Eupatorium cannabinum
Hemp agrimony

Filipendula ulmaria
Meadowsweet

Foeniculum vulgare
Fennel

Galium verum
Lady's bedstraw

Genista tinctoria
Dyer's broom

Hemerocallis fulva
Daylily

Humulus lupulus
Hop

Hypericum perforatum
St. John's wort

Inula helenium
Elecampane

Iris pseudacorus
Yellow flag

Isatis tinctoria
Woad

Linaria vulgaris
Toadflax

Nymphaea alba
White water lily

Phytolacca americana
Pokeweed

Sambucus nigra
Elder

Sanguinaria canadensis
Bloodroot

Tanacetum vulgare var. *crispum*
Crisp tansy

EDIBLE FLOWERS

These herb flowers can be sprinkled on salads to add both flavor and unusual decoration.

Allium schoenoprasum
Chives

Allium tuberosum
Garlic chives

Bellis perennis
Daisy

Borago officinalis
Borage

Calendula officinalis
Pot marigold

Cardamine pratensis
Lady's smock

Cichorium intybus
Wild chicory

Dianthus caryophyllus
Clove pink

Jasminum
Jasmine

Lavandula
Lavender

Lonicera periclymenum
Wild honeysuckle

Malva moschata
Muskmallow

Oenothera biennis
Evening primrose

Ononis spinosa
Spiny restharrow

Origanum
Oregano

Pelargonium
Scented pelargonium

Rosmarinus
Rosemary

Salvia
Sage

Tropaeolum majus
Nasturtium

Viola tricolor
Heartsease

FOLIAGE PLANTS

Essential in mixed plantings, these herbs add interest, structure, and variety with a range of textures and colors.

Achillea millefolium
Yarrow

Ajuga reptans 'Atropurpurea' and *A.r.* 'Burgundy Glow'
Bugle

Alchemilla vulgaris
Lady's mantle

Althaea officinalis
Marsh mallow

Anthriscus cerefolium
Chervil

Artemisia
Artemisia

Atriplex hortensis var. *rubra*
Red orache

Chrysanthemum cinerariifolium
Pyrethrum

Foeniculum vulgare and *F.v.* 'Purpureum'
Green and bronze fennel

Galium verum
Lady's bedstraw

Helichrysum angustifolium
Curry plant

Lavandula
Lavender

Marrubium vulgare
Horehound

Melissa officinalis 'Aurea'
Golden lemon balm

Mentha suaveolens 'Variegata'
Variegated apple mint

Myrrhis odorata
Sweet cicely

Nepeta mussinii
Catmint

Origanum vulgare 'Aureum'
Gold and gold variegated marjoram

Perilla frutescens
Perilla

Polemonium caeruleum
Jacob's ladder

Pulmonaria officinalis
Lungwort

Ruta graveolens 'Jackman's Blue'
Rue

Salvia officinalis 'Icterina'
Gold variegated sage

Salvia officinalis
'Purpurascens'
Purple sage

Sanguisorba minor
Salad burnet

Santolina
Santolina

Tanacetum vulgare
var. *crispum*
Crisp tansy

FRAGRANT HERBS

The flowers or foliage of these herbs are fragrant; all release their scent when touched.

Aloysia triphylla
Lemon verbena

Anthemis
Chamomile

Artemisia abrotanum
Southernwood

Calamintha grandiflora
Garden calamint

Cedronella canariensis
False balm of Gilead

Convallaria majalis
Lily of the valley

Daphne mezereum
February daphne

Dianthus
Pink

Dictamnus purpureus
Burning bush

Helichrysum angustifolium
Curry plant

Heliotropium arborescens
Heliotrope

Hemerocallis fulva
Daylily

Hesperis matronalis
Sweet rocket

Jasminum
Jasmine

Lavandula
Lavender

Lilium candidum
Madonna lily

Lonicera periclymenum
Wild honeysuckle

Melissa officinalis
Lemon balm

Mentha x *piperita* var. *citrata*
Eau de Cologne mint

Pelargonium
Scented pelargonium

Rosa
Rose

Salvia elegans syn. *rutilans*
Pineapple sage

Santolina
Santolina

Tagetes tenuifolia
Citrus-scented marigold

Thymus
Thyme

Viola odorata
Sweet violet

GROUND-COVER HERBS

Provide a dense carpet of decorative foliage and flowers, which also suppresses weeds and helps retain moisture.

Ajuga reptans
Bugle

Alchemilla vulgaris
Lady's mantle

Anthemis nobile
Roman chamomile

Anthyllis vulneraria
Kidney vetch

Arctostaphylos uva-ursi
Bearberry

Calluna vulgaris
Heather

Cymbalaria muralis
Ivy-leaved toadflax

Fragaria vesca
Wild strawberry

Galium odoratum
Sweet woodruff

Galium verum
Lady's bedstraw

Gaultheria procumbens
Wintergreen

Geum rivale
Water avens

Helianthemum nummularium
Rockrose

Lysimachia nummularia
Creeping Jenny

Mentha pulegium
Pennyroyal

Polemonium reptans
Greek valerian

Pulmonaria officinalis
Lungwort

Ranunculus ficaria
Lesser celandine

Satureja montana
Winter savory

Teucrium chamaedrys
Wall germander

Thymus serpyllum
Creeping thyme

Vinca major
Greater periwinkle

Viola odorata
Sweet violet

MEDICINAL HERBS

These, and many other herbs in the "Herb Directory," have been traditionally valued in herbal medicine, and many are still used today. Some herbs are toxic or potentially toxic. Always consult a qualified herbal practitioner before using any herbs for home treatment.

Achillea millefolium
Yarrow

Allium sativum
Garlic

Althaea officinalis
Marsh mallow

Arctostaphylos uva-ursi
Bearberry

Arnica montana
Arnica

Calendula officinalis
Pot marigold

Chrysanthemum parthenium
Feverfew

Cimicifuga racemosa
Black cohosh

Digitalis purpurea
Purple foxglove

Echinacea angustifolia
Coneflower

Hamamelis virginiana
Witch hazel

Humulus lupulus
Hop

Hypericum perforatum
St John's wort

Inula helenium
Elecampane

Lavandula angustifolia
Common lavender

Lobelia inflata
Indian tobacco

Marrubium vulgare
Horehound

Melissa officinalis
Lemon balm

Mentha x *piperita*
Peppermint

Oenothera biennis
Evening primrose

Passiflora incarnata
Passionflower

Pulsatilla vulgaris
Pasqueflower

Ruta graveolens
Rue

Salvia officinalis
'Purpurascens'
Purple sage

Scutellaria lateriflora
Skullcap

Symphytum officinale
Comfrey

Thymus vulgaris
Common thyme

Valeriana officinalis
Valerian

Viola tricolor
Heartsease

ESSENTIAL OILS

These essential oils are used extensively in aromatherapy and are readily available for home use.

Anthemis nobile
Roman chamomile

Jasminum grandiflorum
Jasmine

Lavandula angustifolia
and *L.* x *intermedia*
Lavender

Melissa officinalis
Lemon balm

Mentha x *piperita*
Peppermint

Origanum majorana
Sweet marjoram

Pelargonium graveolens
Scented geranium

Rosa x *centifolia* and
R. x *damascena*
Rose

Rosmarinus officinalis
Rosemary

Useful Addresses

NURSERIES AND GARDENS

United Kingdom

Arne Herbs
Limeburn Nurseries
Limeburn Hill
Chew Magna
Avon BS18 8QW
Tel (01275) 333999

Brin School Fields
The Old School
Flichity
Inverness
IV1 2KD
Tel (01808) 521288

Cheshire Herbs
Fourfields
Forest Road
Little Budworth
Nr Tarporley
Cheshire CW6 9ES
Tel (01829) 760578

Chelsea Physic Garden
Swan Walk,
Off Royal Hospital Road
London SW3 4HS
Tel (0171) 352 5646

The Cottage Herbery
Mill House
Boraston Ford
Boraston
Nr Tenbury Wells
Worcs WR15 8LZ
Tel (01584) 781575

The Herb Garden
Hall View Cottage
Hardstoft
Pilsley
Chesterfield
Derbs S45 8AH
Tel (01246) 854268

Hexham Herbs
The Chesters Walled Garden
Chollerford
Hexham
Northumberland NE46 4BQ
Tel (01434) 681483

Hollington Herbs
Woolton Hill
Newbury
Berks RG20 9XT
Tel (01635) 253908

Iden Croft Herbs
Frittenden Road
Staplehurst
Kent TN12 0DN
Tel (01580) 891432

Jekka's Herb Farm
Rose Cottage
Shellards Lane
Alveston
Bristol
Avon BS12 2SY
Tel (01454) 418878

Lower Severalls Herb
Nursery
Haselbury Road
Crewkerne
Somerset TA18 7NX
Tel (01460) 76105

Norfolk Herbs
Blackberry Farm
Dereham Road
Dillington
Dereham
Norfolk NR19 2QD
Tel (01362) 860812

Norfolk Lavender
Caley Mill
Heacham
Norfolk PE31 7JE
Tel (01485) 570384

Paradise Centre
Twinstead Road
Lamarsh
Bures
Suffolk CO8 5EX
Tel (01787) 269449

Poyntzfield Herb Nursery
Black Isle
Ross & Cromarty
Scotland IV7 8LX
Tel (01381) 610352

Royal Horticultural Society
Gardens
Wisley
Surrey GU23 6XB
Tel (01483) 224234

Ryton Organic Gardens
(Henry Doubleday Research
Association)
Ryton on Dunsmore
Coventry CV8 3LG
Tel (01203) 303517

Unusual Plants
The Beth Chatto Gardens Ltd
Elmstead Market
Colchester
Essex CO7 7DB
Tel (01206) 822007

United States

Brooklyn Botanic Garden
1000 Washington Ave
Brooklyn, NY 11225-1099
Tel (718) 622 4433

Caprilands Herb Farm
534 Silver Street
Coventry, CT 06238
Tel (203) 742 7244

De Baggio Herbs
923 N Ivy St
Arlington, VA 22201
Tel (703) 243 2498

Gilbertie's Herb Gardens Inc
65 Adams Road
PO Box 118
Easton, CT 06612
Tel (203) 452 0913

Logee's Greenhouses
141 North Street
Danielson, CT 06239
Tel (203) 774 8038

Nichols Herbs and Rare Seeds
Nichols Garden Nursery
1190 North Pacific Highway
Albany, OR 97321
Tel (541) 928 9280

Peconic River Herb Farm
310 C River Road
Calverton, NY 11933
Tel (516) 369 0058

Southern Exposure Seed
Exchange
PO Box 170-8
Earlysville, PA 22936
Tel (804) 937 4703

United States National
Arboretum
3501 New York Ave NE
Washington, DC 20002
Tel (202) 475 4865

Australia

Chamomile Farm
79 Monbulk Road
Emerald
Victoria 3782
Tel (059) 684807

The Diggers Club at
Heronswood
Diggers Garden Co Pty Ltd
105 Latrobe Parade
Dromana
Victoria 3936
Tel (059) 871877

Plants Naturally Herbs
PO Box 24
Monbulk
Melbourne
Victoria 3793
Tel (061) 37567 680

Renaissance Herbs
Lot 521, Hakone Road
Warnervale
NSW 2259
Tel (043) 931221

South Africa

Herbal Centre
PO Box 41
De Wildt 0251
Pretoria
Tel (012) 504 1729

"Leipsig" Wine & Herb Farm
PO Box 5051
Worcester 6851
Cape Town
Tel (0231) 21435/6

Sunherbs
PO Box 618
Irene 1675
Transvaal
Tel (011) 316 4609

Heather Hill Nursery
PO Box 19
Rheenendel 6576
Near George
South Cape
Tel (0445) 4873

SEED SOURCES

United Kingdom

John Chambers
15 Westleigh Road
Barton Seagrave
Kettering
Northants NN15 5AJ
Tel (01933) 652562

Chiltern Seeds
Bortree Stile
Ulverston
Cumbria LA12 7PB
Tel (01229) 581137

Suffolk Herbs
Monk's Farm
Coggeshall Road
Kelvedon
Essex CO5 9PG
Tel (01376) 572456

United States

The Cook's Garden
PO Box 535
Londonderry, VT 05148
Tel (802) 824 3400

J. L. Hudson, Seedsman
PO Box 1058
Redwood City, CA 94064
Tel (415) 369 0772

Johnny's Selected Seeds
Foss Hill
Albion, ME 04910
Tel (207) 437 9294

Seeds Blum
Idaho City Stage
Boise, ID 83706
Tel (208) 342 0858

Seeds of Change
621 Old Santa Fe Trail #10
Santa Fe, NM 87501
Tel (505) 438 8080

Shepherd's Garden Seeds
6116 Highway 9
Felton, CA 95018
Tel (408) 335 5216

Canada

Richters
357 Hwy 47
Goodwood
ON L0C 1A0
Tel (416) 640 6677

Japan

Mikasa Engei Inc
3-3-2 Seta
Setagaya-ku
Tokyo 158
Tel (03) 3700 2221

South Africa

Blackwoods Herbs
PO Box 86
Hoekwil 6538
Eastern Cape
Tel (0441) 8501135

HERB SOCIETIES

The herb society of each country will be pleased to provide further information for herb suppliers, and herb gardens to visit.

United Kingdom

The Herb Society
134 Buckingham Palace Road
London SW1W 9SA
Tel (0171) 823 5583

United States

The Herb Society of America
9019 Kirtland Chardon Road
Menton
Kirtland, OH 44094
Tel (216) 256 0514

Australia

The Queensland Herb Society
PO Box 110
Mapleton
Qld 4560
Tel (07) 3397 5405

Canada

Canadian Herb Society
1102-1067 Seymour Street
Vancouver V6B 5S4
Tel (604) 683 2014

Japan

Japan Herb Society
701, 1-5 Saiku-cho
Shinjuku-ku
Tokyo 162
Tel (03) 3267 2105

New Zealand

Herb Federation of
New Zealand
PO Box 4055
Nelson South
Tel (03) 412 8783

South Africa

Herb Association of
South Africa
PO Box 1831
Estcourt 3310
Tel (0363) 24645

The Herb Society of
South Africa
PO Box 37721
Overport
Durban 4067

Index

Page numbers in italic refer to illustrations. Plants are occasionally reclassified by botanists. The index lists both old and new names where they have recently changed.

A

B

C

D

Acknowledgments

I WOULD LIKE TO THANK the following for their kindness in allowing us to photograph their gardens and for their help in many ways: Janet Allan, Natalie Allen, Sir Francis Avery Jones, Penny and Bob Black, Ronald Blyth, Geoff and Sylvia Cassell, Miss J. Courtauld, Sara and Tim Daniel, Maggie and Colin Ellis, Sir Charles and Lady Anne Frazer, Jill Goodwin, Chris and Christine Grey-Wilson, Anne Hoellering, Mrs Hynard, Joy Larkcom, Frank and Margery Lawley, Trant and Alwyn Luard, Margaret Mackenzie, Mr and Mrs Euan Macpherson, Waj and Edna Mirecki, Frances Mount, Jane and Jonathan Newdick, John and Sue Nicol, Louise Stevens, Roger and Angelika Stevens, Mrs Diana Turner, Mrs Williams, and The Chelsea Physic Garden, London; Pamela Cullinan of Sunherbs, South Africa; The Guildhall, Lavenham, Suffolk; Chris Nye of CN Seeds, National Centre for Organic Gardening, Ryton Gardens, Coventry; Duncan Ross of Poyntzfield Herb Nursery, Scotland; Cees and Hedy Stapel-Valk of The Paradise Centre; Parham House and Garden, West Sussex; Hexham Herbs, Northumberland; Iden Croft Herbs, Kent; University Botanic Garden, Cambridge; Clive Blazey of The Digger's Club, Australia; Lyle and Elvie Williams of Chamomile Farm, Australia; Shiro Mishima and Mina Hashimoto of Mikasa Engei, Tokyo.

Many thanks to Jacqui Hurst and Sampson Lloyd for driving long distances in search of herbs and gardens to photograph and for their masterly studio shots. Many thanks also to Jean Saer for being the "hands" in the step-by-steps, for her beautiful flower arrangements, and for preparing so many herbs for photography.

My special thanks to Sarah Davies, who designed the book, for her unstinted dedication and for her calming and cheerful influence. I would also like to thank Eric Thomas for his wonderful illustrations.

My grateful thanks to Catherine Bradley, our first editor, who did all the groundwork for the book and offered such encouragement. Also to Sarah Hoggett and Katie Bent for completing the task and to Jo Weeks for her expert help. Special thanks, also, to Sylvia Cassell for word processing the manuscript so efficiently.

My very special gratitude to my wife Caroline for her constant encouragement and meticulous editing and proof-reading.

Collins & Brown would also like to thank Ruth Baldwin, Joanna Chisholm, Robin Gurdon, Claire Graham, Sue Metcalfe-Megginson, and Barbara Segal for their assistance.

Photographic Credits

Heather Angel 61 (box); **Nigel Cattlin/Holt Picture Library** 41 (all); **Jacqui Hurst Library** 96; **McOnegal Botanical** 92, 112 (left), 113 (left), 121 (middle), 133 (middle), 138 (middle), 151 (left), 174 (right); **Mikasa Engei, Tokyo** 158 (right); **Norfolk Lavender** 143 (bottom middle); **Photoflora** 108 (middle), 109 (left and right), 115 (left), 124 (middle), 125 (right), 129 (middle), 149 (middle), 155 (top left and right), 175 (left); **Harry Smith Collection** 99, 113 (middle), 117 (left), 135 (right), 146 (middle), 159 (top middle); **John Stevens** title page; 6–7, 33, 65 (box), 82, 85, 102 (middle and right), 103 (left), 104 (middle), 105, 107 (middle, top right and bottom right), 112 (right), 115 (right), 116 (left and right), 117 (right), 118 (left), 119 (middle and right), 122 (left), 123 (right), 126 (left and top right), 128 (left), 129 (left and right), 131 (right), 133 (right), 134 (left), 139 (top right), 140 (left and middle), 143 (left), 144 (left and right), 145 (right), 148 (all), 149 (left), 151 (right), 152 (middle top and middle bottom), 153 (right), 154 (left), 155 (middle), 156 (bottom right), 160 (middle), 167 (all), 169 (right), 170 (right), 171 (left), 172 (left and middle), 174 (left and middle), 175 (middle), 177 (right); **John Vanderplank** 158 (left).

All other photographs by Jacqui Hurst or Sampson Lloyd.